Language and Masculinity

D0234016

Language and Masculinity

Edited by
Sally Johnson
and
Ulrike Hanna Meinhof

Copyright © Blackwell Publishers Ltd, 1997

First published 1997

2 4 6 8 10 9 7 5 3 1

Blackwell Publishers Ltd
108 Cowley Road
Oxford OX4 1JF
UK

Blackwell Publishers Inc.
238 Main Street
Cambridge, Massachusetts 02142
USA

British Library Cataloguing in Publication Data

A CIP catalogue record for this book is available from the British Library.

Library of Congress Cataloging-in-Publication Data has been applied for.

ISBN 0-631-19767-2 (hbk)
ISBN 0-631-19768-0 (pbk)

Typeset in 10.5 on 12.5pt Palatino
by Wearset, Boldon, Tyne and Wear.
Printed and bound in Great Britain by Hartnolls Limited, Bodmin, Cornwall

This book is printed on acid-free paper.

Contents

List of Contributors   vii

Acknowledgements   x

Introduction   1
Ulrike Hanna Meinhof and Sally Johnson

1 Theorizing Language and Masculinity*conc* ·
   A Feminist Perspective   8
   Sally Johnson

2 'Box-out' and 'Taxing'   27
   Roger Hewitt

3 Performing Gender Identity: Young Men's Talk and the
   Construction of Heterosexual Masculinity   47
   Deborah Cameron

4 Power and the Language of Men   65
   Scott Fabius Kiesling

5 Masculinities in a Multilingual Setting   86
   Joan Pujolar i Cos

6 One-at-a-Time: The Organization of Men's Talk   107
   Jennifer Coates

7 Do Men Gossip? An Analysis of Football Talk on Television   130
   Sally Johnson and Frank Finlay

8 The Role of Expletives in the Construction of Masculinity   144
   Vivian de Klerk

 9 *'Aceptarlo con hombría'*: Representations of Masculinity
   in Spanish Political Discourse   159
   JoAnne Neff van Aertselaer

10 'Randy Fish Boss Branded a Stinker': Coherence and the
   Construction of Masculinities in a British Tabloid Newspaper 173
   Mary M. Talbot

11 'The Object of Desire is the Object of Contempt':
   Representations of Masculinity in *Straight to Hell* Magazine   188
   John Heywood

12 'The Most Important Event of My Life!'
   A Comparison of Male and Female Written Narratives   208
   Ulrike Hanna Meinhof

Bibliography   229

Index   240

Contributors

Deborah Cameron teaches linguistics at Strathclyde University, Glasgow. She is the author of *Feminism and Linguistic Theory* (2nd edition, Macmillan, 1992) and *Verbal Hygiene* (Routledge, 1995). She is also the editor of *The Feminist Critique of Language* (Routledge, 1990) and co-editor with Jennifer Coates of *Women in their Speech Communities* (Longman, 1989).

Jennifer Coates is Professor of English Language and Linguistics at Roehampton Institute, London. Her publications include *The Semantics of Modal Auxiliaries* (Croom Helm, 1983), *Women in their Speech Communities* (co-edited with Deborah Cameron, Longman, 1989), and *Women, Men and Language* (2nd edition, Longman, 1993). Her most recent book is *Women Talk. Conversations between Women Friends* (Blackwell, 1996), which is an account of her long-term research project on the talk of single-sex friendship groups.

Frank Finlay is a graduate of German and English at Newcastle University and was awarded his Ph.D. in 1993. His publications include *The Rationality of Poetry. Heinrich Böll's Aesthetic Thinking* (Rodopi, 1996). He is Senior Lecturer and Head of German in the Department of Modern Languages at Bradford University.

Roger Hewitt is a senior lecturer at the Institute of Education, University of London, and has conducted research into adolescence, ethnicity and language. He is the author of *White Talk, Black Talk. Inter-racial Friendship and Communication Amongst Adolescents* (CUP,

1986). He is also a contributor to *Text, Discourse and Context* (eds Meinhof and Richardson, 1994) in the Longman Real Language Series, and is currently writing a monograph in the same series entitled *'Culture' and Group Talk.*

John Heywood took his first degree in social anthropology at Cambridge and then worked for fifteen years teaching English as a Second Language in London, where, at various times, he was also involved in both gay and AIDS voluntary organizations. He is currently doing research in stylistics at Lancaster University, after gaining an MA in ELT in 1993.

Sally Johnson studied modern languages at Salford University. Her publications include *Gender, Group Identity, and Variation in the Berlin Urban Vernacular* (Peter Lang, 1995) and various articles on language and gender. She teaches German language and linguistics at Lancaster University, and is currently working on an introduction to German linguistics for Edward Arnold entitled *The Study of German.*

Scott Fabius Kiesling is a Ph.D. candidate in sociolinguistics at Georgetown University in Washington, DC. He is currently writing his dissertation 'Language, gender, and power in a fraternity', an analysis of language variation and discourse at a university in the commonwealth of Virginia.

Vivian de Klerk is Professor and Head of the Department of Linguistics and English Language at Rhodes University, South Africa. She has published widely on language and gender with reference to both English and Afrikaans, and her most recent work is a volume with M. Gorlach entitled *English in South(ern) Africa* (John Benjamins, 1995).

Ulrike Hanna Meinhof is Professor of Cultural Studies in the Department of Modern Languages at Bradford University. She is co-editor (with Kay Richardson) of *Text, Discourse and Context* (Longman Real Language Series, 1994), joint winner of the 1995 Book Prize of the British Association for Applied Linguistics. Her other publications include articles on various media discourses such as the representation of subversive women in the British and German press, and she has also co-authored text books and multi-media packages for German, English and French language learning.

JoAnne Neff van Aertselaer is Head of the Department of English

Philology and Assistant Director of the Master of Arts Programme in Applied Linguistics at the Universidad Complutense de Madrid. She has published widely in Spain on feminism, and has given many in-service training sessions for teachers on sexist language. She is currently working on a project on social change advertising in Spain.

Joan Pujolar i Cos is a research supervisor in the Departament de Filologia Catalana at the Universitat Autonoma de Barcelona. He studied in the Department of Linguistics at Lancaster University, where he gained his Masters degree in 1991 and his Ph.D. in 1995 for his thesis 'The identities of *'la penya'*: voices and struggles of young working-class people in Barcelona'. He has been involved in various political movements devoted to the promotion of the Catalan language as well as working on a project about the use of Catalan in business.

Mary M. Talbot was awarded her Ph.D. at Lancaster University in 1990 for her thesis 'Language, intertextuality and subjectivity: voices in the construction of consumer femininity', and is currently a research fellow in the Centre for Consumer Culture at Southampton Institute. Her recent publications include *Fictions at Work: Language and Social Practice in Fiction* (Longman, 1995) and articles on various aspects of media discourse and consumerism. She is now working on *An Introduction to Language and Gender* for Polity Press.

Acknowledgements

There are a number of people we would like to thank for their various contributions to the production of this volume. First of all, Philip Carpenter, Bridget Jennings and Brigitte Lee at Blackwell Publishers. Second, thanks to Bev Skeggs, Beth Linklater and Andy Stafford at Lancaster University for their support and ideas, especially with respect to the first chapter. Third, we are extremely grateful to Frank Gloversmith for his excellent proofreading. Any remaining errors are, of course, entirely our own.

We would also like to acknowledge the following copyright holders for their permission to reprint certain items: Carfax Publishing Company, Abingdon, Oxfordshire, allowed us to print a revised version of an earlier paper by Sally Johnson entitled 'A game of two halves? On men, football and gossip', which originally appeared in the *Journal of Gender Studies*, 3 (2) in 1994. *The Sun* newspaper granted us permission to reproduce the article '£6,000 bill puts randy fish boss in his plaice', originally published on 19 April 1989. Finally, thanks to Bill Andriette and Edward Hougen at Fidelity Publishing for permission to quote from the *Raunch, Scum* and *Lewd* editions of *Straight to Hell* magazine and the interview with Boyd McDonald published in *The Guide*. Also, we gratefully acknowledge permission from Winston Leyland at Gay Sunshine Press to quote from the *Sex* and *Meat* anthologies of *Straight to Hell*.

Introduction

Ulrike Hanna Meinhof and Sally Johnson

Feminist linguistics has come of age. From marginalized beginnings at the very periphery of what was considered to be the proper and legitimate task of language analysts, there is now barely a linguistics department in the country which does not, in some way or other, address issues of language and gender. The academic literature is substantial, both in quantity and quality. It is also extensive in terms of its objects of analysis, complex in methodology and argument, and critical in the assessment and reassessment of its own output. Furthermore, whilst such work has inevitably – and rightfully – focused on the speech behaviour of women, feminist linguistics has almost always entailed a critical stance on the interactional norms of men. So why, then, a book specifically on language and masculinity?

In chapter 1, 'Theorizing language and masculinity: a feminist perspective', Sally Johnson argues the case for putting the study of male speech behaviour more firmly onto the linguist's – and the feminist linguist's – agenda. In reviewing the literature on language and gender, and the ideas associated with theories of difference and dominance, Johnson suggests that neither of these approaches has tackled the issue of masculinity in a sufficiently rigorous manner. Even though a critique of masculinity may have been implied, many aspects of men's use of language have retained their status as the unproblematized norm, with the consequence that social and linguistic change ultimately remains a female prerogative. She argues that there is much to be gained politically from an explicit, as opposed to an implicit, questioning of male behaviour.

Rather than viewing masculinity as an essentialist opposite to an equally essentialist femininity, Johnson supports those who see masculinity and femininity as mutually dependent constructs in a dialectical relationship. She therefore stresses the variability of masculine identities, and the divergent roles that language plays in the social construction of those identities. However, Johnson leaves open the question of whether this recognition of multiple subjectivities prevents us from making any real generalizations about power and dominance. What she does stress is that, in view of the inherent fluidity of masculine identities, any generalizations that might emerge are unlikely to relate to the use of isolated linguistic structures by men as a group. Instead, she advocates studying the disparate ways in which masculinities express themselves, with conclusions drawn in terms of the content and purpose, rather than the form, of language. This, she believes, is important if feminist linguistics is to gain a broader view of the workings of language and gender with reference to both masculinity *and* femininity.

Despite the relative neglect of masculinity within the field of language and gender, Johnson points out how this topic has been a popular focus for analysis since the 1970s within the social sciences more generally. What marks this book off from other volumes discussing masculinity, however, is its emphasis on language, with spoken or written data forming the core of every chapter. In this respect, the book complements the development of other gender-related work on language, where initial 'armchair' theorizing on female speech (e.g. Lakoff, 1973) was challenged by analyses of authentic linguistic data.

The type of written and spoken data presented covers a wide range of settings. The individual chapters analyse both informal interaction (Cameron, chapter 3; Coates, chapter 6; Pujolar, chapter 5) and various kinds of ritualistic settings (Hewitt, chapter 2; Kiesling, chapter 4) with corresponding degrees of casual or conventionalized forms of talk. There are spontaneously occurring spoken data, as well as written corpora specifically elicited by questionnaires (de Klerk, chapter 8). Some of the chapters discuss texts which are strongly confessional (Heywood, chapter 11; Meinhof, chapter 12), whilst others include language which is mediated by second-order representations in different genres, for example, a printed pamphlet containing political advertising (Neff, chapter 9), a discussion of football on television (Johnson and Finlay, chapter 7), an article from the tabloid press (Talbot, chapter 10), and extracts from reader–editor correspondence in a magazine for gay men (Heywood, chapter 11). Each chapter thus makes its own particular contribution to the discussion of language and masculinity.

Following Sally Johnson's opening contribution, chapters 2 and 3, by Roger Hewitt and Deborah Cameron, respectively, begin with a discussion of two concepts which have been central to debates on language and gender: cooperation and competition. Both authors, however, question and subvert what they perceive to be the unjustifiably gendered use of these terms.

In chapter 2, '"Box-out" and "taxing"', Roger Hewitt describes a game played by adolescent males in a London school, and highlights the complexity of, and interplay between, notions of cooperation and competition. Hewitt demonstrates the ways in which cooperative talk, though very much a part of the ritual surrounding play, also contains sharp elements of contestation. Conversely, he illustrates how the boys' fiercely competitive game is dependent on a high degree of communication and coordination which demands that participants respect the rules of talk. On the basis of his analysis, Hewitt argues that the declarative 'I' and the coordinative 'we' are simultaneously valid for any group exchange, irrespective of the gender of its participants. He thus problematizes the essentializing attribution of cooperation and competition to one gender or the other.

Whereas Hewitt focuses on the codes of understanding that regulate the game of 'box-out' and 'taxing', Deborah Cameron emphasizes the codes of understanding that inform the uptake of conversations. Her analysis in chapter 3, 'Performing gender identity: young men's talk and the construction of heterosexual masculinity', explores casual conversations between a group of male students at a US college, demonstrating that these codes are themselves constructed and relate to a more 'general discourse on gender difference'. Thus, any specific instance of behaviour – and of associated patterns of talk – is indirectly interpreted through conventional filters, that is to say, coloured by the partiality of shared assumptions vis-à-vis gender differentiation.

The next two chapters, by Scott Fabius Kiesling and Joan Pujolar i Cos, respectively, also demonstrate how cooperation and contestation are not necessarily mutually exclusive features of group exchanges.

In chapter 4, 'Power and the language of men', Kiesling, like Cameron, analyses data from male interaction in a US college. Kiesling, however, observes a more structured setting based on an election meeting within a fraternity group, exploring the ways in which individual men perform different roles according to their hierarchical position within the fraternity as a whole. The adoption of differing 'archetypal' male roles by these men might easily be taken as representing the idealized paradigms of masculinity and femininity. But the individual members of the fraternity group display a range of discursive strategies, which cut across the categories of speech behaviour previously assigned to either men *or* women in the language and gender literature. Kiesling shows how the different roles occupied by the men – and the discursive representations of those roles – are highly dependent on the place of each individual within the power structure of the fraternity.

In chapter 5, 'Masculinities in a multilingual setting', Joan Pujolar i Cos looks at two groups of working-class youth in Barcelona and, like Kiesling, demonstrates the variability of masculine identities. Pujolar shows how the formation and expression of these identities are very much in evidence in the multiplicity of voices that group members playfully adopt. The construction of such voices draws on changes in speech style, language choice and – intriguingly – code-switching between Catalan and Spanish. But the signification of these switches is locally determined, differing from group to group, and from one situation to the next. Thus, even though Pujolar highlights the role played by language in the construction of masculinities, he underlines the fact that ways of speaking cannot be characterized in terms of fixed meanings attached to male (or female) interaction.

By way of contrast, the data analysed by Jennifer Coates in chapter 6 point to a more regular differentiation between male and female conversational behaviour. In 'One-at-a-time: the organization of men's talk', Coates compares the turn-taking patterns of all-male and all-female conversations, finding a marked difference between the two. Whereas women create a collaborative floor in their conversations, preferring a more polyphonic way of talking, men pursue a strictly one-at-a-time floor. Coates' conclusions, backed by detailed analysis of an extensive corpus, avoid essentialist oppositions since she sees the underlying linguistic resources as shared by both sexes. But she argues that there is a significant contrast in the way in which men and women typically draw upon those resources in their respective interactive styles.

Several of the authors in this volume suggest, implicitly or explicitly, that male speech behaviour serves as a form of male bonding. In chapter 7, 'Do men gossip? An analysis of football talk on television', Sally Johnson and Frank Finlay look at one episode of the popular football programme *Saint and Greavsie*, and propose that the 'female' speech genre of gossip is also used by men as a form of bonding through talk. This occurs, however, in relation to the different – and ultimately less personal – topic of football. Using stylized para-social interaction on television as a basis for commenting on authentic speech is always problematical, but Johnson and Finlay argue that the programme attempts to imitate, in the public arena, men's talk in the private sphere. Hence, the discursive structures of these exchanges provide data for testing the hypothesis of 'male gossip'.

Johnson and Finlay explore what is often perceived to be a 'female' form of talk, and show how it is equally used by men. Conversely, in chapter 8, 'The role of expletives in the construction of masculinity', Vivian de Klerk focuses on the traditionally male domain of swearing, and discovers that this kind of 'male' talk is increasingly being used by females. Conventional sex role theory is thus no longer able to account for the use of expletives by either men or women. Instead, de Klerk proposes that the underlying meanings of unconventional and taboo-breaking behaviour need to be reassessed. Even if swearing is no longer seen as a symbol of taboo-breaking for males, it is still possible that the desire for non-conformity might produce different styles of swearing or perhaps an absence of expletives altogether.

The following chapters by JoAnne Neff van Aertselaer and Mary Talbot discuss two very different forms of public language – a government pamphlet and a newspaper article – both of which would appear to take account of changing relations between men and women. Yet in their analyses, each author underlines how this semblance of change is no more than an illusion.

In chapter 9, '"*Aceptarlo con hombría*": representations of masculinity in Spanish political discourse', Neff looks at a Spanish Socialist comic 'Por el futuro de todos' ('For the Future of All') as an example of social advertising. She explores the messages of the text, which appeared before the 1993 national elections in Spain, and analyses the ways in which political language and male identity formation interrelate. However, whilst the comic claims to support feminist demands for greater equality in a popular and seemingly more progressive manner than the conventional political rhetoric of the past, Neff argues that its language and imagery continue to construct male identity in terms of conventional protective and commanding roles. Ultimately, she proposes, the text is no more than a ploy to attract votes.

Like Neff, Mary Talbot also traces the persistence of conventional attitudes in an article that purports to be in favour of change. In chapter 10, '"Randy fish boss branded a stinker": coherence and the construction of masculinities in a British tabloid newspaper', Talbot looks at a feature in *The Sun* newspaper, which reports on the successful conviction of a male boss for the sexual harassment of two female workers. The very act of covering such a case might well appear to be an implicit challenge to notions of hegemonic masculinity. Yet Talbot argues that the sub-text of this article draws heavily on class antagonism and scapegoating (the comical middle-class boss versus his pretty employees) in order to affirm, rather than reject, traditional assumptions about sexual relations between men and women. Interestingly, elements of the oppositional discourse of feminism seem to have been incorporated, though without dislodging the stability of hegemonic masculinity. Talbot thus points out how the assimilation of feminist ideas, along with the appearance of flexibility, may be working in a way which actually reinforces and stabilizes male dominance.

Whereas most of the other contributions to this volume treat male dominance in the context of male/female relations, chapter 11 by John Heywood sees this hegemony as similarly contained in the sexual discourses of gay men. In ' "The object of desire is the object of contempt": representations of masculinity in *Straight to Hell* magazine', Heywood analyses sexually explicit readers' letters to a gay magazine, which were published during the 1970s and 1980s, and which purport to be authentic narratives of the writers' experiences. Many of the texts from *Straight to Hell* (*STH*) were anthologized in pornographic collections, and Heywood acknowledges the way in which some of the narratives blur the border between authentic experience and fictional pornography. He argues nevertheless that these texts offer valuable insights into the way in which the writers construct their identities as gay men. Heywood shows that these men express their masculinity in forms which draw upon the full range of sexual identities, thus subverting the traditional oppositions employed in the construction of heterosexuality, e.g. passive/active, masculine/feminine, gay/straight. Although he suggests that the blurring of these categories sets the writers apart from hegemonic masculinity, such binary oppositions are still fundamental to the construction of gay men's identities. Heywood thus shows how the gay men he analyses are – paradoxically – still very much a part of the system of hegemonic masculinity which they appear to reject.

The analysis of confessional, first-person narratives also constitutes the focus for chapter 12, the final contribution to this volume. In ' "The most important event of my life!" A comparison of male and female written narratives', Ulrike Hanna Meinhof looks at narratives describing 'the most important event' in the lives of male and female academics and students, and shows how all the texts follow an underlying structural pattern consisting of three distinct discourse units. However, whilst the similarity in surface structure illustrates the way in which related narrative processes are at work, the linguistic form and content of the texts reveal a different approach to the disclosure of self by certain individuals and groups of writers. The way in which the most important event is narrated, hidden or displaced in the writing suggests a contrasting predisposition between the men and women academics (though not the students) towards the acceptance and retelling of the tensions and contradictions inherent in their lives. Whereas the female academics seem to embrace the ambivalences of their everyday existence, the male academics in Meinhof's sample displace the core of the question by various stylistic and rhetorical means. The fact that both groups produce poetic and often very moving accounts should be seen as an indication of the considerable linguistic resourcefulness of the writers. However, it is their very ability to control the narratives which, according to Meinhof, renders the emergence of contradictions in the men's writing doubly suggestive.

Viewed in their totality, the contributions to this volume illustrate a range of positions regarding the conceptualization of masculinities. The methods of analysis, the objects and genres of study, and the conclusions drawn, are entirely attributable to the authors of each chapter. As a result, some very real differences emerge. Having said this, all contributors to this volume would agree, in principle, that gender is to be seen as constructed, rather than fixed or innate. But the extent to which linguistic structures can be marked off as essentially masculine or feminine remains contested. Similarly, there are genuine differences of emphasis regarding how much overlap and similarity can be inferred from the linguistic analysis of data, both in terms of men versus women, and men versus other men. As editors, however, we have made no attempt to homogenize the individual contributions, nor indeed, to censor them, even if the language reproduced in some of the chapters may disturb or shock. Our aim has not been to produce consensus, but to stimulate debate.

1

Theorizing Language and Masculinity: A Feminist Perspective

Sally Johnson

Introduction

When the North American journal *Language in Society* published Robin Lakoff's 'Language and woman's place' in 1973, the article was accompanied by the following editorial footnote:

> A focus on women brings to light an aspect of language in social life that has its counterpart for men [...] 'Men's language' needs study too. (Dell Hymes in Lakoff, 1973, p. 79)

Many feminist linguists would argue that the study of language in society has always been about men, given that global relevance has traditionally been attributed to what are potentially *masculine* norms of discourse (Coates, 1986, p. 6). Indeed, it is from this vantage point that feminist critiques of linguistics originally emerged, providing the impetus for theorists to contest the implied universality of male verbal behaviour, and to put forward alternative paradigms within which the voices of women could be explored and acknowledged in their own right.

Yet despite the emergence of a comprehensive critique of androcentric methodologies, and extensive investigation into the speech of women since the 1970s, what have we really learned about language with specific – and explicit – reference to *men* and *masculinity*? Moreover, in what ways might such an insight contribute to feminist linguistic theory, or indeed, feminist practice generally? These are the kinds of issues which this chapter sets out to explore.

Men and Women: Difference or Dominance?

Feminism is founded upon critiques of male power, and one of the aims of feminist work is to throw light on the various structures that underpin the systematic oppression of women in society. But feminist practices themselves are not homogeneous. Theoretical approaches inevitably mirror differing perceptions of female oppression, and, more importantly perhaps, also reflect divergent strategies of resistance and opposition.

In order to pursue the question of how the study of men and masculinity might benefit feminist linguistic practice, it is essential to begin by looking closely at the theoretical and political positions that have traditionally informed work in this field. Two main approaches can be identified: the first founded upon a theory of *dominance*, the second upon a theory of *difference* (see Cameron, 1992a, 1992b, 1995b).

The agenda for early feminist linguistics was, in many ways, framed by the *dominance* approach. Robin Lakoff (1973), for example, suggested that women speak a 'powerless language', characterized by a tentativeness that conveys a lack of authority. This female style – or 'genderlect' as it later became known – was exemplified by women's assumed preference for a variety of so-called weakening devices: softer expletives, hesitant intonation, statements formed as questions or, in particular, accompanied by tag questions. As critics have variously noted, however, these claims were based on the author's own intuition as opposed to empirical data gathered from real speakers.

Subsequent work, included in such volumes as *Language and Sex* (Thorne and Henley, 1975) and *Language, Gender and Society* (Thorne et al., 1983), presented a number of case studies based on actual recordings of men and women talking. In their contributions to these volumes, Candice West and Don Zimmerman (1975, 1983), for example, analysed cross-sex conversations, and concluded that women fare poorly in comparison with men in terms of turn-taking, interruptions and holding the floor. Similarly, Pamela Fishman (1983) explored what she referred to as the 'unequal distribution of work in conversation', arguing that, whilst women invest considerable effort in maintaining interaction and supporting the conversational needs of men, they do so at their own expense. 'Men compete, women cooperate' has become the familiar catch-phrase where such work is concerned.

These early studies on gender and language usage can still be said to form part of the feminist linguist's 'canon', although many of their conclusions have since been questioned or refined. For instance, the work of William O'Barr and Bowman Atkins (1980) on courtroom procedures suggested that 'powerless language' is not necessarily a female prerogative, but may be used by any speaker of a lower status than his or her interlocutor(s). Similarly, Janet Holmes (1984a) and Deborah Cameron et al. (1989) illustrated how the use of tag questions must be considered in terms of function as well as form, demonstrating that it is problematical to claim that tags are inherent in the speech of one sex only, in this case, women. With the advantage of hindsight, such conflicting evidence comes as no surprise. Why should all women speak in the same or even similar ways, and why should the same linguistic structures convey identical meanings in different contexts?

An alternative approach to language and gender is the *difference* view, which emerged at least partly in critical response to the dominance view, and hence somewhat later. Here, theorists seek to distance themselves from the dominance concept. Politically, it is felt that work on women should avoid the perpetual comparison of female with male norms, which invariably places women in a position of deficit. Instead, the aim is to study women's use of language on its own terms (see Jones, 1980; Coates, 1986; 1995a). To a certain extent, the difference view explores the linguistic behaviour of women in a more positive light, and explanations are sought in the context of the distinctive subcultures within which gender-specific patterns of verbal interaction are thought to be acquired. Many studies of gender and dialect variation (though not always conducted from an explicitly feminist standpoint) can also be viewed within this framework. Since it is difficult to account for variation in the usage of dialect or standard language in terms of male dominance, such work has tended to stress the different types of groups or social networks in which men and women interact (Cheshire, 1978, 1982a, 1982b; Coates and Cameron, 1989; Milroy, 1980).

Theoretical approaches to a subject as complex as language and gender can never, of course, be as straightforward as this brief outline implies. As Deborah Cameron shows (1992a, p. 37), both the concepts of dominance and difference permeate feminist linguistics today, and the two are not mutually exclusive – aspects of Robin Lakoff's work, for example, can be analysed from either perspective. However, there are elements of both the difference and the dominance approaches which, in my opinion, reveal weaknesses where the theoretical conceptualization of gender is concerned.

First of all, both the dominance and the difference views are characterized by almost exclusive *problematization of women*. As a result, we know very little about men or masculinity, and what we do learn is largely by implication. Within the dominance paradigm, despite the mandatory reference to informants of both sexes, we are left with a fairly one-dimensional view of the male of the species. A kind of 'all-purpose male oppressor' is constructed in the guise of a mysterious individual who talks too much, interrupts and generally dominates conversations with women. The difference paradigm, with its conscious focus on all-female groups of informants, only really allows us to guess as to what the male and his patterns of verbal behaviour might be like. Significantly, this latter approach also fails to address satisfactorily the crucial question of why it is that women and men should belong to different subcultures in the first place.

A second – though not unrelated – weakness is the way in which both the dominance and difference approaches appear to work with a concept of gender based on *binary opposition*. The tacit hypothesis of many studies seems to be that men and women are essentially different, and that this difference will be reflected in their contrasting use of language. But many linguists have become so preoccupied with the need to uncover statistically significant gender differences that they frequently seem to overlook one important fact: the two sexes are still drawing on the same linguistic resources. Ultimately, there must be some degree of similarity or overlap in the speech of men and women, otherwise it would be impossible to envisage a situation where they could ever communicate.[1] As I hope to show, the implicit assumption that men and women are binary opposites, and that speech constitutes a symbolic reflection of that opposition, is inherently problematical both from the point of view of language *and* gender.

Perhaps the most intriguing point about the two shortcomings I have outlined, however, is the fact that they do not only concern feminist linguistics. It is axiomatic, I believe, that both criticisms could be levelled similarly at mainstream sociolinguists and their work. This is because both mainstream and feminist approaches, though from very different perspectives, have consistently employed 'gender' as synonymous with 'women', thus defining women as in greater need of problematization than men. And, like many mainstream studies, much feminist work is predicated upon a concept of gender where the main objective is to verify presumed oppositions between male and female language usage. As Deborah Cameron (1992a, p. 8) has suggested, is it not possible that some aspects of feminist linguistics are more mainstream in their approach than their authors might like to think?

Problematizing Men

History has given women every reason to want to talk and write about their own gender. It is a truism, therefore, to point out that feminism chooses to focus on women because it is primarily women – and not men – whose lives are marginalized and obscured by male power. So, for example, in the early 1970s, when much of the work on social aspects of language usage was either a *de facto* study of men, or constructed women in an unacceptably androcentric fashion, work *by* women and *on* women was both apposite and crucial. Some two decades later, however, we find ourselves in a different position: a large body of data has been gathered, and a considerable amount has been learned about women and language. Although it would be clearly inappropriate to suggest that we now know all that we need to know, it is useful nonetheless to take stock and reconsider the direction of feminist linguistics today.

It seems to me that what we often find in language and gender work is the following scenario: whilst women continue to be the object of problematization, men adhere to a position characterized by *normalization*. Yet it is precisely men's status as 'ungendered representatives of humanity' that is the key to their hegemony. Antony Easthope, for example, points out that: 'Despite all that has been written over the past twenty years on femininity and feminism, masculinity has stayed pretty well concealed. This has always been its ruse to hold on to its power' (1986, p. 1). One might argue that men are more able to sustain an indifference to feminism as long as women remain the primary focus of such theorizing.

Early debates on 'powerless language' provide a good example of the way in which work on language and women has lent a normative status to male verbal behaviour. Thus, when Lakoff and others implied that women's language was perhaps too indirect or hesitant for women to be taken seriously, one of the by-products was professional advice to women that they should be more 'upfront', clear and objective. This, in turn, led to the rise of a huge industry cashing in on women's perceived need for 'assertiveness training' courses.[2] The corollary for women is a self-image based on deficit; for men, however, it is a tacit and effortless reconfirmation of their own behaviour as the 'default mode' for both sexes. Men have little need to modify their ways, and male behaviour continues to set the standards for the rest of us. The problem is, of course, that as long as this perception goes unchallenged, any attempt to transform the extant gender order will remain a distinctly female prerogative – a Sisyphean task if ever there was one.

Thus, even though it can be argued that much of the mainstream work undertaken in linguistics has constituted a study of male norms of interaction, it is nonetheless essential to discriminate between men as unelected representatives of humanity, on the one hand, and as constructed, gendered individuals, on the other. We need to differentiate between the *implicit* and *explicit* study of masculinity. To me, it seems inevitable that if it is male power we wish to contest, then it is all aspects of the male order that we must comprehend. Though all feminist work is ultimately (and rightfully) concerned with the effects on women of life within a patriarchal world order, I would argue that to concentrate exclusively on women and femininity is insufficient. What is needed *in addition* is informed study of the mechanisms of oppression, that is, of the specific ways in which men construct a world which so manifestly excludes and undermines women. How else can such structures be contested? And whether feminists find the prospect of such work attractive or interesting is perhaps secondary – it must be conceded that the construction of the extant gender order takes place frequently (though not exclusively) in all-male contexts.

To propose, as a feminist, that masculinity should form an integral part of feminist research is not uncontroversial. Is there not already enough dubious literature on masculinity 'in crisis'? Is it not the case that too much understanding of men will diminish the struggle for equality as the concept of the 'oppressor' gradually slips out of focus? Surely such work is a waste of precious feminist energy and resources? As Christine Griffin (1989) has convincingly argued, the answer to feminist methodological dilemmas by no means rests with the burgeoning field of 'men's studies', and in her biting review of three related publications, she illustrates how many male academics working on masculinity have sustained a remarkable indifference to feminist positions on gender and power relations.

Clearly, these are contentions which must be taken seriously. Nonetheless, I still hope to show how the study of masculinity can provide a vital input where feminist work on *language and gender* is concerned. This is not simply because masculinity might be interesting in itself but, more importantly, because the issues which it raises have significant implications for the way in which we conceptualize the field of language and gender *per se*.

The Structuralist Legacy of Sociolinguistics

So far I have questioned the way in which many linguistic studies, whether mainstream or feminist, appear to have been predicated upon a view of men and women as binary opposites. One outcome of this approach has been the way in which it has been possible to separate the study of men and women so clearly within a discipline which nonetheless conceives of itself in terms of language and *gender*. But why has such work adopted this type of binary model as its theoretical base, and how does this ultimately relate to the study of men and masculinity?

The positing of men and women as opposites, and therefore essentially different, needs to be seen within a much broader tradition in linguistic thinking generally, the roots of which are to be found in structuralist approaches to language. Within the Saussurean paradigm, for example, language is conceptualized in terms of a series of contrasting sounds, which, when linked to form words, still only acquire meaning in the context of their opposition to other lexemes. Language is therefore seen as a closed system generating its meanings internally, and without reference to external influences in the form of 'society'. The 1960s, however, saw a phase where many Anglo-American linguists began to question this notion of language as a closed system (as, indeed, others had before them). Linguists emphasized the need for an approach which would stress the status of language as a living entity used in the real world by real speakers. It was within this emergent tradition of sociolinguistics that many early studies of language and gender were undertaken.

Yet despite a willingness to recognize and explore the relationship between language and society, the new discipline of sociolinguistics was still firmly grounded in the structuralist tradition. The early work of William Labov (1966), for example, was primarily concerned with the introduction of 'social' variables into quantitative studies, the ultimate aim of which was nonetheless to complete the Chomskyan project of generating a finite set of rules for a finite set of grammatically acceptable sentences (Chomsky, 1965). For many, 'the social' remained little more than a 'bolt-on' element to be used in the formulation of such 'variable rules'.

Thus, even though the new sociolinguistics undoubtedly questioned the concept of language as a totally closed system, it continued to perpetuate the view of language as something fundamentally different, and so separate from, society. This binary opposition was underpinned by variationist studies, which attempted to correlate the use of linguistic variables, on the one hand, with the social characteristics of their speakers, on the other. Furthermore, *language* remained the primary focus, with social factors integrated only insofar as they might 'explain away' that which could not be accounted for within the language system itself. Needless to say, such an approach is incapable of addressing the possibility of a more complex view of language and society, where society might be characterized in terms of a dialectical relationship with language. This would be more typical of the work of Marxist and some post-structuralist theorists as well as 'critical discourse' analysts such as Norman Fairclough (1989, 1992a, 1992b).[3]

With hindsight, it would seem that early work on language and gender might have benefited from an acuter awareness of these kinds of theoretical issues. Even for those researchers for whom gender, rather than language, may have constituted the point of departure, there does not seem to have been very much concern with the intricacies of theorizing gender itself. Of greater import has been the way in which gender could be used to explain variation in what are essentially linguistic phenomena. This, in turn, has entailed a simplified understanding of gender as it relates to language, characterized by the view: if women talk one way, then men must do the opposite. It is only when thinking in these terms, I believe, that it is possible to align not only the use of isolated phonological variables to a single sex, but ultimately whole discourse genres such as 'gossip' to women.

As both Toril Moi (1985) and Chris Weedon (1987) have made patently clear, however, excessive preoccupation with male/female difference always has its roots in essentialist notions of gender. For women and men to be opposites, they must, of course, be different. The problem is that it is not only mainstream researchers, but also many feminist theorists working on language and gender, who have remained quite comfortable with notions of essential womanhood. This is evident from those studies concerned with the identification of a 'typically female language' or 'genderlect'. Yet although such feminists would be unlikely to defend the way in which biological difference is used to justify social inequality, the celebration of the 'essentially female' and/or the 'female subculture' comes remarkably close in theoretical terms to the very ideas which are used to oppress women.[4] As Moi argues with specific reference to language and gender research: 'Politically, this projection of male and female as unquestioned essences is surely always dangerous for feminists: if any sex difference were ever to be found it could always (and always would) be used against us, largely to prove that some particularly unpleasant activity is "natural" for women and alien to men' (1985, p. 154).

To put it simply, an over-celebration of the essentially female always runs the risk of appropriation by the oppressor, who is inevitably quite comfortable with such conceptualizations of gender.

This is because they can easily be distorted to uphold the most mysogynistic adage of all: *Vive la différence*. It is precisely for this reason that it comes as no surprise to discover an equally strong tradition of maintaining binary concepts of gender within certain sectors of 'men's studies'.

'Men's Studies' – The Inexpressive Man and Other Stories . . .

Whilst masculinity remains relatively unexplored in linguistics, its problematization within the social sciences led to the emergence of a new field of research in the 1970s, now generally referred to as 'men's studies'.[5] This predominantly *male* interest in masculinity can be seen as a response to critiques of male power afforded by women's studies, on the one hand, and gay studies, on the other. Although the various influences from beyond the confines of academe (e.g. therapy/men's consciousness-raising groups) should not be overlooked, such work has frequently been located within such disciplines as sociology and cultural studies (Brittan, 1989; Connell, 1987, 1995; Easthope, 1986; Edley and Wetherell, 1995; Hearn, 1992; Morgan, 1992; Segal, 1990; Seidler, 1989).

But despite the wealth of literature now available, it would be unrealistic to overlook the considerable scepticism of a number of academics towards any attempt to develop a new field of study which focuses specifically on men and masculinity. Inevitably, any move towards men's studies is viewed with concern by many feminists engaged in 'women's studies' as long as they must continue to fight for institutional recognition. Given that feminists still struggle to obtain – and maintain – the limited resources available for their own work *on women*, they have every reason to be anxious about the potential 'siphoning off' of those resources by men keen to 'get in on the act' (Griffiths, 1992). The weight of this concern is underpinned by historical experience: white, heterosexual men have a better track record when it comes to monopolizing the means of academic production. As Christine Griffin (1989) has convincingly demonstrated, such monopolization does not cease merely because masculinity has become the object of study.

Robert Connell (1995) provides an excellent review of the numerous so-called 'Books about Men' published since the 1970s, showing how much of the popular and academic writing that has appeared on the topic is both dubious in content and anti-feminist in substance. In

Robert Bly's *Iron John* (1990), for example, epithets such as 'Zeus energy' abound, and the concept of male power is marginalized by biological and mythopoetic narratives, which leave little scope for feminist contestation. Men are called upon to reclaim their masculinity, and reassert their innate and essential difference from women. Even in those texts where masculinity is seen as bearing some relation to the social order, men frequently emerge as either 'victims' of their own male roles or, worse still, of feminist castration threats.

Indeed, in the limited coverage of masculinity within linguistics, the notion of men as victims of their own social roles is already present. Consider, for example, the complete quotation from Dell Hymes, cited only partially in the introduction to this chapter:

> A focus on women brings to light an aspect of language in social life that has its counterpart for men. *Pre-emption of the 'serious' sphere of life by a certain style of 'maleness' is not without its cost for many men.* The association of male creativity in the arts with effeminacy is a well-known instance. The channelling of the range of human attributes into stereotypes for a 'lady' and a 'man' *harms identity and individuality for many of both sexes,* as the younger generation widely recognizes. 'Men's language' needs study too. (Hymes in Lakoff, 1973, p. 79 – my italics)

Though such a call may not be the product of an explicitly anti-feminist perspective, it is precisely this kind of claim which many feminists fear as the upshot of excessive preoccupation with men and masculinity. The pressure of gender roles, so the argument goes, places not only women but also men under torturous strain, denying *both* sexes the freedom to express their true needs and desires. Men, too, are casualties of a society dominated by the competitive masculine ethos.

The notion of men's suffering the constraints of their own prohibitive gender roles also relates to one of the few claims regarding a typical male verbal style. Men, it is proposed, are unable to express their emotions with the same lucidity as women due to the pressure of a patriarchal society which demands that they appear rational and unemotional (see Seidler, 1989). If only they could free themselves of such constraints, men too could be more contented and fulfilled human beings. Yet as Jack Sattel rightly points out in one of the rare early pieces on language and masculinity: 'What better way is there to exercise power than *to make it appear* that *all* one's behaviour seems to be the result of unemotional rationality. Being impersonal and inexpressive lends to one's decisions and position an apparent autonomy and "rightness"' (1983, p. 120 – author's own italics). Deborah

Cameron similarly dismisses this 'male confessionalist' view as the 'Women can't vote/Men can't cry' syndrome, finding it both 'trivial and banal' (1992a, p. 77).

If one is to make a plea for the study of language and masculinity, it is important to consider why the idea of men's own emotional torment is problematical from a feminist point of view. One obvious – though superficial – objection is to the idea of men's suffering the consequences of a social order of which they are constitutive agents. At a simple level, there is nothing to prevent men from changing if they are so dissatisfied with the roles 'prescribed' to them. The reality is more likely to be that, in doing so, they have far too much to lose in terms of the privileges enjoyed within patriarchy. This is also why the concept of a 'men's movement' is so misleading. As Jack Sattel emphasizes: 'Men are not oppressed *as men*, and hence are not in a position to be liberated *as men*' (1983, p. 123 – author's own italics).[6]

But there is a more complex angle to this issue. This is because the idea of the isolated rational male out of touch with his own, more expressive alter ego is politically suspect. The image is one of the emotional male locked away inside his own rational Self, waiting to be teased out by the humanizing forces of his environment (read: women?). Yet this is alarmingly reminiscent of the rationalist ideologies which have characterized male-dominated Western thinking since the Enlightenment. Indeed, it is the very fissure that obtains between the rational and the emotional, Self and Other, the public and private, which has traditionally been employed in the construction of male power and the concomitant oppression of women. We are dealing with the one mechanism which has been used, above all others, to define women as emotional, irrational beings in order to exclude them from the public domain, and confine them to the private sphere of the family and domesticity (see Brittan, 1989; Morgan, 1992).

This does not mean to say, of course, that the opposition of the rational and emotional does not also have very real, and sometimes problematical, consequences for men. The fact that such a dichotomy exists, and may influence some men's perceptions of the roles open to them, cannot be ignored. What is important is the relationship between the dichotomization of the rational and emotional, on the one hand, and the construction of gender, on the other. Thus, feminist approaches are (or should be) concerned with the *politicization* of this dichotomy, demonstrating the way in which it functions as an instrument of men's power vis-à-vis women. However, the confessionalist view within men's studies problematizes the rational/emotional divide not in terms of male power over women, but reclaims it as a source of men's own oppression within the extant gender order. In doing so, it *depoliticizes* the very mechanism which has defined and limited women so severely across the centuries.

To a certain extent, it comes as no surprise that much of the literature on masculinity is in the business of implicitly legitimizing, rather than explicitly challenging, the gendered status quo. This occurs primarily where writers are unable or unwilling to work with the idea of gender as power relations. What is interesting is the strategy employed in such cases. Thus, the *Iron John*-type study calls upon men to reclaim the identity which has been savaged by feminism – an identity which ultimately resides in *essential* masculinity. This essence of the masculine, it is argued, is rooted in natural or biological states. And the problem with such pre-determined states is, of course, that it is meaningless to contest them. So when men and masculinity come under attack, it is clear who or what is at fault – not the objects of criticism, but its perpetrators. It does not really matter whether this anti-feminist agenda is framed within structuralist, psychoanalytic or mythopoetic discourses. The issue is simple: difference is used to justify inequality and, in the struggle to maintain power, men must assert, and reassert, their innate and essential distinction from women.

There's More than One Kind of Man – Pluralizing Masculinity

Fortunately, not all studies of masculinity have been based on the kind of essentialist and/or anti-feminist approaches discussed so far. Indeed, there is a strong tradition of writing on men within which the rejection of such views is central (Brittan, 1989; Connell, 1987, 1995; Morgan, 1992; Segal, 1990). The main concern of anti-essentialist approaches is then to deconstruct the notion of a single, distinctive form of masculinity across time and space. Instead, theorists emphasize the nature of masculinity as socially constructed, highly contextualized, hence fluid and variable.

Thus, in the same way that feminist theorists have stressed the diversity of female experience by showing, in particular, how the concept of 'woman' cannot be divorced from issues of class, race and sexuality, the same can be said of masculinity. Work within pro-feminist approaches to masculinity has explored men in terms of 'multiple subjectivities', and this has led writers to abandon the idea of 'masculinity' in the singular, in preference for the pluralized 'masculinities'. The concept of 'male power' is then dislodged by the notion of 'hegemonic' or 'hierarchical' masculinities, perhaps best characterized as those forms of masculinity able to marginalize and dominate not only women, but also other men, on the grounds of, say, class, race and/or sexuality (Connell, 1987).

According to this view of masculinities, where gender identities and power relations are seen as highly contextualized practices, it becomes rather more difficult to make clear and generalizable statements about how men are, or what they do. This is even more problematical when we look for inherent distinctions between the practices of men, on the one hand, and women, on the other. Indeed, it is evident from the issues raised by the various contributions to this volume that whatever the relationship between language and masculinity, it is not as simple or straightforward as might originally have been assumed. Probably the two most important realizations are that men do differ from one another in their use of language, and that the way men employ language does not simply constitute a mirror image of whatever it is we think we understand by 'women's language'.

However, the notion of variable, contextualized 'masculinities', and the difficulty in formulating generalizations regarding men's behaviour, may seem additionally vexing for feminists. This is because the very acknowledgement of diversity might be adduced by some as evidence of the fact that there is no clear case of men's oppression of women. This is especially problematical where we can see obvious examples of men's exerting power over one another. Ultimately, it might be argued that if men oppress each other, why should women complain? It becomes apparent in this context, as Nigel Edley and Margaret Wetherell (1995) point out, how the more simplified notion of generalized and generalizable forms of male power has certain advantages for feminism. Too much understanding may seem like 'letting men off the hook' (p. 195), such that, superficially, there is a lot to be said for holding on to your 'all-purpose male oppressor'.

But good research is not easy, and simplistic explanations will usually reveal themselves to be unsatisfactory. It is with this in mind that both Lynne Segal (1990) and Robert Connell (1995) have argued in favour of a more complex view of masculinities. The key to theorizing hegemonic power, they argue, rests precisely with an understanding of the differences between men as a group, and the way in which these differences work together as a coherent system of power: 'To recognize diversity in masculinities is not enough. We must also recognize the *relations* between the different kinds of masculinity: relations of alliance, dominance and subordination. These relationships are constructed through practices that exclude and include, that intimidate, exploit, and so on. There is a gender politics within masculinity' (Connell, 1995, p. 37 – author's own italics).

According to Robert Connell, then, it is not so much a question of appreciating that there is variation, but of understanding the way in which such variation plays a part in the overall construction of hegemonic masculinity. This is, in fact, precisely what both Deborah Cameron and Scott Fabius Kiesling do in their respective chapters in this volume. For example, in chapter 3, Deborah Cameron is able to show how, through straight men's characterization and oppression of gay men, heterosexual masculinity is constructed as the norm. On the other hand, whilst Scott Kiesling's fraternity members in chapter 4 are using power to gain control over other men, they are doing so in preparation for a world beyond college, that is, a professional environment in which they anticipate dominance and control over others, presumably women and working-class men. Furthermore, in a study of the way in which male DJs try to justify the lack of women on daytime radio, Rosalind Gill (1993) shows how the discursive strategies employed by men are more than just varied and flexible – they are frequently inconsistent and contradictory. Not only do the male broadcasters offer different explanations for the inherent sexism operating in their place of work, but the same men contradict themselves in the course of their own accounts.

Thus, it becomes apparent how flexibility, inconsistency and contradiction must not be seen as irritations which distract from feminist accounts of hegemonic male power. As Beverley Skeggs (1993) has argued, of central importance is the recognition that the obvious fragmentation of male subjectivities across time and space, and the differing structural mediations thereof, in no way dissipates the power that men enjoy over women (as some post-modern theorists would have us believe . . .). There is no underlying reason why *men as a group* should be linguistically homogeneous. And there is no inherent reason why the discursive strategies used by *individual men* should be consistent – either from one situation, or even from one utterance to the next. On the contrary, such tenacity would be counter-productive. This is quite simply because rigid, monolithic and predictable systems of power are far more open to attack than the kinds of 'flexible sexism' described by Rosalind Gill (1993).

Gender is a Verb

From the moment we begin to explore language in terms of men as well as women, we realize the futility of searching for simplistic

ls between language, on the one hand, and gender, on the
By painting the other half of the picture as it were, it becomes
clear that there are probably very few generalizations which can be
made about formal, *structural* aspects of the language of one sex as
opposed to the other. The status of traditional binary oppositions
such as language/gender and masculinity/femininity is, therefore,
severely in need of recalibration. But does this imply that there is no
longer anything meaningful to be said about men, women and language? I believe the answer is no, although we may need to re-think
the fundamental research questions we wish to ask.

One of the main points stressed by pro-feminist texts that have
dealt with men is the way in which concepts of masculinity and femininity are not in fact opposites, but *mutual* constructs. Arthur Brittan
(1989), for example, draws upon psychoanalytic and post-structuralist theories to elucidate this view. Within the symbolic order of language, he argues, women are defined by men in terms of their own
negative relation to a positive male construct, signified by the phallus. But whereas women have traditionally been constructed as
'minus male', what has been frequently overlooked is the way in
which masculinity is equally dependent on femininity for the purpose of self-definition. Thus, it is not only the feminine which is
defined *ex negativo*, but also the masculine. This means that one
important element in the construction of heterosexual masculinity
will be the perpetual denial, subjugation and exclusion of the feminine – as symbolized by both women and homosexual men.

In theoretical terms then, although we are still dealing with a view
of masculinity and femininity as somehow *different*, the relationship
between the two is dialectical – neither construct is ultimately feasible
without the other. This dialectical view of gender also has important
implications for the apparent immutability of gender identities. This
is because, if masculinity is constructed at least partly in terms of its
opposition to femininity, the very omnipresence of the feminine
means that those men who have a stake in hegemonic masculinity
must constantly reassert their symbolic opposition to femininity in
order to confirm their own sense of masculinity. By implication,
therefore, gender identities can never be complete. Masculinity and
femininity are not character traits or social roles which are learned
during childhood and adolescence, and which are fixed and intransi-
gent in adult life. Instead, they are ongoing social processes dependent upon systematic restatement, a process which is variously
referred to as 'performing gender' or 'doing identity work'.
According to Arthur Brittan: 'Every social situation [...] is an occasion for identity work' (1989, p. 36). Since we can realistically assume

that virtually every 'social situation' and 'occasion for identity work' which he has in mind will somehow involve language, the centrality of linguistic issues for theorizing gender is indisputable.)

Thus, language does not simply mirror gender; it helps constitute it – it is one of the means by which gender is enacted (bodily practices, for example, are another). In the same way that the anthropologist Brian Street (1993) has argued that 'culture' is not simply a state of being but a series of practices, the same can be said of gender: to borrow his linguistic analogy, gender is not a noun, it is a *verb*. Moreover, when exploring the linguistic processes involved in the construction of gendered identities, language need not be defined in the narrow sense of the spoken, *parole*-oriented construct which has typified much sociolinguistic work – in itself another artificially imposed in binary opposition. As several chapters in this volume demonstrate, the written or visual text is an equally valid arena for 'doing masculinity' (see Johnson and Finlay, chapter 7; Neff, chapter 9; Talbot, chapter 10; Heywood, chapter 11; Meinhof, chapter 12; see also Mills, 1995).

If we accept that language is one of the resources drawn upon in the construction of gender, and that gendered identities are themselves ongoing processes, this has important implications for the way in which we theorize the question of *difference* where the language of men and women is concerned. This is because, if gender identities are not fixed, then it is difficult to imagine how the linguistic resources used in their construction can be the same from one situation to the next. What cannot be overlooked is that performances of gender will certainly involve many men and women drawing upon linguistic resources which they *perceive* to be appropriate to their gender group – in the same way that the two sexes may dress in a manner which conforms to gender expectations. This is why, over time, ways of speaking or dressing will come to be associated with one sex or the other, although they may, of course, be resisted by some groups or individuals. In this particular sense, the binary oppositions traditionally associated with masculinity and femininity are very real, and highly pertinent to any discussion of gendered behaviour. Thus, men who invest heavily in hegemonic masculinity will inevitably try to talk in ways which they consider to be typical of, and appropriate to, men. More significantly, perhaps, they will also aim to avoid those ways of talking which they perceive to be typically feminine (see Coates, chapter 6), or typically feminine in certain contexts (see Cameron, chapter 3). However, the important point regarding the gendered meanings which become associated with certain linguistic resources over time is that they are *not* inherent in the structures of language themselves. We are able to say this for two reasons using examples from this volume.

First, it is possible for different meanings to be attached to the same linguistic resources. So whereas gossip has traditionally been characterized as a female genre, both Deborah Cameron (chapter 3) and Sally Johnson and Frank Finlay (chapter 7) illustrate that men do know how to talk in ways which can be labelled as gossip – if the researcher chooses to do so. Similarly, whereas women's and girls' talk has typically been classified as cooperative, Roger Hewitt (chapter 2) shows how men and boys can be seen to talk in ways which can also be described as cooperative. All in all, it would seem that it is perfectly possible for men and women to do the same thing, but for it to be labelled and valued differently – an idea which is familiar, for example, to anyone engaged in the struggle for equal pay.

The second reason why the gendered meanings associated with certain linguistic resources cannot be considered intrinsic to those forms is because we can see examples of how both meanings and forms may change. Thus, Vivian de Klerk (chapter 8) describes the way in which the use of expletives and slang (traditionally male linguistic territory) can no longer be considered a typically masculine way of talking, given that females have increasingly come to use such forms over the years. On the other hand, Joan Pujolar i Cos (chapter 5) shows how, in some situations, individuals and groups can actively intervene in the construction of the meanings which are attributed to certain types of language.

I have thus argued why I believe the conceptualization of gender identities as ongoing social processes to be central to the study of language and masculinity. But this emphasis on fluidity also has a bearing on the political stance which might be adopted towards masculinities in more general terms. On the one hand, this is because working with a notion of masculinities as non-fixed brings with it a possibility of change. If men's identities evolve (as they clearly do), then there is at least some degree of hope that this will be for the better where women are concerned. On the other hand – and rather than end on a note of unadulterated feminist optimism – it is important to consider the same phenomenon from a different angle. Hegemonic masculinity, and the linguistic resources drawn upon in its construction, are highly contextualized, inconsistent and unpredictable. However, this is not because men are necessarily in the business of relinquishing power, but because of their struggle to consolidate it . . .

Conclusion

Chris Weedon has argued that: '[feminist] theory must also be able to account for resistance to change' (1987, p. 9). In this chapter, I have tried to show how the study of masculinities is one way of exploring such resistance. To this end, I have argued that a focus on the highly variable ways in which masculine identities are formed, and in particular the role of language in the construction of those identities, is a worthwhile feminist project.

But linguists who choose to pursue this topic should, I believe, also be prepared to go a step further. An important aim will be to learn more about the precise discursive strategies employed by men in their attempts to resist change, and hold on to power. Are these strategies so highly contextualized that there are no meaningful generalizations that can be made? Or will it be possible to recognize discursive typologies, which, even though they differ in their localized character, can still be identified as part of an overall system of power?

Whatever the answer to these questions, one thing is clear: in order to pursue them, we must abandon the search for trivial structural reflections of whatever we believe to be typically 'male' or 'female' language. There is no such thing as a 'men's language'. This does not mean that the notion of 'difference' has no part to play in the study of language and gender. But it would undoubtedly be more appropriate, as Deborah Cameron (1992b) has argued, to shift the emphasis from 'gender difference' to 'the difference gender makes'. What we really need is to know more about the complex role played by 'difference' *in the construction of* 'dominance'. The study of language and masculinities is not simply one way of exploring such a role – I find it difficult to envisage how this can be done *without* looking at men.

Notes

1 See Cynthia Fuchs Epstein (1988) for a general discussion of this issue within feminist theory, and Sally Johnson (1995) for a critique with specific reference to sociolinguistics.
2 See Deborah Cameron (1995a) for a detailed survey and analysis of what she refers to as 'Verbal hygiene for women'. Above all, Cameron shows how this kind of professional training has created the ideal market, that is to say, one which can never be saturated because women will always be judged (and dismissed) as *women*, irrespective of their ability to adapt their use of language. Furthermore, such training has the advantage of placing the responsibility for gender inequality in the workplace firmly

back on the shoulders of individual women, who must then take the blame for their own inability to achieve.

3   See Glyn Williams (1992) for a trenchant critique of sociolinguistic methods from a sociological point of view.

4   See Diana Fuss (1989) for a more detailed discussion of essentialism as it relates to feminist debates on gender difference.

5   See Robert Connell (1995) for a survey of work on masculinity before the 1970s, particularly within the context of psychoanalysis in the first half of the twentieth century.

6   This is also why Robert Connell argues that where men do become able and willing to question their own position of power vis-à-vis women, this is most likely to occur within a framework of what he refers to as 'alliance politics' (1995, pp. 225–43). Like Jack Sattel, he does not see a 'men's movement' as the locus of potential change since the only factor which unites men in such a context is their collective status as the object of feminist criticism. Instead, Connell proposes, men are probably more able to reflect upon their power *as men* within the framework of other political struggles in which they might engage, e.g. class, ethnic, environmental etc.

2

'Box-out' and 'Taxing'

Roger Hewitt

Introduction

The points at which individualistic wants come into conflict with a
set of rules designed to serve some collectivity can be revealing about
the systems humans set up and their social dynamic. The game that
this chapter describes, known as 'box-out' and 'taxing', was created
by 14-year-old boys in a south London secondary school.[1] It is extra-
ordinary for a number of reasons. As it was created more or less col-
lectively but not completed, it was in a constant state of refinement,
revision and – because it developed a certain *systemic* quality – exploration. It had not stabilized and perhaps never would. Thus, although
the broad outline of the game, a number of rules and certain rituals,
were generally agreed, there was also much fluidity of interpretation
and innovation, where individual players would attempt to establish
for themselves special advantages. Some of these attempts were of
naked egos, wilfully, and against any claim to reasonableness, 'trying
it on' with the collectivity and running foul of the brute fact that, just
as a street of car drivers would soon get into trouble if they abandoned any form of cooperation and obedience to rules, so some level
of coordination needs to be in place in any game or other system for
individuals to derive benefit within it.

Conflicts between an individual's self-interested wishes and the
constraints of the system, delineate an underlying split in the nature
of selves-at-play. It is the split between what we might call the 'self-
driven self' and the 'player-self'. The former may, in the case of most
players of most games, remain tactfully out of the picture, while the
player-self will engage in all those activities which a particular game

delineates and permits to the individual player. The theoretical existence of the self-driven, autonomous and essentially asocial self may,
perhaps, always be left to one side when thinking about the ways in
which a game is a *social* activity, but not always, and certainly not in
the case of the game I describe here. Autonomous, asocial egos were
often evident as ghostly forms present in the room as the game these
boys had created was explored and elaborated.

However, the ludic – and sometimes ludicrous – explorations of
the game-system did not always or only display Man's fallen nature.
What was even more evident was how social constraint itself was
constructed by the boys. The little rituals, verbal formulae developed
and rapidly extrapolated as shared currency, the system of collective
deliberation on disputes etc., all served collective ends, regulating
behaviours and setting parameters within which the legitimate
player-selves could function. Thus there were (1) the player-selves,
(2) the collectivity of player-selves and (3) the Big Bad Wolf of
the autonomous, asocial ego circling round in the background.
Whether the Big Bad Wolf behind games and systems is essentially or
even characteristically male is a question that will not be addressed
here. Instead, I shall consider the extent to which the categories
traditionally employed in the characterization of male and female
interaction are relevant to the boys' talk that surrounds this particular
game.

Cooperation and Competitiveness

Before proceeding to describe the game in more detail, I will make a
small excursion into a set of more general issues relating to language,
and especially to face-to-face communication in talk. Although within
the liberal paradigm of sociolinguistics a moral/political commentary
can often be heard in the background on the use of the terms 'cooperative' and 'competitive', the discussion on these issues (often asserting women's cooperativeness and men's individualism) could have
benefited – both politically and academically – from sharper definition (Coates, 1989; Goodwin, 1980; Kalcik, 1975; Maltz and Borker,
1982; Sheldon, 1993). When such a case is made, the difference
between the cooperation that is necessary to enter into and sustain
talk, and cooperative *style* in talk, is often given short shrift, and, as
has been argued by Graddol and Swann (1989) and by Cameron et al.
(1989), discriminations made *within styles of talk* relating to different
forms of 'cooperation' tend to get ironed out (see also Cameron,

chapter 3; Johnson, chapter 1). 'Cooperation' becomes more a moral/political term than an analytical one.

It is perhaps too obvious to say that there are many ways in which, quite outside the domain of language, cooperative behaviour is observable. Very demonstrative warmth – hugging, for example – is one way of showing support. The asking of friendly questions and keeping up a flow of 'hmms' and other 'minimal responses' are kinds of linguistic hugging (Fishman, 1983; Hirschman, 1994; Leet-Pellegrini, 1980). Here interconnectedness and cooperation are being loudly affirmed. On the other hand, 'cooperation' can also be performed by demonstrably *distancing oneself from any potential implication of self-assertion*. 'Modesty', for example, would be the moral face of this cooperative virtue. Performing the cooperative by undermining, down-playing, attempting to delete one's self as ego rather than as member, might be achieved through hedges, apologies, qualifications and other mitigations of self and self-responsibility; the leaving open of opportunities for others to speak; inviting others to speak and employing facilitative tags. It is linguistically evident in mitigations of many kinds, including the 'epistemic modals' identified by Jennifer Coates (1989), yielding utterances such as 'I believe you may not be entirely right about that', and 'I think it's time to go'.

Already, therefore, it is apparent that 'cooperativeness' can be stylistically enacted by either asserting the collectivity, the 'We' of even just two interlocutors, or by denying the differentiated 'I'. The negative and positive aspects to coordination clearly also relate to the description of politeness phenomena by Brown and Levinson (1987), although the categories described here are more inclusive than the Brown and Levinson schema, and do not rely on the concept of 'face'. I call these social dimensions to utterance the 'declarative' (I) and the 'coordinative' (We).[2] In different guises and aspects they have been discussed many times. It is an interesting attribute of each dimension that it can be enacted by assertion *or* by the denial of its opposite. Thus, just as the coordinative could be performed both by assertion of the mutuality of interactional talk or by a denial of the declarative, as described above, so the declarative (self-assertive) dimension can be enacted both directly in, for example, bald, unqualified and unmitigated statements; in emphatics, exclamations, imperatives, topic initiation; certain kinds of interruptions, 'long turns' etc., and by *denials of the coordinative dimension* in ways such as: failing to respond to or ratify other speakers when face issues may be at stake; the wilful use of socially taboo words in contexts where they are known possibly to give offence; rudeness/insults; challenges, and certain uses of silence – i.e. the withholding or strategic suspension of communication.

It is obvious that all speech has both a declarative dimension – that for which the individual takes sole responsibility, the daring of the high-wire performer extending, step by step above the crowd, the syllables of their exposed being (they might be wrong, foolish, absurd) – and *in the same moment* a coordinative dimension (because the individual is, after all, 'communicating' and not alone). The nuances of interpersonal communication, politeness, camaraderie, cool distancing, etc., are largely built out of the play of these features and the handling of the complex ground of assertion and denial of the declarative and the coordinative.

This social logic could be represented within the following quadrant:

	Declarative	Coordinate
Assert		
Deny		

What might count as an item in any of the available positions could be different for different cultures or different social groups. In some cultures, for example, declarative assertions are performed simultaneously with considerable coordinative assertion: the 'affable command' of the friendly corporate employer. A smile can be doing the coordinative work, while the words can do the rest; or intonation itself might be performing some of the labour. Furthermore, the same item may serve more than one interactional purpose, conveying, say, declarative denial (modesty) and at the same time declarative assertion. Because of the cultural variability of (1) the predominant range of quadrant combinations across interactional contexts, and (2) the communicational *forms* that become the instruments of the different quadrant positions, examples of the ways in which this social logic is performed are necessarily culture-specific and not universal. As Cameron et al. ask: 'How far is it possible to identify a recurrent form – say the tag question, or a rising nucleus – with some specific function or meaning?' They continue:

> It seems to us problematic to suggest that the communicative function of a syntactic form is either invariant or analytically transparent in all cases.

Studies like our own, which deal with natural data, indicate the absolute necessity of considering forms in their linguistic and social context, not in general, and suggest that we should regard multifunctionality as the unmarked case – that is, in real talk most utterances do many things at once. (Cameron et al., 1989, p. 77)

(It is for this reason that ethnographies of communication are able to come closer to interactional meanings than formal linguistic descriptions.)

Where the declarative dimension is performed through the denial of the coordinative (abuse, unacceptably obscene language, refusal to speak, etc.), communicative danger is clearly lurking. Here is the very edge of the communicative system. Such behaviour threatens the breaking off of communication, the abandonment of the game of talk and its willed coherence of Gricean 'cooperation' – in Grice a systemic *not* a moral matter. To use an obscene word directed in hostility at someone is still to be 'in the game' of talk. To use silence pointedly is similarly to communicate. But to be silent and unhearing without intent is not to be in the game of communication at all. Those simple elements of coordination – the reciprocal directing of signs between entities, at the very least (and those other features identified by Goffman (1976) as 'system constraints') – constitute the play and the existence of players. How the game of communication is played, however, the interweave of declarative and coordinative possibilities, includes what Goffman called the 'ritual constraints', the flesh of social particulars.

I theorize the language of both men and women as equally involving the coordinative and declarative dimensions within the realm of the 'ritual constraints' that constitute the social particularity of language use. These are necessary, in-built features of face-to-face communication and operate with regard to interactional (affective) *and* semantic dimensions. (They may also obtain in the theoretically broader dimension of discourse – in the post-Foucaudian sense – but that is a different issue.) One consequence of this is that the surface forms of expression do not necessarily give access to knowledge of which dimension is in play. This means that, for example, cooperative *style* is not necessarily tied to cooperative/coordinative interaction. A brief contrastive example, drawn from research in mathematics and collaborative computer-assisted learning, involving LOGO, may demonstrate the point. In this study, a pair of girls whose modality of interaction was highly mutually cooperative, repeatedly failed to coordinate their efforts to understand a series of maths problems presented to them on the computer. It was not until

the girls fell out with each other and subsequently worked individually that both girls succeeded in making headway with the problems.
By contrast, two boys involved in a similar set of tasks behaved in a
highly competitive way, failing explicitly to acknowledge each
other's contributions to the solution of the problem and behaving as
apparently autonomous individuals, yet analysis of their actual contributions showed a high degree of acceptance of and building upon
each other's utterances (Hoyles and Sutherland, 1989, pp. 159–78).
The coordination of effort was effectively taking place and cooperation being achieved *de facto* through an interactive modality that was
far from 'cooperative'. Thus it is possible that in a given interaction
the cooperative ('We') aspect may be occurring even where an osten-
sibly competitive ('I') aspect appears to be foregrounded. For this reason, simple classifications of interactions into cooperative or
competitive are misleading.

Beyond this stark contrast, how men and women, young/old, people from here/people from there, this person/that person, this person today/this person yesterday, this person with him/this person
with her, etc. *combine* the dimensions of self-assertion and coordination, is where difference is established, and where the social life of
talk has much of its richness. However, the deeper social logic lying
within the contours of this profusion are often difficult to see. The
boys' game that this chapter describes does, in its stumbling, prospective simplicity, capture some powerful dimensions of this dynamic,
permitting a momentary glimpse beneath the puppeteer's cloth at a
social logic that I believe encompasses face-to-face game and face-to-
face communication alike.

The Game

The game, or perhaps it could be called a system of playful
behaviours, that I am going to describe here is one in which (1) individual gain, (2) coordination through sharing a relation to a set of
rules, and (3) the boundaries of the system and of coordination, were
all evident in clear relief. It was never played by girls in the mixed
secondary school where it was recorded. It was made up of two
aspects, the 'box-out' and the 'taxing'. 'Boxing-out' was the practice
of boxing (striking) any item out of another player's hand. The boxer
could then claim possession either of the object boxed or of an
equivalent value in cash. Such a 'box-out' could happen at any time
during the school day and anywhere within the school. A boy could
be writing in class when suddenly his pen might be boxed out of his

hand. The boxer would then call 'box-out!', thus making a formal claim to the nature of the event – it was not an accident; it was not merely to be annoying; it was an act within the game.

The game was not played by all of the boys in the class or year group. The ability to play the game well was said to involve a watchfulness, quickness and opportunism that not all could boast. It was played by approximately thirty of the sixty boys in the year group. These were subdivided into smaller groups of about four to eight members each. Membership was constituted by a pact established through a short ritual in which each boy wishing to join would hook the little finger of either hand with the hooked little finger of one member of the existing group of players. This was referred to as 'joining in'. If a boy no longer wished to be a player he would have to 'join out' using the same ritual. Boys would not usually be members of more than one 'box-out' group.

The 'taxing' part of the game came about whenever a debt incurred through a box-out was not met by a stipulated time. It happened only rarely that a boy boxing an item out of a player's hand wanted to have the object. More normally he would strike the object out, calling 'box-out!', and then add, say, '25 pence by tomorrow', or '50 pence by Wednesday'. Most of the groups allowed three days of grace before the debt had to be paid. If the debtor failed to produce the money at the stated time he would then fall foul of a severe interest system, the 'tax' levied on any debt. This could be something like 10 pence per day while the debt was unpaid, or might itself increase on a daily or weekly basis. Never would boys pay on the spot because they would soon seek an opportunity to box-out the person to whom they owed the money, and thereby remove the debt with a counter-debt. They would alternatively seek to box-out another boy and place *him* in debt, hoping to persuade the second boy to pay and thereby offset the original debt. Those who did not manage this would start to fall into debt during the course of a week and then might gradually slip further as the term progressed. Some boys amassed debts of 'several thousands of pounds' which were then wiped off with a settlement of £3.00 or £5.00. Beside such dramatic cases, most boys sought to end each week owing less than they were owed, so that they would enter the following week ahead. Thus the game did not have visible winners and losers. Rather, the box-out and taxing worked as a total system within which small gains and losses were continually made by all players to some degree. Not all found this process appealing. The following was a discussion between two boys in which Boy B was invited by Boy A to become part of the box-out circle; Boy B declined, giving his reasons:

Episode 1

BOY A: Join in box-out, right?
BOY B: No. It's all right, guv.
BOY A: It's easy to box people out.
BOY B: Then you'll get boxed-out yourself, then there'll be taxes, innit?
BOY A: So? You got three days to pay.
BOY B: Yes, and you've got three days to get boxed-out again and get the amount doubled. I don't play them stupid games, man.

Although Boy B was not interested in box-out, he was a formidable taxer, lending frequently at high interest. He earned a regular if small income from this, and would not put this income at risk from being involved in box-out. However, he was often consulted on appropriate rates of interest by box-out players.

There were several aspects to this game that struck me as intriguing. The first was that the boys who were 'joined in' to the system really did 'pay up' their debts. Real cash, of however small an amount, did change hands at certain points, although this was, as described, as infrequently as the boys could make it. Second – and this is how the game came to my attention in the first place – the game generated an enormous amount of talk of different kinds between the boys, who spent much of their school lunch periods in arguing, disputing and discussing the exact nature of particular box-outs, debts or game rules. The boys believed themselves to have invented the game. They credited the initial idea to one boy in particular, apparently during the previous school year, but all shared some responsibility for its elaboration.[3]

The talk about and within the game comprised, for example, the *ludic performatives* that were part of the game; *arguments* about possible exceptions to general rules; *appeals* by individuals to the group at large for some judgement or opinion concerning a dispute between players, and so on. Then there were the arguing about rates of tax and the endless *pestering* for payment that went on between players. The following are some examples.

Ludic Performatives

The most common performatives were 'box-out!' itself, which accompanied the deed, and a performative to achieve exemption from being boxed-out: 'No box-out. No nothin'. The 'nothin' here referred to other ways of getting something out of someone's hand such as by grabbing – although there was also: 'No grab-out, no nothin!' These kinds of exemptions were sought in particular settings, such as in the school dining hall, or any other context where players could agree they should not be disturbed. There were also some non-standard performatives attempted and disputed. One of these is discussed later in this chapter.

Arguments

Because, in the system as it was created, there were numerous points of possible dispute, an endless range of argument and discussion was generated which was part of the process of attempting to come out on top. Players were continually looking for loopholes which would allow them to outwit or otherwise get the better of the other participants in the system. Arguments seemed endless:

Episode 2

An object is boxed out of B's hand by A.

A: That was in your hand! Box out!
B: Yeah, but it ain't come out.
A: Yes it did, you cheatin' whore!
B: Fuck off. It ain't come out. No way! You owe me five.* It never come out.
A: You're a cheat. You make me sick.

* When a box-out failed the perpetrator incurred a debt of 5 pence to his intended victim.

Frequently disputes were settled by appeals to bystanders who acted as witnesses to a particular box-out or deal struck, or as adjudicators. In the following example Boy B had earlier had a schoolbook grabbed out of his hand. The book got torn in the process and a bystander suggested that the boy who had done the boxing (Boy A) owed Boy B some damages. This matter was left until a little later when a return box-out happened and the roles were reversed. This time the box-out, of a newspaper, was deemed to have failed, although the boxer was not happy to accept this. Boy A returned to the theme of his own original box-out.

Episode 3

A: You still owe me ten, though.
B: Ten?
A: You missed that paper.
B: Yeah.
A: I know what I'll do. I'll just . . .
B: Damages later. Damages. I fuckin' didn't even let go of this. I didn't let go of it!

At this point two bystanders (C and D) also entered the discussion with judgements and suggestions of various kinds aimed at settling the dispute:

C: But it's not your book. It's not your book anyway, is it?
B: No, but it was like that, right? (*demonstrating*) He didn't box it out. He just pulled this off it.
C: So? It's still boxed-out, innit? It still came out your hand.
D: It's true, Gary. Right, if you do a pen, right, and the top, and you . . .
C: (*to B regarding his failed/disputed box-out*) Don't charge for it. Don't charge a thing for it. Try him. Try him.
B: Yeah. Call it evens.
A: Yeah. You just owe me seven then, right? (*from a previous occasion*)

It was very common for appeals to bystanders to be made, both for judgements and to act as witnesses to events or agreements. Thus an agreement about a reciprocal payment of debt was followed by an appeal to the onlookers by one of the parties:

Episode 4

A: Did you all hear that?
B: Yeah.
C: Yeah.
D: Yeah.

This kind of thing was routine and it was clear that however much disputing took place between parties, the acceptance of the collectivity, especially in some public way, as with the above, was treated as vital to the system.

Sometimes hypothetical cases were also discussed in this public way. For example:

Episode 5

A: (*to the group in general*): If you box-out money out of somebody's hand can you keep it?
B: Yes.
C: No.
D: No. It ain't a box-out.
A: But if you box money out of someone's hand, you ain't gonna charge 'im 5 pence, you're gonna keep it . . .

Empty classrooms during the lunch breaks took on the aspect almost of a public forum for the hearing of disputes, discussion of the applications of rules, and the testing of suggested innovations by the assembled sages.

Pestering

At a more person-to-person level was the talk relating to particular debts. Those who owed money became subjected to an endless stream of pestering and wearing down. When I asked what would happen if someone refused to pay I was told that 'things would start to go missing. Expensive things, like coats and bags', but my informants knew of no instances of this kind of thing actually happening as people generally did pay up. Indeed, the system seemed to flourish on the voluntary, widespread circulation of many small amounts of cash, varying from between 10 pence to £3.00 on average, sometimes extending to larger amounts of £5.00 and above. The following was a fairly typical pestering episode:

Episode 6

A: I want my money. I'm taxin' you.
B: Why you so happy for?
A: I said 'dinner time', didn't I?
B: So what?
A: What do you mean 'So what?' It's dinner time. Give me my money. (*To an onlooker*): Look at how long I gave him. Over Saturday and Sunday to raise 25 pence and he can't do it. You give me 25p! (*B pays him ten pence.*)

> And the other. And the rest. And the rest. You owe me 15. I'm taxin' ya.
> It's not half.
> B: I'm givin' you that.
> A: 15 pence by tomorrow.

When the talk really became revealing, however, was when the constraints of the system, which these boys had themselves set up, bore
in upon individual players. Here a basic conflict would emerge
between the wants of the individual player, and the viability of the
game-system to support both the collective coherence and the reasonable level of personal gain that made participation of value to individuals. There are a number of issues with regard to this that are
worth dwelling on. The bringing together of the box-out component
with the debt/taxing element constituted the game as a mechanism
for the conversion of quick wits and dexterity into cash. The period
between the box-out and the payment of the debt, however, was
what brought the two aspects into a systemic union, for it was here
that the offsetting counter-box-outs occurred, and the web of debting
relationships was made more complex. A system was called into
being which, because of the interlocking of agreed rules around
shared competitive objectives, was, to some extent, independent of
the will of the players to shape.

There was, however, no universally accepted concept of what was
and was not negotiable. The unnegotiable, objective part of the system was discovered continually, the limits of negotiability tested by
argument and discussion. Here what was obviously objective to some
players was not obvious to others – especially those *so* concerned
with the individualistic, competitive drive to best the others, that
they believed implicitly that it was *all* negotiable. Some, in other
words, understood the 'system constraints' better than others. At the
same time players progressively learned about the constraining features, and some practices found consistently to lead to trouble
became, by consensus, modified by the introduction of new rules.

Disputes, other than those relating to matters of fact (whether such
and such a thing happened etc.), might have one of two outcomes.
Either a claim was deemed to be consistent with the basic constraints
of the game and therefore was permissible, or at least open to negoti-
ation with individual players, or it was found to be inconsistent with
the basic constraints.

Such a case as the latter was one in which a boy who was a sea-
soned player attempted to create a special set of terms unique to himself with the group of boys with whom he was already 'joined in'. He

attempted this by the utterance of an improvised performative – 'Join in whatever I choose' – which he claimed established his right to charge whatever he chose for a box-out. As too high a charge for box-outs had been a feature of the game when it was first invented and had been abandoned by general consent, this individualistic move was doubly unacceptable. It was obvious that part of the viability of the game resided in the fact that the basic reason anyone might have for playing was the *reasonable hope* that he might come out on top. This *reasonable hope* must be equally available to all players. The attempted new condition, in being only available to one player, was clearly inconsistent with this constraint.

A second rather different example of behaviour that was inconsistent with an underlying constraint of the game was the threat of violence as a sanction to ensure payment of a debt. Such a threat contradicted the voluntary nature of the game. The game could only be played if players agreed that when an object was knocked out, a debt was incurred. The debt was only incurred by agreement, not by any right beyond the game. The practice of collecting debts by nagging and pestering until payment was made rested on the shared knowledge that if people did not pay up, the game could not exist and no one could profit. The imperative, therefore, lay in the mutual, overall benefit to players, despite any particular setback or disadvantage. If a player was threatened with real violence if he did not pay, he could simply make the choice that the game was not worth it. He could leave as voluntarily as he had joined.[4]

Although, therefore, a certain air of menace sometimes pervaded pestering episodes when repayments were being exacted, this was actually more part of the drama of the pestering, a certain style of pressure and a part of the fictional structure of the game.[5] Boys foolish enough to take themselves seriously when occupying this theatrical role found themselves ridiculed by the chorus of sages. The acceptance of the boundary of play was itself part of the culture of the school within which the game existed.

The kind of inconsistency inherent in threats of real violence is clearly different from the 'box-out whatever I could choose' example, which related to the internal coherence of the game. The threat of violence related to the status of the game *as a game* for, although adult debts incurred in gambling might be subject to sanctions of this kind in some circles, the idea of actually using violence contradicted common sense about school games and how widely any debt incurred through such a game would be recognized beyond its community of players.

These two kinds of constraints, the first perhaps akin to Goffman's notion of 'system constraints', the second, more circumstantial, to do with the cultural context of the game, were, despite their differences, part of that objective state of affairs with which players had to come to terms or, if they did not, become involved in continual friction.[6]

Constructing the Social

If one were to sketch the different modalities of 'the social' evident in this game, one unavoidable reference point would have to be the ferocious levels of competitive individualism it displays. This aspect is evident in many very obvious ways, starting with the act of box-ing-out itself. This last would be true of any non-team competitive game, of course, but many of the other features would not. In looking at much of the talk we find it given over to the following: re-inter-preting rules; bending rules; creating/trying to create new rules – all of these being attempts to influence the grounds of play to gain advantage in specific transactions. It also includes: threatening; argu-ing against the legitimacy of other claims; pestering for payment; and setting tax-rates. These constitute an exploration of achieving the maximum gain for the self that is commensurate with the continued existence of the game, but as the game was also what created the pos-sibility of individual gain there was, at one level at least, one dimen-sion of 'the social' that was generated from individual need. What this schoolboy culture had here created was, therefore, a mechanism in which the simplest basis of social coherence was derived from the collective exploration of individual gain.[7]

The game also had an associated imagery that drew on connota-tions of the adult world of the street hustler. The basis of the box-out itself was the exploitation of the momentary weakness or inattention of others. Furthermore, the severity of the taxing system was based on the principle that the debtor had no choice, although the three-day rule balanced a limited amount of benefit with the heavy penalties. It became a form of sanctioned victimization. The game thus acted out in shadow form the street-level perception of success at the expense of others, the merciless ethic of pawnbroker economics, of victim against victim. Nevertheless, it did hang together and did offer a number of recognizable roles and, in different terms, subject posi-tions for players.

What the above discussion, concerning attempts to infringe the constraints on players, suggests, is that, as well as the subject posi-tions allowed and determined by the game itself, there was a metaludic level – negatively evident where individual, naked egos scrabbled for advantage at the edge of the system, and positively evident in such things as the essentially socialized behaviour related to the entry and exit ritual – from which players might speak of what was and was not socially reasonable or acceptable.

If we leave to one side the naked egos for one moment, we have the following levels of the social:

1   The game-transcending social world of bonds which underwrite ritual elements, promises, and the illegitimacy of the threat of actual violence.
2   The social world of the game itself, its rules, practices and permitted subject positions – the player-selves.

This second world is itself broken down into the subject positions of (a) the individual player-selves; and (b) what we might call the *choric* player-selves – that most social of all dimensions within the game where players discussed and adjudicated, witnessed and pronounced on disputes.

Now if we consider the nature of rule-breaking in each of these levels of the social, we find some interesting parallels with a division in the types of trickster figures found in the oral cultures of a number of different societies. On the one hand, there are trickster figures who are particularly involved in various forms of gross and unreasonable behaviour which affront the rules and norms of their society – Pisiboro of the !Kung Bushmen would be one, Coyote of the Winnebago Indians would be another (Biesele 1976; Radin, 1956). They are often gluttonous, and sometimes have gargantuan sexual appetites. They violate even the strictest taboos, they sow confusion everywhere they go, and frequently contradict common sense. The other type of trickster – Anansi as found in west Africa and in the Caribbean would be one example, and Robin Hood would be another – is commonly concerned with overcoming those more powerful than himself and with outwitting people. He is generally intelligent and strategic in his thinking, and admired for his ability, as with Anansi the spider-man, to wriggle and limbo dance through the cracks in the system.

Thus one type of trickster is concerned with melting the glue that holds society together,[8] the other with using the system to his own best advantage. It seems to me that these correspond with both of the levels of the social identified above, and also illuminate, if only by analogy, the social underlay of face-to-face communication that I outlined at the start of this chapter.

At the level of the social glue, the 'denial of the coordinative' potential, through the deliberate use of unacceptable utterances – this may include swearing in some social groups, using latinate expressions in others, or strategic switching to certain dialects in yet others – or the use of wilful silences and the withholding of ratifications, seems to correspond to the taboo-breaking trickster who specifically seeks to disrupt people and things. Unlike the tricksters, however, both language users and box-out players do keep at least one foot in the door of the social.

The strategic and intelligent trickster, however, is very much a gamesman, and operates at the second level of the social identified above: working within systems, not seeking to undo them. His intentions are self-centred but he needs the system and therefore plays it. Being nice to people (being emphatically coordinative) is often part of this strategy. (Indeed, these kinds of tricksters, like Ture of the Zande, are often said to be 'engaging rogues', Evans-Pritchard, 1967, p. 30.) But he is first and foremost a declarative, egocentric being and his strategies therefore are always in need of devious interpretation.

The parallel with the taboo-breaking trickster is not made to suggest that certain of the boys who played box-out were deliberately attempting to cause trouble. They were not. But, like this type of trickster, they annunciated a certain asocial naivety, and by their actions caused the social to become explicitly and defensively articulated. Hence they also correspond, in this respect, to that part of the quadrant outlined at the start of this chapter, where the declarative (I) dimension is performed through the denial of the coordinative (We) dimension. It is not surprising to find that their language in such interactions is loaded with direct, unritualized abuse.

At the same time, corresponding to the strategically social trickster, the less wilful player-selves of box-out were also often abusive to each other. However, there were, importantly, genuine moments of resolution and agreement, as in Episode 3, where, partly through the intercession of the chorus of the bystanders, differences were settled. These display *declarative assertion*, but with the coordinative dimension achieved simultaneously through *declarative denial* in the form of mitigations (italicized below). The egos were played down, the social bond was affirmed and agreement reached:

Episode 7

A: Yeah. Call it evens.
B: You *just* owe me seven, *then, right?*

Indeed, the game of box-out was largely conducted through the interaction of these fairly well-socialized player-selves. Clear glimpses of the autonomous, asocial selves, at odds with the system, were infrequent even if their presence lurked.

Whatever these players did or did not do with regard to coordinative work at the *interactional* level, it is evident that all of the disputes found in the game of box-out displayed considerable *semantic* coordination.[9] Indeed, the extrapolation of meaning and the continual digging for subtle differences that might yield an advantage were primary in many of these exchanges. Nevertheless, in the terms of the I/We quadrant, the *interactional style* could still be based on declarative assertion and the denial of the coordinative. The following is an extreme case in this respect, and one where the Big Bad Wolf is clearly visible. It involves the boy who wished to demand for himself charging rules not open to others. He had just boxed-out something from Boy A:

Episode 8

1	A:	What d'you mean, 'whatever you could charge'?
2	B:	I said, 'Join in whatever I could charge', so I can charge you what I like.
3		Thank you.
4	A:	No.
5	B:	Well *that* ain't a box-out then (*referring to a counter-box-out performed*
6		*by A*), cos if I can't 'ave my things why should you have box-out?
7	A:	That's a new game.
8	B:	It ain't a new game. It wasn't a new game. It i'n't a new game.
9	A:	No.
10	B:	If I box you out
11	A:	No.
12	B:	I can charge you what I like, innit.
13	A:	No.
14	B:	Simple as that.
15	A:	No. No.
16	B:	Well *that* ain't a box-out, then. Still 95 pence. Either take that or take,
17		well then you 'ave to take one of them.
18	A:	'Ere, I'll take my one.
19	B:	Right, and I'll take my one. So we're even.
20		(*Inaudible*)
21	B:	If I box you out I'll charge a pound.
22	A:	No way. No way.
23	B:	(*Inaudible*) . . . you tight arse.

There is not much here in the way of mitigation to accompany the stream of assertion and counter-assertion, although with *"Ere'* and *'Right, and'* (lines 18–19) there is some degree of oblique mitigation. Possibly even 'you tight arse' (23) simultaneously both denies and asserts (as familiarity and insulting rights) the interactional coordinative. The dominant form of coordination, however, is at the semantic level and in particular in the logical connectives. Here we find, if somewhat buried, the forms: 'if p then q' (2–3); 'if not p then not q' (5–7); 'if not p and not q then y' (5–8); and the whole passage is a fairly unrelenting drive of focused argumentation shared between the speakers. Furthermore, there also seems to be a kind of mutual self-congratulation involved in lines 21–2, as well as these lines having an almost stagey coordinative effect.

Conclusion

Even in an interaction where 'cooperation' is likely to be at its weakest, and embedded in a game which seems to conform to the most negative stereotype of boys' behaviour, cooperation is very much present, both at the level of the social organization of the talk generated by/sustaining of the game, and at the levels of ritual and social organization within the game structure itself. Furthermore, there were also often 'asides' between players seeking private advice or consultation on game events. These were intimate and personal, perhaps contributing to a bond which remains implicit in more public contexts. It is difficult to be sure about such matters. For this reason it seems arbitrary whether 'minimal responses' are claimed to 'demonstrate (women's) sensitivity to interactional processes' (Coates, 1989, pp. 106–7) or to demonstrate an anxious attempt to create cooperative unity. Likewise, boys' putative *lack* of activity in this respect could be taken positively as the secure reliance on bonds known to be already in place. This arbitrariness demonstrates the problem with moving from the descriptive to the moral/political.

It was not part of my primary objective to question the belief that cooperation as a communicative attribute is unequally distributed between males and females, but it has been a by-product of my characterization of communication in terms of the coordinative and declarative dimensions, and their realization by negative or positive means. This clearly also puts the above approach at some distance from the sorts of conclusions drawn by Sheldon (1993) in her study of game-related disputes amongst pre-school boys and girls.

I *have* been primarily concerned to document a moment of spontaneous exploration of the social by these adolescent boys, and to elucidate a framework within which certain dimensions of the social that are relevant for interaction can be mapped. It is relevant that for the most part the game functioned well for most of the boys, that it came to be a social activity in its own right of endless interest, and that, despite the fact that there was no actual grand design which guaranteed the system to work, they did well in creating the rituals, rules, appeals processes, and so on to make it do so. They did so collaboratively and cooperatively, despite the game's fiercely competitive and individualistic nature, and in the interplay of ego and collectivity evident through the uncertain exploration of fragmentary rules – an ordering of both game and communication that was distinctly social.

Notes

1   The data came to me, as it were, by accident. I was conducting a series of recordings of boys and girls using radio-microphones in school lunch periods for purposes quite unrelated to this chapter. Exchanges that were unintelligible to me began to occur in the recordings. I conducted several interviews with the boys about these and the broad outlines of the game appeared. The data continued to be gathered and included many exchanges relating to box-out and taxing.

2   This formal interactional structure is related to, but is not identical with, the opposition of the terms 'egocentric' and 'sociocentric' in the work of Basil Bernstein (1959; 1962). In Bernstein they are used to describe linguistic realizations of different orientations and speaker positions which derive from mediations of macro-social relations.

3   I have heard reports of games similar to the 'box-out' part being played in schools elsewhere in London and in east Kent; while 'taxing' – both in the form of boys extorting money with menaces from other boys, and in the form of simple high-interest credit – is not uncommon in secondary schools according to anecdotal reports. I know of no examples of the two aspects being brought together in this way, however, with its 'systemic' total structure.

4   Indeed, there was even a discussion of this very point when the boy first cited at the start of this chapter (who was, essentially, the classroom usurer) advised another boy who was *owed* an unpaid box-out debt to 'join out'. However, that boy insisted that it was the *non-paying* boy's responsibility to 'join out' if he couldn't pay. This was clearly an important principle, and he was surely right, for it was the non-paying player who had failed the game, in the sense that he failed to take seriously the responsibilities that made the game possible.

5   This is reminiscent of Bateson's (1985) discussion of meta-communication with regard to paradoxes in the message 'this is play'.

6   Perhaps at a social level related to the second of these was whatever it was that underwrote the status of the entering/exiting ritual. One boy, following a frustration at having one of his box-outs deemed faulty, declared, 'Right. I'm not playing any more box-out'. To which another replied: 'You ain't gonna join out, boyo. You ain't gonna get my little finger.' The first answered: 'You wish.' This reply implicitly agreed to the need to catch the little finger of the other player, i.e. the ritual was treated as binding despite one boy's desire simply to cease to play.

7   This is not to argue for any form of psychological reductionist approach to social relations and processes.

8   It is interesting that this trickster type has been associated with extreme autonomous psychological states, in particular certain forms of schizophrenia (see Layard, 1958; Metman, 1958).

9   The notion of coordination cannot be restricted to the interpersonal stylistics of interaction. It is evident that attempts to make meaning clear to interlocutors, for example, or their neglect, also involve the coordinative dimension. Indeed, for Sperber and Wilson's spare definition (1986), the semantic attribute of 'relevance' describes the formal limit of 'cooperation'.

3

Performing Gender Identity: Young Men's Talk and the Construction of Heterosexual Masculinity

Deborah Cameron

Introduction

In 1990, a 21-year-old student in a language and gender class I was teaching at a college in the southern USA tape-recorded a sequence of casual conversation among five men; himself and four friends. This young man, whom I will call 'Danny',[1] had decided to investigate whether the informal talk of male friends would bear out generalizations about 'men's talk' that are often encountered in discussions of gender differences in conversational style – for example that it is competitive, hierarchically organized, centres on 'impersonal' topics and the exchange of information, and foregrounds speech genres such as joking, trading insults and sports statistics.

Danny reported that the stereotype of all-male interaction was borne out by the data he recorded. He gave his paper the title 'Wine, women, and sports'. Yet although I could agree that the data did contain the stereotypical features he reported, the more I looked at it, the more I saw other things in it too. Danny's analysis was not inaccurate, his conclusions were not unwarranted, but his description of the data was (in both senses) *partial*: it was shaped by expectations that caused some things to leap out of the record as 'significant', while other things went unremarked.

I am interested in the possibility that Danny's selective reading of his data was not just the understandable error of an inexperienced analyst. Analysis is never done without preconceptions, we can never be absolutely non-selective in our observations, and where the object of observation and analysis has to do with gender it is extraordinarily difficult to subdue certain expectations.

One might speculate, for example, on why the vignettes of 'typical' masculine and feminine behaviour presented in popular books like Deborah Tannen's *You Just Don't Understand* (1990) are so often apprehended as immediately *recognizable*.[2] Is it because we have actually witnessed these scenarios occurring in real life, or is it because we can so readily supply the cultural script that makes them meaningful and 'typical'? One argument for the latter possibility is that if you *reverse* the genders in Tannen's anecdotes, it is still possible to supply a script which makes sense of the alleged gender difference. For example, Tannen remarks on men's reluctance to ask for directions while driving, and attributes it to men's greater concern for status (asking for help suggests helplessness). But if, as an experiment, you tell people it is women rather than men who are more reluctant to ask for directions, they will have no difficulty coming up with a different and equally plausible explanation – for instance that the reluctance reflects a typically feminine desire to avoid imposing on others, or perhaps a well-founded fear of stopping to talk to strangers.[3]

What this suggests is that the behaviour of men and women, whatever its substance may happen to be in any specific instance, is invariably read through a more general discourse on gender difference itself. That discourse is subsequently invoked to *explain* the pattern of gender differentiation in people's behaviour; whereas it might be more enlightening to say the discourse *constructs* the differentiation, makes it visible *as* differentiation.[4]

I want to propose that conversationalists themselves often do the same thing I have just suggested analysts do. Analysts construct stories about other people's behaviour, with a view to making it exemplify certain patterns of gender difference; conversationalists construct stories about themselves and others, with a view to performing certain kinds of gender identity.

Identity and Performativity

In 1990, the philosopher Judith Butler published an influential book called *Gender Trouble: Feminism and the Subversion of Identity*. Butler's essay is a postmodernist reconceptualization of gender, and it makes use of a concept familiar to linguists and discourse analysts from speech-act theory: *performativity*. For Butler, gender is *performative* – in her suggestive phrase, 'constituting the identity it is purported to be'. Just as J. L. Austin (1961) maintained that illocutions like 'I promise' do not describe a pre-existing state of affairs but actually bring one into being, so Butler claims that 'feminine' and 'masculine' are not what we are, nor traits we *have*, but effects we produce by way of particular things we *do*: 'Gender is the repeated stylization of the body, a set of repeated acts within a rigid regulatory frame which congeal over time to produce the appearance of substance, of a "natural" kind of being' (p. 33).

This extends the traditional feminist account whereby gender is socially constructed rather than 'natural', famously expressed in Simone de Beauvoir's dictum that 'one is not born, but rather becomes a woman'. Butler is saying that 'becoming a woman' (or a man) is not something you accomplish once and for all at an early stage of life. Gender has constantly to be reaffirmed and publicly displayed by repeatedly performing particular acts in accordance with the cultural norms (themselves historically and socially constructed, and consequently variable) which define 'masculinity' and 'femininity'.

This 'performative' model sheds an interesting light on the phenomenon of gendered *speech*. Speech too is a 'repeated stylization of the body'; the 'masculine' and 'feminine' styles of talking identified by researchers might be thought of as the 'congealed' result of repeated acts by social actors who are striving to constitute themselves as 'proper' men and women. Whereas sociolinguistics traditionally assumes that people talk the way they do because of who they (already) are, the postmodernist approach suggests that people are who they are because of (among other things) the way they talk. This shifts the focus away from a simple cataloguing of differences between men and women to a subtler and more complex inquiry into how people use linguistic resources to produce gender differentiation. It also obliges us to attend to the 'rigid regulatory frame' within which people must make their choices – the norms that define what kinds of language are possible, intelligible and appropriate resources for performing masculinity or femininity.

A further advantage of this approach is that it acknowledges the instability and variability of gender identities, and therefore of the behaviour in which those identities are performed. While Judith Butler rightly insists that gender is regulated and policed by rather rigid social norms, she does not reduce men and women to automata, programmed by their early socialization to repeat forever the appropriate gendered behaviour, but treats them as conscious agents who may – albeit often at some social cost – engage in acts of transgression, subversion and resistance. As active producers rather than passive reproducers of gendered behaviour, men and women may use their awareness of the gendered meanings that attach to particular ways of speaking and acting to produce a variety of effects. This is important, because few, if any, analysts of data on men's and women's speech would maintain that the differences are as clear-cut and invariant as one might gather from such oft-cited dichotomies as 'competitive/cooperative' and 'report talk/rapport talk'. People *do* perform gender differently in different contexts, and do sometimes behave in ways we would normally associate with the 'other' gender. The conversation to which we now turn is a notable case in point.

The Conversation: Wine, Women, Sports . . . And Other Men

The five men who took part in the conversation, and to whom I will give the pseudonyms Al, Bryan, Carl, Danny and Ed, were demographically a homogeneous group: white, middle-class American suburbanites aged 21, who attended the same university and belonged to the same social network on campus. This particular conversation occurred in the context of one of their commonest shared leisure activities: watching sports at home on television.[5]

Throughout the period covered by the tape-recording there is a basketball game on screen, and participants regularly make reference to what is going on in the game. Sometimes these references are just brief interpolated comments, which do not disrupt the flow of ongoing talk on some other topic; sometimes they lead to extended discussion. At all times, however, it is a legitimate conversational move to comment on the basketball game. The student who collected the data drew attention to the status of sport as a resource for talk available to North American men of all classes and racial/ethnic groups, to strangers as well as friends, suggesting that 'sports talk' is a typically 'masculine' conversational genre in the US, something all culturally competent males know how to do.

But 'sports talk' is by no means the only kind of talk being done. The men also recount the events of their day – what classes they had and how these went; they discuss mundane details of their domestic arrangements, such as who is going to pick up groceries; there is a debate about the merits of a certain kind of wine; there are a couple of longer narratives, notably one about an incident when two men sharing a room each invited a girlfriend back without their room-mate's knowledge – and discovered this at the most embarrassing moment possible. Danny's title 'Wine, women, and sports' is accurate insofar as all these subjects are discussed at some length.

When one examines the data, however, it becomes clear there is one very significant omission in Danny's title. Apart from basketball, the single most prominent theme in the recorded conversation, as measured by the amount of time devoted to it, is 'gossip': discussion of several persons not present but known to the participants, with a strong focus on critically examining these individuals' appearance, dress, social behaviour and sexual mores. Like the conversationalists themselves, the individuals under discussion are all men. Unlike the conversationalists, however, the individuals under discussion are identified as 'gay'.

The topic of 'gays' is raised by Ed, only a few seconds into the tape-recorded conversation (6):[6]

ED: Mugsy Bogues (.) my name is Lloyd Gompers I am a
      homosexual (.) you know what the (.) I saw the new
      Remnant I should have grabbed you know the title? Like
      the head thing?

'Mugsy Bogues' (the name of a basketball player) is an acknowledge-ment of the previous turn, which concerned the on-screen game. Ed's next comment appears off-topic, but he immediately supplies a ratio-nale for it, explaining that he 'saw the new Remnant' – *The Remnant* being a deliberately provocative right-wing campus newspaper whose main story that week had been an attack on the 'Gay Ball', a dance sponsored by the college's Gay Society.

The next few turns are devoted to establishing a shared view of the Gay Ball and of homosexuality generally. Three of the men, Al, Bryan and Ed, are actively involved in this exchange. A typical sequence is the following (14–16):

AL: gays=
ED: =gays w[hy? that's what it should read [gays why?
BRYAN: [gays]   [I know]

What is being established as 'shared' here is a view of gays as alien (that is, the group defines itself as heterosexual and puzzled by homosexuality ('gays, why?'), and also to some extent comical.

Danny comments at one point, 'it's hilarious', and Ed caps the sequence discussing the Gay Ball (23–5) with the witticism:

ED: the question is who wears the boutonnière and who wears
      the corsage, flip for it? or do they both just wear
      flowers coz they're fruits

It is at this point that Danny introduces the theme that will dominate the conversation for some time: gossip about individual men who are said to be gay. Referring to the only other man in his language and gender class, Danny begins (27):

DANNY: My boy Ronnie was uh speaking up on the male
         perspective today (.) way too much

The section following this contribution is structured around a series of references to other 'gay' individuals known to the participants as classmates. Bryan mentions 'the most effeminate guy I've ever met' (29) and 'that really gay guy in our Age of Revolution class' (34). Ed remarks that 'you have never seen more homos than we have in our class. Homos, dykes, homos, dykes, everybody is a homo or a dyke' (64). He then focuses on a 'fat, queer, goofy guy ... [who's] as gay as night' [*sic*] (78–80), and on a 'blond hair, snide little queer weird shit' (98), who is further described as a 'butt pirate'. Some of these references, but not all, initiate an extended discussion of the individual concerned. The content of these discussions will bear closer examination.

'The Antithesis of Man'

One of the things I initially found most puzzling about the whole 'gays' sequence was that the group's criteria for categorizing people as gay appeared to have little to do with those people's known or suspected sexual preferences or practices. The terms 'butt pirate' and 'butt cutter' were used, but surprisingly seldom; it was unclear to me that the individuals referred to really were homosexual, and in the one case where I actually knew the subject of discussion, I seriously doubted it.

Most puzzling is an exchange between Bryan and Ed about the class where 'everybody is a homo or a dyke', in which they complain that 'four homos' are continually 'hitting on' [making sexual overtures to] one of the women, described as 'the ugliest-ass bitch in the history of the world' (82–9). One might have thought that a defining feature of a 'homo' would be his lack of interest in 'hitting on' women. Yet no one seems aware of any problem or contradiction in this exchange.

I think this is because the deviance indicated for this group by the term 'gay' is not so much *sexual* deviance as *gender* deviance. Being 'gay' means failing to measure up to the group's standards of masculinity or femininity. This is why it makes sense to call someone *'really* gay': unlike same- versus other-sex preference, conformity to gender norms can be a matter of degree. It is also why hitting on an 'ugly-ass bitch' can be classed as 'homosexual' behaviour – proper masculinity requires that the object of public sexual interest be not just female, but minimally attractive.

Applied by the group to men, 'gay' refers in particular to insufficiently masculine appearance, clothing and speech. To illustrate this I will reproduce a longer sequence of conversation about the 'really gay guy in our Age of Revolution class', which ends with Ed declaring: 'he's the antithesis of man'.

BRYAN: uh you know that really gay guy in our Age of
         Revolution class who sits in front of us? he wore
         shorts again, by the way, it's like 42 degrees out he
         wore shorts again [laughter] [Ed: That guy] it's like
         a speedo, he wears a speedo to class (.) he's got
         incredibly skinny legs [Ed: it's worse] you know=
ED: =you know
         like those shorts women volleyball players wear? it's
         like those (.) it's l[ike

BRYAN: [you know what's even more ridicu[lous? when
ED: [French cut spandex]

BRYAN: you wear those shorts and like a parka on . . .
(5 lines omitted)

BRYAN: he's either got some condition that he's got to
         like have his legs exposed at all times or else he's
         got really good legs=
ED: =he's probably he'[s like
CARL: [he really likes

BRYAN: =he
ED: =he's like at home combing his leg hairs=
CARL: his legs=

BRYAN: he doesn't have any leg hair though=   [*yes* and oh
ED: =he *real*[*ly* likes

ED: his legs=
AL: =very long very white and very skinny

BRYAN: those ridiculous Reeboks that are always (indeciph)
         and goofy white socks always striped=   [tube socks
ED: =that's [right

ED: he's the antithesis of man

In order to demonstrate that certain individuals are 'the antithesis of man', the group engages in a kind of conversation that might well strike us as the antithesis of 'men's talk'. It is unlike the 'wine, women, and sports' stereotype of men's talk – indeed, rather closer to the stereotype of 'women's talk' – in various ways, some obvious, and some less so.

The obvious ways in which this sequence resembles conventional notions of 'women's talk' concern its purpose and subject-matter. This is talk about people, not things, and 'rapport talk' rather than 'report talk' – the main point is clearly not to exchange information. It is 'gossip', and serves one of the most common purposes of gossip, namely affirming the solidarity of an in-group by constructing absent others as an out-group, whose behaviour is minutely examined and found wanting.

The specific subjects on which the talk dwells are conventionally 'feminine' ones: clothing and bodily appearance. The men are caught up in a contradiction: their criticism of the 'gays' centres on their unmanly interest in displaying their bodies, and the inappropriate garments they choose for this purpose (bathing costumes worn to class, shorts worn in cold weather with parkas which render the effect ludicrous, clothing which resembles the outfits of 'women volleyball players'). The implication is that real men just pull on their jeans and leave it at that. But in order to pursue this line of criticism, the conversationalists themselves must show an acute awareness of such 'unmanly' concerns as styles and materials ('French cut spandex', 'tube socks'), what kind of clothes go together, and which men have 'good legs'. They are impelled, paradoxically, to talk about men's bodies as a way of demonstrating their own total lack of sexual interest in those bodies.

The less obvious ways in which this conversation departs from stereotypical notions of 'men's talk' concern its *formal* features. Analyses of men's and women's speech style are commonly organized around a series of global oppositions, e.g. men's talk is 'competitive', whereas women's is 'cooperative'; men talk to gain 'status', whereas women talk to forge 'intimacy' and 'connection'; men do 'report talk' and women 'rapport talk'. Analysts working with these oppositions typically identify certain formal or organizational features of talk as markers of 'competition' and 'cooperation' etc. The analyst then examines which kinds of features predominate in a set of conversational data, and how they are being used.

In the following discussion, I too will make use of the conventional oppositions as tools for describing data, but I will be trying to build up an argument that their use is problematic. The problem is not merely that the men in my data fail to fit their gender stereotype perfectly. More importantly, I think it is often the stereotype itself that underpins analytic judgements that a certain form is cooperative rather than competitive, or that people are seeking status rather than connection in their talk. As I observed about Deborah Tannen's vignettes, many instances of behaviour will support either interpretation, or both; we use the speaker's gender, and our beliefs about what sort of behaviour makes sense for members of that gender, to rule some interpretations in and others out.

Cooperation

Various scholars, notably Jennifer Coates (1989), have remarked on the 'cooperative' nature of informal talk among female friends, drawing attention to a number of linguistic features which are prominent in data on all-female groups. Some of these, like hedging and the use of epistemic modals, are signs of attention to others' face, aimed at minimizing conflict and securing agreement. Others, such as latching of turns, simultaneous speech where this is not interpreted by participants as a violation of turn-taking rights (cf. Edelsky, 1981), and the repetition or recycling of lexical items and phrases across turns, are signals that a conversation is a 'joint production': that participants are building on one another's contributions so that ideas are felt to be group property rather than the property of a single speaker.

On these criteria, the conversation here must be judged as highly cooperative. For example, in the extract reproduced above, a strikingly large number of turns (around half) begin with 'you know' and/or contain the marker 'like' ('you know like those shorts women volleyball players wear?'). The functions of these items (especially 'like') in younger Americans' English are complex and multiple,[7] and may include the cooperative, mitigating/face-protecting functions that Coates and Janet Holmes (1984a) associate with hedging. Even where they are not clearly hedges, however, in this interaction they function in ways that relate to the building of group involvement and consensus. They often seem to mark information as 'given' within the group's discourse (that is, 'you know', 'like', 'X' presupposes that the addressee is indeed familiar with X); 'you know' has the kind of hearer-oriented affective function (taking others into account or inviting their agreement) which Holmes attributes to certain tag-questions; while 'like' in addition seems to function for these speakers as a marker of high involvement. It appears most frequently at moments when the interactants are, by other criteria such as intonation, pitch, loudness, speech rate, incidence of simultaneous speech, and of 'strong' or taboo language, noticeably excited, such as the following (82–9):

ED: he's I mean he's **like** a real artsy fartsy fag he's
         like (indeciph) he's so gay he's got this **like** really
         high voice and wire rim glasses and he sits next to
         the ugliest-ass bitch in the history of the world

ED: [and
BRYAN: [and they're all hitting on her too, **like** four

ED: [I know it's **like** four homos hitting on her
BRYAN: guys [hitting on her

It is also noticeable throughout the long extract reproduced earlier how much latching and simultaneous speech there is, as compared to other forms of turn transition involving either short or long pauses and gaps, or interruptions which silence the interruptee. Latching – turn transition without pause or overlap – is often taken as a mark of cooperation because in order to latch a turn so precisely onto the preceding turn, the speaker has to attend closely to others' contributions.

The last part of the reproduced extract, discussing the 'really gay' guy's legs, is an excellent example of jointly produced discourse, as the speakers cooperate to build a detailed picture of the legs and what is worn on them, a picture which overall could not be attributed to any single speaker. This sequence contains many instances of latching, repetition of one speaker's words by another speaker (Ed recycles Carl's whole turn, 'he really likes his legs', with added emphasis), and it also contains something that is relatively rare in the conversation as a whole, repeated tokens of hearer support like 'yes' and 'that's right'.[8]

There are, then, points of resemblance worth remarking on between these men's talk and similar talk among women as reported by previous studies. The question does arise, however, whether this male conversation has the other important hallmark of women's gossip, namely an egalitarian or non-hierarchical organization of the floor.

Competition

In purely quantitative terms, this conversation cannot be said to be egalitarian. The extracts reproduced so far are representative of the whole insofar as they show Ed and Bryan as the dominant speakers, while Al and Carl contribute fewer and shorter turns (Danny is variable; there are sequences where he contributes very little, but when he talks he often contributes turns as long as Ed's and Bryan's, and he also initiates topics). Evidence thus exists to support an argument that there is a hierarchy in this conversation, and there is competition, particularly between the two dominant speakers, Bryan and Ed (and to a lesser extent Ed and Danny). Let us pursue this by looking more closely at Ed's behaviour.

Ed introduces the topic of homosexuality, and initially attempts to keep 'ownership' of it. He cuts off Danny's first remark on the subject with a reference to *The Remnant*: 'what was the article? cause you know they bashed them they were like'. At this point Danny interrupts: it is clearly an interruption because in this context the preferred interpretation of 'like' is quotative (see note 7) – Ed is about to repeat what the gay-bashing article in *The Remnant* said. In addition to interrupting so that Ed falls silent, Danny contradicts Ed, saying 'they didn't actually (.) cut into them big'. A little later on during the discussion of the Gay Ball, Ed makes use of a common competitive strategy, the joke or witty remark which 'caps' other contributions (the 'flowers and fruits' joke at 23–5, quoted above). This, however, elicits no laughter, no matching jokes and indeed no take-up of any kind. It is followed by a pause and a change of direction if not of subject, as Danny begins the gossip that will dominate talk for several minutes.

This immediately elicits a matching contribution from Bryan. As he and Danny talk, Ed makes two unsuccessful attempts to regain the floor. One, where he utters the prefatory remark 'I'm gonna be very honest' (20), is simply ignored. His second strategy is to ask (about the person Bryan and Danny are discussing) 'what's this guy's last name?' (30). First Bryan asks him to repeat the question, then Danny replies 'I don't know what the hell it is' (32).

A similar pattern is seen in the long extract reproduced above, where Ed makes two attempts to interrupt Bryan's first turn ('That guy' and 'it's worse'), neither of which succeeds. He gets the floor eventually by using the 'you know, like' strategy. And from that point, Ed does orient more to the norms of joint production; he over-laps others to produce simultaneous speech but does not interrupt; he produces more latched turns, recyclings and support tokens.

So far I have been arguing that even if the speakers, or some of them, compete, they are basically engaged in a collaborative and solidary enterprise (reinforcing the bonds within the group by denigrating peo-ple outside it), an activity in which all speakers participate, even if some are more active than others. Therefore I have drawn attention to the presence of 'cooperative' features, and have argued that more extreme forms of hierarchical and competitive behaviour are not rewarded by the group. I could, indeed, have argued that by the end, Ed and Bryan are not so much 'competing' – after all, their contributions are not antagonistic to one another but tend to reinforce one another – as engaging in a version of the 'joint production of discourse'.

Yet the data might also support a different analysis in which Ed and Bryan are simply *using* the collaborative enterprise of putting down gay men as an occasion to engage in verbal duelling where points are scored – against fellow group members rather than against the absent gay men – by dominating the floor and coming up with more and more extravagant put-downs. In this alternative analysis, Ed does not so much modify his behaviour as 'lose' his duel with Bryan. 'Joint production' or 'verbal duelling' – how do we decide?

Deconstructing Oppositions

One response to the problem of competing interpretations raised above might be that the opposition I have been working with – 'com-petitive' versus 'cooperative' behaviour – is inherently problematic, particularly if one is taken to exclude the other. Conversation can and usually does contain both cooperative and competitive elements: one could argue (along with Grice, 1975) that talk must by definition involve a certain minimum of cooperation, and also that there will usually be some degree of competition among speakers, if not for the floor itself then for the attention or the approval of others (see also Hewitt, chapter 2).

The global competitive/cooperative opposition also encourages the lumping together under one heading or the other of things that could in principle be distinguished. 'Cooperation' might refer to agreement on the aims of talk, respect for other speakers' rights or support for their contributions; but there is not always perfect co-occurrence among these aspects, and the presence of any one of them need not rule out a 'competitive' element. Participants in a conversation or other speech event may compete with each other and at the same time be pursuing a shared project or common agenda (as in ritual insult sessions); they may be in severe disagreement but punctiliously observant of one another's speaking rights (as in a formal debate, say); they may be overtly supportive, and at the same time covertly hoping to score points for their supportiveness.

This last point is strangely overlooked in some discussions of women's talk. Women who pay solicitous attention to one another's face are often said to be seeking connection or good social relations *rather than* status; yet one could surely argue that attending to others' face and attending to one's own are not mutually exclusive here. The 'egalitarian' norms of female friendship groups are, like all norms, to some degree coercive: the rewards and punishments precisely concern one's status within the group (among women, however, this status is called 'popularity' rather than 'dominance'). A woman may gain status by displaying the correct degree of concern for others, and lose status by displaying too little concern for others and too much for herself. Arguably, it is gender-stereotyping that causes us to miss or minimize the status-seeking element in women friends' talk, and the connection-making dimension of men's.

How to do Gender with Language

I hope it will be clear by now that my intention in analysing male gossip is not to suggest that the young men involved have adopted a 'feminine' conversational style. On the contrary, the main theoretical point I want to make concerns the folly of making any such claim. To characterize the conversation I have been considering as 'feminine' on the basis that it bears a significant resemblance to conversations among women friends would be to miss the most important point about it, that it is not only *about* masculinity, it is a sustained performance *of* masculinity. What is important in gendering talk is the 'performative gender work' the talk is doing; its role in constituting people as gendered subjects.

To put matters in these terms is not to deny that there may be an empirically observable association between a certain genre or style of speech and speakers of a particular gender. In practice this is undeniable. But we do need to ask: in virtue of what does the association hold? Can we give an account that will not be vitiated by cases where it does *not* hold? For it seems to me that conversations like the one I have analysed leave, say, Deborah Tannen's contention that men do not do 'women's talk', because they simply *do not know how,* looking lame and unconvincing. If men rarely engage in a certain kind of talk, an explanation is called for; but if they do engage in it even very occasionally, an explanation in terms of pure ignorance will not do.

I suggest the following explanation. Men and women do not live on different planets, but are members of cultures in which a large amount of discourse about gender is constantly circulating. They do not only learn, and then mechanically reproduce, ways of speaking 'appropriate' to their own sex; they learn a much broader set of gendered meanings that attach in rather complex ways to different ways of speaking, and they produce their own behaviour in the light of those meanings.

This behaviour will vary. Even the individual who is most unambiguously committed to traditional notions of gender has a range of possible gender identities to draw on. Performing masculinity or femininity 'appropriately' cannot mean giving exactly the same performance regardless of the circumstances. It may involve different strategies in mixed and single-sex company, in private and in public settings, in the various social positions (parent, lover, professional, friend) that someone might regularly occupy in the course of everyday life.

Since gender is a relational term, and the minimal requirement for 'being a man' is 'not being a woman', we may find that in many circumstances, men are under pressure to constitute themselves as masculine linguistically by avoiding forms of talk whose primary association is with women/femininity. But this is not invariant, which begs the question: under what circumstances does the contrast with women lose its salience as a constraint on men's behaviour? When can men do so-called 'feminine' talk without threatening their constitution as men? Are there cases when it might actually be to their advantage to do this?

When and Why do Men Gossip?

Many researchers have reported that both sexes engage in gossip, since its social functions (like affirming group solidarity and serving as an unofficial conduit for information) are of universal relevance, but its cultural meaning (for us) is undeniably 'feminine'. Therefore we might expect to find most men avoiding it, or disguising it as something else, especially in mixed settings where they are concerned to mark their difference from women (see Johnson and Finlay, chapter 7). In the conversation discussed above, however, there are no women for the men to differentiate themselves from; whereas *there is* the perceived danger that so often accompanies Western male homosociality: homosexuality. Under these circumstances perhaps it becomes acceptable to transgress one gender norm ('men don't gossip, gossip is for girls') in order to affirm what in this context is a more important norm ('men in all-male groups must unambiguously display their heterosexual orientation').

In these speakers' understanding of gender, gay men, like women, provide a contrast group against whom masculinity can be defined. This principle of contrast seems to set limits on the permissibility of gossip for these young men. Although they discuss other men besides the 'gays' – professional basketball players – they could not be said to gossip about them. They talk about the players' skills and their records, not their appearance, personal lives or sexual activities. Since the men admire the basketball players, identifying *with* them rather than *against* them, such talk would border dangerously on what for them is obviously taboo: desire for other men.

Ironically, it seems likely that the despised gay men are the *only* men about whom these male friends can legitimately talk among themselves in such intimate terms without compromising the heterosexual masculinity they are so anxious to display – though in a different context, say with their girlfriends, they might be able to discuss the basketball players differently. The presence of a woman, especially a heterosexual partner, displaces the dread spectre of homosexuality, and makes other kinds of talk possible; though by the same token her presence might make certain kinds of talk that take place among men *im*possible. What counts as acceptable talk for men is a complex matter in which all kinds of contextual variables play a part.

In this context – a private conversation among male friends – it could be argued that to gossip, either about your sexual exploits with women or about the repulsiveness of gay men (these speakers do both), is not just one way, but the most appropriate way to display heterosexual masculinity. In another context (in public, or with a larger and less close-knit group of men), the same objective might well be pursued through explicitly agonistic strategies, such as yelling abuse at women or gays in the street, or exchanging sexist and homophobic jokes. *Both* strategies could be said to do performative gender work: in terms of what they do for the speakers involved, one is not more 'masculine' than the other, they simply belong to different settings in which heterosexual masculinity may (or must) be put on display.

Conclusion

I hope that my discussion of the conversation I have analysed makes the point that it is unhelpful for linguists to continue to use models of gendered speech which imply that masculinity and femininity are monolithic constructs, automatically giving rise to predictable (and utterly different) patterns of verbal interaction. At the same time, I hope it might make us think twice about the sort of analysis that implicitly seeks the meaning (and sometimes the *value*) of an interaction among men or women primarily in the style, rather than the substance, of what is said. For although, as I noted earlier in relation to Judith Butler's work, it is possible for men and women to performatively subvert or resist the prevailing codes of gender, there can surely be no convincing argument that this is what Danny and his friends are doing. Their conversation is animated by entirely traditional anxieties about being seen at all times as red-blooded heterosexual males: not women and not queers. Their skill as performers does not alter the fact that what they perform is the same old gendered script.

Transcription conventions

Horizontal sequencing of utterances represents (impressionistically) their relative arrangement in time.
    Other symbols used:

=	latching
[	turn onset overlaps previous turn
[]	turn is completely contained within another speaker's turn
?	rising intonation on utterance
(.)	short pause
(indeciph)	indecipherable speech
italics	emphatic stress on italicized item

Notes

1 Because the student concerned is one of the speakers in the conversation I analyse, and the nature of the conversation makes it desirable to conceal participants' identities (indeed, this was one of the conditions on which the data were collected and subsequently passed on to me), I will not give his real name here, but I want to acknowledge his generosity in making his recording and transcript available to me, and to thank him for a number of insights I gained by discussing the data with him as well as by reading his paper. I am also grateful to the other young men who participated. All their names, and the names of other people they mention, have been changed, and all pseudonyms used are (I hope) entirely fictitious.

2 I base this assessment of reader response on my own research with readers of Tannen's book (see Cameron, 1995a, ch. 5), on non-scholarly reviews of the book, and on reader studies of popular self-help generally (e.g. Lichterman, 1992; Simonds, 1992).

3 I am indebted to Penelope Eckert for describing this 'thought experiment', which she has used in her own teaching (though the specific details of the example are not an exact rendition of Eckert's observations).

4 The German linguist Karsta Frank (1992) has provocatively argued that so-called gender differences in speech-style arise *exclusively* in reception: women and men are heard differently, as opposed to speaking differently. I do not entirely accept Frank's very strong position on this point, but I do think she has drawn attention to a phenomenon of some importance.

5 I mention that this was 'at home' because in the United States it is also common for men, individually or in groups, to watch televised sports in public places such as bars and even laundromats; but this particular conversation would probably not have happened in a public setting with others present. It appears to be a recurrent feature of male friends' talk that the men are engaged in some other activity as well as talking. The Swedish researcher Kerstin Nordenstam, who has an impressive corpus comprising data from twelve different single-sex friendship groups, has found that the men are far less likely than the women to treat conversation as the exclusive or primary purpose of a social gathering. Many of the women's groups recorded for Nordenstam were 'sewing circles' – a traditional kind of informal social organization for women in Sweden – but they frequently did not sew, and defined their aim simply as 'having fun'; whereas the men's groups might meet under no particular rubric, but they still tended to organize their talk around an activity such as playing cards or games. (Thanks to Kerstin Nordenstam for this information.)

6 Numbers in parenthesis refer to the lines in the original transcript.

7 For example, *like* has a 'quotative' function among younger US speakers, as in 'and she's like [= she said], stop bugging me, and I'm like, what do you mean stop bugging you?'. This and other uses of the item have

become popularly stereotyped as markers of membership in the so-called 'slacker' generation.

8   It is a rather consistent research finding that men use such minimal responses significantly less often than women, and in this respect the present data conform to expectations – there are very few minimal responses of any kind. I would argue, however, that active listenership, involvement and support are not *absent* in the talk of this group; they are marked by other means such as high levels of latching/simultaneous speech, lexical recycling and the use of *like*.

4

Power and the Language of Men

Scott Fabius Kiesling

Introduction

Power is usually cited as the most important factor when discussing the ways in which men's identities are constructed.[1] For example, in 'Men, inexpressiveness, and power', Jack Sattel argues that: 'the starting point for understanding masculinity lies, not in its contrast with femininity, but in the asymmetric dominance and prestige which accrues to males in this society' (1983, p. 119). In this chapter, I aim to show how issues of power and dominance as they relate to male identities are more complex than previously suggested. I will provide examples of some of the discursive strategies used by individual men in order to create and demonstrate power, showing how each man adopts a unique and personal approach when doing so. In particular, I will demonstrate how sequentiality and activity type must be taken into account when exploring the construction of men's identities through language.

It cannot be denied that men have more power than women in modern Western society. Men still dominate the upper echelons of government and business, and women continue to perform most of the unpaid labour of housework and child care. In addition, women still frequently earn less than men for comparable work, and professions dominated by women are less valued monetarily than those dominated by men (see Hewlett, 1986). Along with the freedom brought by power, however, comes the expectation (or requirement) that a man will somehow embody this power in his identity. This expectation is by no means as restrictive as those which obtain where women's identities are concerned; when a man constructs a powerful identity, it is usually connected in some way to 'real' power. Thus, the expectation of a 'powerful' identity for men is not symmetrical to the expectation of a 'powerless' identity for women, since a man's powerful identity is *rewarded* (with power), whereas a woman's non-powerless identity may be *punished*.

Following Sattel's suggestion, therefore, I take the power of men as a starting point for investigating how men construct their identities through language; I unpack the concept, describe different kinds of power, and show how these work with specific regard to four individual men.

My analysis is based on data gathered during a continuing ethnographic study of a fraternity in the United States. A fraternity is an all-male social club at a university, in which membership is selective. Typically, the fraternity becomes the central organization around which members structure their college lives, especially socially. It is a 'community of practice' (Eckert and McConnell-Ginet, 1992), defined sharply from the rest of the university through various means – initiation rituals, secret ceremonies and exclusive social events. Cynthia McLemore (1991) has worked on intonation in the female counterpart to the fraternity – the sorority. She showed that this type of community is ideal for studying language and society, especially the language of society's privileged members, because it is an intensely social, well-defined community, and its activities are based primarily on talk (e.g. meetings and parties). In addition, fraternities exhibit processes typical of other social groups more intensely: entrance into the community is carefully guarded, its members change completely every four years, and yet it manages to retain a unique history and ideology. Finally, fraternities are important to study because they prepare their members for the world of work after college. By analysing the strategies that men learn in fraternities, we can therefore gain insights into how men acquire, construct, and reproduce certain social practices in anticipation of dominance over others in later life.

In this chapter, I will explore how the fraternity's ideology and the immediate speech situation work together to constrain the members' identities. I use the term 'constrain', rather than 'affect' or 'determine', because identity construction is, to some extent, a creative endeavour. In theory, the men are free to create any identity they want, but in practice, they are pushed (and push themselves) towards identities which do not challenge the perceived values of the fraternity or of dominant US society. Each man also has different discursive resources (e.g. storytelling ability, joking ability, a powerful structural role, a loud voice, etc.) in order to draw upon disparate types of power. And crucially, each member has his own personal history within the fraternity, which further constrains the kind of identity he can display at any given time. Each time he speaks, then, the man must produce an utterance (and posture, gaze, etc.) that satisfies these constraints as far as possible. At the same time, he must make the utterance coherent within each current speech situation.

Because I am focusing on power, I will begin by outlining the framework of power used in my analysis. I will then discuss the specific ideology of power at work in the fraternity in question, exploring, for example, the kinds of constraints which the community places on a member's presentation of self. Finally, I will analyse excerpts from my corpus in order to illustrate how men draw upon, and construct, different types of power through their use of language.

A Framework for Power

Before applying a concept to any analysis, it should be well defined. When power is used as an explanation in sociolinguistic analyses, however, it is frequently undefined and unanalysed. Because I am taking power as the starting point for my work, I will briefly sketch the theoretical approach which is to be employed.

Following Foucault (1982), power is action that modifies action. The effect of this action need not be immediate, direct or even real. So, for example, because power takes place in actions, it is exercised to the extent that people *believe* that they should perform an action because of another action. However, power is not something that individuals may suddenly pull out and use. It must be salient to the situation; the people being acted on must believe in it. Thus, illusions can be powerful motivators. People believe that they should act in certain ways with certain people because they feel that not acting in these ways would have serious consequences. The reasons for performing a given action might therefore seem irrational, such as the avoidance of embarrassment, or the appearance of foolishness or 'weakness'. But what constitutes a serious consequence is, in turn, dependent on the community in question and its own particular values. This means that any analysis exploring issues of power must be based on a primary analysis of the local community's values and its ideology.

Whilst this view of power is flexible, it lacks analytical force. At a practical level, therefore, I assume that people have power because they occupy roles – some so enduring as to seem eternal and necessary, some fleeting and unnoticed, and some newly created within specific interactions. People place themselves in roles by using language because different ways of speaking are associated with such roles. A new role may be thrown together out of bits of others, and, in some cases, a single role may dominate a personality. But such roles can only really be discovered by analysing the discourse of community members, and by examining the community's formal and informal structures through ethnographic observation and interviewing.

On the basis of my own study, I have identified seven types of power processes from which local roles may be built: physical (coercive and ability), economic, knowledge, structural, nurturant, demeanour and ideological. I distinguish between two types of physical power: *coercive physical power* is the power of the mugger, while *ability physical power* is an action made possible by physical ability or skill. *Economic power* is the process that rewards one action (e.g. labour) with the possibility of another action (e.g. purchasing goods). *Knowledge power* is the process of gaining knowledge in order to perform an action. *Structural power* is the power of a place within a structure, classically (but not necessarily) a hierarchy. *Nurturant power* is the process of helping another, as in teaching or feeding. *Demeanour power* is the power of solidarity: moral authority, being liked, being 'a good guy'. The process of demeanour is not normally addressed by views of power, because the actions in this type of power act on emotions. Thus a person exhibits demeanour power when others feel happy, entertained, involved, respectful, etc.

But it is the ideological process which is the most important. This is a 'defining process', because individuals evaluate the other types of power processes through the ideological process. This defining process – which I will refer to as *ideological power* – ratifies certain traits as powerful, and determines which of the other processes are available (i.e. identifies the roles in the community). Within each of the other processes, ideological power identifies what is, and what is not, powerful. Thus, ideological power is the process of power whereby ways of thinking about the world are naturalized into a community's behaviour.

Each of the seven types of power outlined is not isolated from the others, but all are closely connected to form what Foucault refers to as: 'a net-like organization [...] something which circulates, or rather (as) something which only functions in the form of a chain' (1980, p. 98). In this way, an ideology such as the competitive, hierarchical, group ideology frequently identified as typical of all-male interaction is likely to affect the way in which men structure their groups, change their demeanour and learn disciplines. Men may be inclined to form hierarchical communities, act in ways that always seem competitive, and see education and work as a competition. The success with which they learn to think and act in these ways will, in turn, affect their ability to use economic, structural, physical, knowledge and demeanour processes of power.

Power is therefore a way of viewing local practices globally: an etic framework filled in by emic values. Power in this view (as a role focused on – or created in – a community-defined structure) is similar to concepts of footing and alignment (see Goffman, 1981). However, by using the framework I have outlined, we can identify the types of roles which are available and created vis-à-vis power. As a consequence, we will not be limited to analyses using broad, universal categories. Moreover, we can approach some comparability across communities by looking at the ways in which different communities deal with similar ideologies of power, and similar communities deal with different ideologies of power.

'Ideology Power' in a Fraternity

In the light of the framework I have outlined, I need to discuss the ideology of the fraternity in question before analysing how power works in the fraternity's discourse. The way a man presents himself within a fraternity is of ultimate importance because he becomes a member of and gains status in the fraternity by projecting the right kind of identity.

Gaining membership to a fraternity is contingent upon successfully negotiating the process of 'rush', which is not unlike courtship. In this process, current members meet prospective members (known as 'rushes') at organized social functions; they also socialize informally, for example, by talking in dormitory rooms. Prospective members gauge whether they want to be a part of the fraternity, and current members consider whether they want to invite the prospective members to join. The rushes selected by the current members are then offered an invitation for membership, and can accept or reject the 'bid', as the offer is known. Once they have accepted a bid, the rushes become probationary members, or 'pledges'. During the 'pledge period', which lasts for six to eight weeks, pledges learn the fraternity's traditions, and pledge education activities take place in unofficial secret ceremonies, which are similar to military 'boot camps'. Pledges are treated as second-class citizens, subordinating their autonomy and identities to the fraternity as an institution, and to individual older 'brothers', as members are called. Pledges 'earn respect' and the privilege to become members themselves. They also learn the fraternity's customs, traditions and oral history. During this time, a strong bond tends to form between so-called 'pledge brothers', who are members of the same 'pledge class', because of their common adversity as second-class citizens.

The pledge period culminates in initiation, a formal clandestine ceremony where the secrets, rights and responsibilities of membership are imparted. However, the newly initiated brother – known by the acronym 'nib' – is still inexperienced in the eyes of the fraternity. He lacks knowledge and past accomplishments in order to prove that he will function well in a fraternity office. In the social sphere, nibs normally follow the older brothers' lead, show respect to them, and defer to their judgement. But nibs still have more latitude here than in the fraternity's 'business' sphere, which will be discussed below. As a brother becomes older, he has a chance to prove himself by performing services for the fraternity. Also, simply by becoming older, he gains the respect of younger 'generations' of members.

In the fraternity I studied for over a year, which I will call Gamma Chi Phi (ΓΧΦ), almost all of the men were Caucasian. Out of fifty-seven members, one was Korean-American, and four were Arab-American. Most were of college age (17–22 years old); three alumni members were in their late twenties. By comparison, the university as a whole is 88 per cent Caucasian, 10 per cent Asian and 6 per cent African-American.

I was able to gain entry into this fraternity because, as an undergraduate, I was a member of the same national fraternity. I first contacted the national fraternity to describe my project, attending several meetings of the steering committee, the National Council. Once I had chosen the local chapter, I contacted the president of that chapter (whom I had met previously at the National Council meeting), and described the project to him in detail in a letter. I told him that I was interested in studying interaction among men, and that I would be observing and audio-tape-recording, as well as conducting interviews with members. He then asked the members for permission to allow me to go ahead with my research at a general meeting of the fraternity, and the members approved. I was permitted to attend any function and visit any individual member. I was also allowed to attend secret ritual ceremonies, but not to tape the ceremonial portion of the ritual activities. The names of the fraternity and all members are aliases.

At ΓΧΦ, there is an overt distinction between the formal, governing sphere of the fraternity, on the one hand, and the social sphere, on the other. However, the border between the two is fuzzy; older, office-holding members tend to associate together, and personality plays a large role in deciding who is elected into fraternity offices. Nonetheless, the ideological organization is the same throughout the fraternity, and can best be described as hierarchic.[2]

The hierarchical nature of the fraternity is already evident in the stages of acquiring membership outlined above. First, because only certain men are accepted into membership, the fraternity experience begins by valuing one identity over another. In ΓΧΦ, demeanour and physical power are highly valued. If someone is rich, caring or gets good grades, they are not more likely to be offered membership. The current members value skill at playing sports[3] – so a prospective member who played baseball in high school will be highly respected because he can help the fraternity win at intramural softball. Demeanour power is, however, most important in terms of gaining membership.[4] Members told me in interviews that the main reason they joined was because they thought the fraternity was 'a good group of guys'; similarly, bids are offered because a prospective member seems like 'a good guy'.

But what is 'a good guy'? Members themselves had difficulty defining this characteristic. For them, a good guy would seem to be someone who others enjoy being with, and someone who would appear to exemplify the members' own ideology. Thus, it may be someone who tells funny stories, or who is the subject of funny stories. Because of the hierarchic, competitive ideology of the organization, a man who acts strong, competitive and quick is valued. Friendship and community is shown through what seems like competitive talk filled with insults, boasts, orders, and embarrassing jokes and stories. A 'good guy' is someone who exemplifies powerful, competitive traits in all spheres: he works hard, gets things accomplished, is seen as a leader, and is verbally skilled in the 'competitive cooperative' style through which the men build solidarity. By selecting only men with certain characteristics, the fraternity creates a hierarchy between its members and outsiders (although non-members are also ranked).

Once access to the fraternity has been gained, there is still an implicit hierarchy evident in all stages of membership. The pledges begin their fraternity experience by being treated as unknowledgeable, childlike servants, and even when the pledges become full members, they are still not valued as highly as older members. Usually, only after at least one year of membership does a man have the power to affect, through his own actions, the actions of the fraternity and its members. When attempting to influence the fraternity in this way, ability and demeanour power are highly valued, along with knowledge power. This is especially evident during elections, for example, where members evaluate candidates' work ethic, experience, personality and skills.

Thus, the main constraint that the men place on each other is to present a competitive, successful, confident identity. The fraternity ideology also values hard work, especially work that promotes the good of the group. In this way, members are taught to protect and care for each other.

Data Analysis: Power and Identity in Practice

In this section, I will explore how four men employ different discursive means in order to construct powerful identities. The excerpts I analyse come from an election meeting involving the entire fraternity membership. Ordinary meetings are held every Sunday evening in a campus classroom, but elections are held only once a year, usually in the autumn.

Because they are speaking in a meeting, the four men in question have much at stake. Initially, they must show that they have the authority to speak. But because their identities are on public display in the business sphere, the men are more constrained than usual by the competitive, hierarchic ideology of the fraternity. Through the varying employment of mitigation, mood, pronoun use and personal experience, these members orient themselves towards different processes of power. The processes they draw upon are consistent with the identities that they have constructed previously in the fraternity, but are nevertheless specific to the time of speaking.

The excerpts I analyse are taken from a discussion during elections for the office of chapter correspondent, whose job it is to communicate with the national fraternity through letters published in the fraternity's national magazine. The position traditionally goes to a younger member because it requires little experience or knowledge of how the fraternity works. After the four candidates – Kurt, Ritchie, Mullin and Ernie – give their speeches, they leave the room so that other members can discuss the candidates' strengths and weaknesses. The four members I shall focus on are: Darter, Speed, Ram and Mack.

Darter

The first speaker I consider is Darter, a newly initiated brother. He no doubt still feels deferential to those men who, until a few weeks ago, had almost total control over his life. Although he was the president of the pledge class, and is recognized as a possible future leader of the fraternity, he is not in a position to exercise demeanour or structural power because he is a nib, and does not hold a high position. In his comments, the first he has made in the elections, Darter bases his argument on his knowledge of the candidates' abilities. Two of the candidates are his pledge brothers, Ritchie and Ernie. Kim is Korean-American; Speed is an older brother.

Excerpt 1

```
48   DARTER:   Um Ri:tchie may come off like he's really like a dumb ass
49             and everything but uh
50             he's like one of the smartest people
51             I know y'know
52             I went to high school with him
53             and he was like ranked fifth in our class.
54             and he can he can write like rea:lly well
55   KIM:                              He's A:sian man, what
56             do you expect?
57   SPEED:    (sarcastic) Is he really?
58   DARTER:            I mean he he types like unbelievably ... quick.
59             um I just think this would be a good position for him
60             to hold because he's a really good writer,
61             I mean I've read a lot of papers of his.
```

Because he is young and a new brother, Darter does not normally speak in meetings. But in this comment Darter draws from his specialized knowledge – his high school friendship with Ritchie – to assert his right to speak. He begins by acknowledging the identity that Ritchie has in the fraternity (line 48).[5] Darter then contrasts this identity with the identity he remembers from high school (lines 50–4). He then states his position: 'I just think this would be a good position for him to hold.' He mitigates his statement through the use of 'I just think', which suggests his opinion is not very valuable. By using 'I think' and the conditional 'would', he frames his statement as a suggestion, rather than a fact (e.g. 'this is a good position for him'). Instead of simply making this more direct statement, he includes a dependent clause that explicitly highlights his reasoning ('because he's a really good writer'), which is implicit from his statements in lines 50–4. (I show below that the older brothers do not need to provide this kind of justification.) Darter then emphasizes once again how he knows that Ritchie is a good writer. He thus explicitly justifies his support for Ritchie through his knowledge of the latter's writing abilities. His power is therefore not based on his demeanour or position in the fraternity, but on knowledge, which he is careful to highlight extensively. He presents himself as holding information important to the debate, but as unsure of its worth.

Speed

The next speaker I introduce is Speed, a third-year member. Of the four men I am considering, he speaks next in the meeting. His statement is short and to the point.

Excerpt 2

```
83  MICK:  Speed.
84  SPEED:        Ri:tchie. I like Ritchie 'cause he's smart
85          and he probably writes really good too:
86          so let him do it dude.
```

Speed at first does not justify his statement. He merely states Ritchie's name. Then he notes that Ritchie is smart and (extrapolating from line 84) that Ritchie is capable of doing the job. His short statement indicates that for him the choice, based on Ritchie's ability, is simple. It is just a matter of 'letting him do it'. In addition, by first only uttering Ritchie's name, Speed implies that members should be swayed by the mere fact that he is for Ritchie.

Ram

Ram presents his powerful identity in a different way. An older brother, he has just finished a year as treasurer. He creates a fatherly, 'wise elder' identity through his comment:

Excerpt 3

```
119  Ram:  um I'd like to endorse David here, surprisingly
120        I mean the kid–
121        I don't want to see him fall into another–
122        and I'm not saying that he would
123        Kevin Fierst type thing,
```

124	I think we need to make him–
125	we need to strongly involve him *now*
126	I think he's pretty serious about it, y'know
127	and with a little guidance I mean he'll do a fine job.

Ram creates a powerful identity by putting himself in the role of a person with age and experience: he refers to David as 'the kid', and he shows off his knowledge of past members of the fraternity (Kevin Fierst was a member who dropped out of school because of substance abuse problems). He further highlights his position through his use of the phrase 'with a little guidance', suggesting that he is qualified to give that guidance. He also shows concern for David ('I don't want to see him fall into another . . . Kevin Fierst type thing'), which suggests a fatherly position. Thus, he draws on the part of the fraternity ideology that stresses 'looking out for' another brother. Finally, he also uses the device of speaking on behalf of the fraternity ('we need to strongly involve him now'), although he mitigates his statement more than Mack, in the next section, by embedding it in 'I think'.

Mack

Contrast Darter and Speed's comments with those made by Mack, a fourth-year member, who was Darter's pledge educator (in charge of the programme and activities during the pledge period). Mack affects actions through his demeanour, using little mitigation in his statements, and through the imperative mood. Mick is the president, Pencil is the graduate advisor.

Excerpt 4

184	MICK:	Mack.
185	MACK:	*Okay* . . .
186		This is *it* . . .
187		Somebody said something about=
188	PENCIL:	=Again, we need to reorganize (?).
189	MACK:	yeah somebody's–
190		we need to look at what we have left here,
191		and there are certain positions
192		that everybody fits into perfectly.
193		Ernie does *not* fit into this: (0.1)
194		I'm not sure where Ernie fits in just yet.
195	?:	historian

196	Mack:	*but* I: a:m afraid that we are going to *waste* uh
197		one of the few brains *left*. in someplace that that
198		uh historian has potentially been a
199		non-existent position. uh I think for a couple
200		semesters yahoo took some pictures,
201	Pencil:	We're talking about chapter correspondent now
202	Mack:	what's that? I know
203	Pencil:	and he can hold *both* positions
204	Mack:	I understand that. (0.3)
205		But he won't.
206		(0.5)
207		I see– I see *Kurt*– I see Kurt– I see *Kurt*–
208	Pencil:	Then talk about chapter correspondent.
209		point of order.
210	?:	we have we have four left.
211	Pencil:	point of order.
212	Mack:	I see Kurt as chapter correspondent.
213		not Ritchie damn it.

Mack begins by serving notice that his word is gospel: 'This is it'. It is
unmitigated and imperative. Unlike Darter, Mack does not justify his
statement at all. This non-mitigation and non-justification presents a
role of someone who can make a proclamation – someone with
power. In line 190, he emphasizes this view by instructing the members on how to go about making a decision ('We need to look at what
we have left'). He does this by using the first person plural subject
without any hedges (or 'I think', as Darter does), and by using 'need'
instead of 'should'. Contrast his statement with what might be
termed its 'opposite': Mack might have said 'I think we should look
at what's left'. By using a bald imperative, then, Mack implicitly puts
himself in a role of structural power. However, Mack is not constructing a new place for himself in the fraternity, but continuing in a carefully constructed role: that of the elder, wise, behind-the-scenes
manipulator. In an interview, he indicated this manipulator role was
the one he seeks for himself. Although he has held few fraternity
offices, he goes to other members before elections, and suggests that
they run for certain positions, then makes comments in their favour
during elections.

Mack was also the pledge educator for the newly initiated brothers,
which may affect his comments in two ways. First, he has had a position of supreme authority over the new members until recently – he
was their teacher and 'drill sergeant' – so that they perceive him as an
authority within the fraternity. Second, he can claim to know the new
members better than any other member (except perhaps the new mem-

bers themselves). Thus, he can claim to be qualified to make these pronouncements. He can use his structural and demeanour power to influence the new members, many of whom will vote in the election, and he can employ his knowledge power to influence older brothers.

Mack also demonstrates his role by where he sits in the classroom in which the meeting is held. Older members sit on the right-hand side of the room, and Mack sits as far to the right as possible. Darter, in contrast, sits on the 'younger' left-hand side, towards the middle (the extreme left-hand side is empty). Mack's cadence is also significant. Though not evident in the transcript, he speaks with a slow, pause-filled cadence that gives the impression of thoughtfulness and wisdom, while Darter speaks very quickly.

Mack continues to use unmitigated, authority-laden devices throughout his comments. In lines 191–4, he sets up a system in which each member has his place, and Mack knows who belongs where. He presents his statements as axiomatic truths by using 'there are' without any indication that he is actually voicing a personal opinion. Had he used modality markers, such as 'may', he would be implying that members can decide the issue for themselves. Instead, he leaves no room for doubt. In line 196, he presents himself as advisor to the fraternity ('I am afraid'). In contrast, instead of using these devices to speak for the collective in a leader-like role, he might have said something like 'I think Ritchie is overqualified for this position'. It is unclear where his argument is going from line 197 forward, because he stops his sentence, and begins to discuss the historian position. It looks as if he planned to highlight his age, by discussing the past worth of the historian position in lines 198–200 ('historian has potentially been a non-existent position'). Pencil then argues with him about discussing one position at a time (lines 201–11), which prompts Mack to finish his statement. Mack ends by simply stating that 'he sees' Kurt as correspondent, again without any justification (in fact, with less justification than at the beginning of his comments). This construction, 'I see', is used by other brothers to create a similar air of authority, as though the speaker were a visionary, who speaks with the wisdom of the ages.

Thus, there is a large difference between the way in which the older brothers and a younger brother present themselves. The older brother has a position of experience and respect that he can implicitly draw upon, while the younger brother, lacking this structural and demeanour power, is explicit about his reasoning to sway votes in his direction. While both are under similar general pressures to present a 'powerful' identity, each has different resources and solves the problem in his own way.

Speed

Now contrast Mack and Ram's remarks with a later comment by
Speed. After Mack speaks, other older members have taken up the
discussion of finding offices for the newly initiated brothers. Speed
responds to this trend, and returns to his utilitarian theme. Speed's
comments are given in a hurried, shouting voice, as if he is angry.

Excerpt 5

```
245   SPEED:   All right look.
246            first of all, you guys need to realize we do not
247            ha:ve to ne– necessarily make a:ll the new
248            brothers, put them in positions right away.
249            a lot of the new brothers already have positions.
250            they can get elected next year or next semester.
251            there are some positions that are semesterly.
252            we don't have to make sure that every one of them
253            has a position. they need time to learn and grow–
254            it's better that//they're– that they're=
255   ?:           I need an assistant
256   SPEED                                    =shut the fuck up.
257            it's better that they're–
258            that they're almost like I was with Tex.
259            I was Tex's like little bitch boy . . . graduate
260            affairs, and I learned a lot more there,
261            than I would if I got stuck in some leadership
262            role, so fuck 'em,
263            I don't care if any of 'em don't get a position.
264            but I'm telling you right now,
265            I think Ritchie should do it because like Kim
266            said, people are gonna read this shit,
267            Kurt might get ha:mmered and write some shitty . .
268            fuckin' letter, Ernie can't write,
269            fuckin' Mullin already has a position,
270            so put Ritchie in there,
271            and stop fuckin' trying to . . set everybody up in
272            a position. Christ.
273   MICK:    Alex.
274   SPEED:      I:'d like one
275            (laughter)
```

Speed is an older brother, but he has created an adversarial identity
in the fraternity, resisting those in formal offices. He relies on a differ-

ent presentation of power, one that sets him up in opposition to others. Even though he is a third-year member, he always sits on the 'non-powerful' left-hand side, in the back of the room, thus showing his contempt for the fraternity hierarchy. Speed's argumentative identity is evident in this speech, but he uses some of the same linguistic devices as Mack. Like Mack, Speed uses the imperative. He begins by saying 'All right look', which is similar in tone to Mack's 'This is it'. In line 246, Speed states that 'you guys need to realize', which is similar to Mack's 'we need to look at what we have left'. Speed then shows his knowledge of the fraternity, continuing in an imperative mood, saying 'we don't have to make sure that every one of them has a position', which contrasts with Mack's 'we need to look at what we have left here'.

Speed then draws on his personal experience (as Ram did) in the fraternity for an example in lines 259–62 (notably in a low position – 'I was Tex's like little bitch boy'). This statement disparages 'leadership positions', and implicitly the organizational structure of the fraternity. Next, he uses an aggravated, bold statement to show his indifference to the brothers' aspirations in lines 262–3 ('*so fuck 'em* . . .'). Speed then again presents a utilitarian argument for voting for Ritchie by pointing out why other candidates are unqualified (lines 264–70). In line 264, he uses a pedagogic tone similar to Mack's ('I'm telling you right now'). Note that this rhetoric is consistent with his argumentative, impatient identity: he sums up each person quickly, with aggravation and profanity. Then, at the very end (line 274), he injects some self-directed humour. Throughout the elections, he has been unable to get elected, and this has become a running joke. When he says 'I'd like one', he adds to his demeanour with a joke making fun of himself. Ending with a joke is a common device used by the members in these comments; it builds demeanour power by easing the tedium that accompanies the election meetings.

Thus Speed, while staying within the constraints of the hierarchic fraternity ideology, manages to construct an identity that appears to reject the manipulative structural power used by some of the older brothers. He accomplishes his identity by focusing on the value of competing against a structure of power; rebellion and independence are consistent with the fraternity's competitive ideology. He also focuses on the need to do what is best for the group by highlighting why Ritchie is best qualified for the position. Thus, Speed, Mack and Ram, while using similar linguistic devices to convince the members and present their identities, nevertheless construct very different identities. Because he is younger, Darter, on the other hand, has different constraints on the identity he presents in the meeting. He does not have a demeanour or structural power process working in his favour, so the problem presented to him – of creating an identity consistent with the fraternity ideology – is much different than the problem presented to Speed, Mack and Ram. Darter must create a means of influencing voting (an action that will affect other actions) without any prior history of being able to do so. He must also construct a role for himself that fits within the constraints of being a nib, but nevertheless convinces people to vote for his favoured candidate. Darter therefore draws on his specialized knowledge of the candidate.

It is important to notice also that Speed was genuinely impatient with the discussion at the time of his second statement, as seen by a comparison of his two utterances. In the first statement, he simply says why Ritchie is qualified for the position. In the second, however, he is arguing *against* other members – especially Mack – as much *for* Ritchie, in addition to arguing about the progress of the debate generally. This place in the discussion (he is nearly the last speaker) sets up a context in which he can position himself as the defender of ability power over structural power for its own sake. In other words, he can make clear his dislike of voting members into structural positions without any clear functional reason for doing so. This secondary argument was not possible in Speed's first comments because none of the older members had suggested considering all the new members, and what offices they should occupy. His identity construction in the second statement therefore shows the situated, sequence-dependent nature of identity.

Speed also exhibited this adversarial identity in an interview, however. The semester before the interview, Speed had been the pledge educator, but was ousted because of what he sees as his 'independence':

Excerpt 6

```
1   SCOTT:   Did you keep it ((the pledge period)) the way
2            you had it?
3   SPEED:   I tried to, man, but they wouldn't let me so:
4            I had to I had to succumb to their rules
5            th th– th– they got all pissed off at me and tried to take my
6            position away from me and all that shit,
7            man. (1.0) Bunch a dicks.
```

Speed's independence shows through in this excerpt when he says 'I had to succumb to their rules'. Speed also sees that he lost his position because he didn't follow the dominant ideology, but evaluates that ideology – or its proponents – negatively ('Bunch a dicks'). Thus, Excerpt 6 provides more evidence for an ideological clash between Speed's alleged independence, and the fraternity's expectation of sacrifice in return for structural power.

All the men discussed create powerful identities, but they each use disparate strategies in order to achieve a different kind of power. Differences can be seen in how the men orient themselves to various features of the fraternity ideology. Most appeal to what will be best for the fraternity. Darter and Speed focus on the ideology of being rewarded for ability. They both argue that Ritchie is simply the most qualified candidate, and voting for him will benefit the fraternity the most. They therefore appeal to the part of the ideology that puts the group before the individual. Ram also appeals to this value, but in another way. He argues that the fraternity will lose Kurt if they don't involve him in it. Mack, however, focuses on the fraternity's hierarchical nature; for him, some jobs are more important than others, and must be 'assigned' to more important members. Thus, he wants Ritchie to have a job other than chapter correspondent. Mack also sees his own role as that of manipulator, and uses his structural position of age to put members in the offices that he 'sees' for them. Finally, Speed fights against this focus on structural power.

The elections are very important to the members. They care deeply about the fraternity and its future. Who they elect very much affects what happens in the fraternity. In addition, the outcomes affect their own power within the fraternity and, even more important perhaps, their ability to affect the actions of others in the future.[6]

Discussion

I have thus shown how four men employ both similar and varied discursive devices in order to construct a particular kind of identity, given certain constraints on that identity. All four manage to present some kind of identity valued by the competitive, hierarchic fraternity ideology. Darter had to justify his statements overtly. Ram created a fatherly image. Mack spoke with a voice of the elder. Speed 'resisted' the dominance of structural power over ability, and the good of the fraternity and its members over trying to control every detail of the fraternity's future. While being men in a fraternity affected their language in similar ways, their individual solutions in time and space were unique. It is worth pointing out, however, that I have only had sufficient space to consider one speech activity here; in fact, the men's identities vary even more when other speech activities are analysed.

Sociolinguists often group people together based on criteria external to the community, and focus on how people of certain groups use language in a similar way. Generalizations about men and women are among the most common. But within these generalizations we find many variations. Within the fraternity community, for example, we can group older members together, because they tend to use less mitigation and justification and, more importantly, because age is one way the members group themselves. Clearly, then, it is essential, when considering the language of men, to explore how gender is mediated by age, status, and so on, in the same way that this has been necessary when analysing the speech of women. But even grouping Speed, Ram and Mack together as elder members of the fraternity ignores their very different individual presentations of self.

Meaningful generalizations are, however, still possible and necessary. We can still say that, in some general sense, many men in the United States construct powerful, competitively oriented identities. Moreover, due to the ideology of difference in US society, the motivation for men to construct these identities is of a different nature than for women, and the outcomes for 'resistance' are different for each of the two sexes. Men who construct the 'preferred' gender identity are rewarded with power, while women are not rewarded in the same sense when they construct the identity that society 'prefers' for their gender. In fact, a 'powerless' identity that many researchers have shown to be the 'preferred' identity for a North American woman could actually be seen as punishing women. Real resistance to the gender order, for instance a 'powerful female' identity or a 'powerless male' identity, may have similar consequences. But many men arguably have little motivation for such resistance. Speed, for example, appears to be resisting 'the establishment', but he is nevertheless using that 'resistance' as an alternative way of constructing a powerful, individualistic identity that is ultimately ratified by the fraternity ideology.

The way in which the fraternity men create different yet powerful identities suggests that particular roles, such as workplace and family roles, may be the specifics that make up what people idealize as 'masculinity' and 'femininity'. The men discussed here adopt elements of archetypal male roles: loyal friend, concerned father, wise elder, pragmatic individualist. In addition, two of the men identify *themselves* as having the identities they present in the election.

As Sattel (1983) points out, many men are expected to take on positions of leadership. But the direction of the indexing of men's identities and leadership is not clear; we might also say that society expects leadership positions to be held by men. Work such as Bonnie McElhinny's (1993) study of female police officers in Pittsburgh similarly highlights the importance of work and family roles in society's view of masculinity and femininity. Further research is needed in this area to learn more about such roles and their relationship to the construction of gender. In my research, I plan to return to the fraternity to test whether new members take on the same kinds of roles as older members who have left. Does Darter become a 'wise elder', a 'concerned father figure', an 'impatient individualist'? Or does he create an entirely new role, or a combination of all?

Conclusion

In this chapter, I have explored the way in which the identities of four fraternity members are constructed through interaction in an election meeting. My findings have, however, a number of implications for work on language and gender in more general terms. For example, I have shown how the four men construct their own identities, drawing upon both the same, and different, types of power processes through the language they use. Thus, although all the men manage to evoke some type of power with their language, it would be extremely difficult to draw specific conclusions on the types of linguistic structures (e.g. tag-questions, hedging etc.) used by men 'as a group' on the basis of my data since their usage is highly contextualized. In this sense, my findings compare with those of both Cameron (chapter 3) and Pujolar (chapter 5).

Transcription conventions

Turn-taking

//	Bounds simultaneous speech.
=	Connects two utterances that were produced with noticeably less transition time between them than usual.
(number)	Silences timed in tenths of seconds.
(.)	Noticeable silence less than 0.2 second.
#	Bounds passage said very quickly.

Sound production

^	Falsetto.
TEXT	Upper-case letters indicate noticeably loud volume.
*	Indicates noticeably low volume, placed around the soft words.
text	Italics indicate emphatic delivery (volume and/or pitch).
–	Indicates that the sound that precedes it is cut off, stopped suddenly and sharply.
:	Indicates that the sound that precedes it is prolonged.
,	Indicates a slight intonational rise.
?	Indicates a sharp intonational rise.

Breathiness, laughter, comments

h	An audible outbreath.
'h	An audible inbreath.
he, ha	Laughter.
(text)	Transcript enclosed in single parentheses indicates uncertain hearing.
((comment))	Double parentheses enclose transcriber's comments.

Notes

1 I have chosen the term 'men's identities', rather than 'masculinity', for several reasons. First, 'masculinity' is not a neutral term; it connotes a single stereotype of male identity, for example, John Wayne and Arnold Schwarzenegger in their movie roles. However, the majority of men in Western culture do not present themselves as copies of these movie heroes (Kessler and McKenna, 1978; Segal, 1990). Some men even contradict this view of men's identities. Thus, masculinity, as I use the term, is but one possible (idealized) type of male identity. Similarly, that there is no 'natural', single identity to which men aspire is an important point; hence, I use the plural 'identities'. Men's (and women's) identities are constructed, negotiated and changing, but they are also constrained by social structures that value some types of identities over others. Furthermore, I use the term 'men' rather than 'male' or 'masculine' in order to highlight the fact that the identity is a social as opposed to biological construction; it is gender, not sex. 'Identity' is an intersection between a social presentation of self, and a psychological understanding of that self.

2 This hierarchic ideology is similar to Connell's characterization of hegemonic masculinity (1987, 1995).

3 Interest in sports, of course, is also connected to competition; in this case, the desire is to be the best fraternity on campus in intramural sports.
4 The fact that demeanour is of primary importance in the fraternity supports its inclusion as a type of power, and not something other than power.
5 Line numbers match those from a complete transcript.
6 Ritchie won the election.

5

Masculinities in a Multilingual Setting

Joan Pujolar i Cos

Introduction

During the dictatorship of General Franco in Spain (1939–75), the public use of the Catalan language was forbidden and severely prosecuted. Following Franco's death, a new democratic constitution was established which granted Catalonia[1] a degree of self-rule. An autonomous government was set up in 1980, and one of its key policies has been the reintroduction of Catalan into schools as a medium of instruction. This chapter summarizes an ethnographic study of two groups of young people from working-class districts of Barcelona, most of whom attended school in the 1980s during this period of linguistic transition.

Initially, I was interested in investigating the impact of these recent language policies in Catalonia in quite general terms. I wanted to see how young people had responded to such changes, and what attitudes and discursive practices they had developed in their peer groups as a result. It soon became clear to me, however, that gender played a crucial role in structuring many of the groups' activities, along with their attitudes towards language-related issues. Many games, tastes and ways of talking, for example, appeared to be gender-specific.

In the first half of this chapter, I will look at a number of discursive features that I found to be typical of my male informants in face-to-face interaction, and I will focus on the different types of masculinity that were constructed by the two groups I observed. In the second half, I shall use this understanding of masculine identities to explore the way in which speech styles, language choice and code-switching between Catalan and Spanish also relate to the formation of those identities. I shall not, therefore, be dealing with the relationship between masculinity and *language* in the singular, but between various masculinities and *languages* in the plural, that is to say, the role played by multilingualism in the construction of gendered identities.

The Study

In Catalonia, most speakers of Spanish are immigrant workers or their children. This is why, as Woolard (1989) has pointed out, the Catalan language is usually associated with the most prestigious social groups in spite of its subordinated political status within Spain as a whole. In my study, however, I was keen to explore the effect of the new language policies on working-class speakers. In order to do this, I sought to build a context-sensitive account of the ways in which my informants constructed their identities within the peer groups, and then find out how these were linked to patterns of language use.

The participants in my study were between 17 and 23 years old, and lived in various working-class neighbourhoods of Barcelona. I gave each group a name: the 'Rambleros' and the 'Trepas' (see table 1). My fieldwork consisted in joining these two groups in their leisure activities as they went to pubs, cafés, discos or on holiday. During this time, I took notes, recorded spontaneous conversations, and organized group discussions and interviews where I encouraged participants to talk about issues of gender, language use, job prospects, politics, music and other hobbies. With the exception of the youngest, who still attended school, most members of the groups had given up their studies at secondary level.

Table 1 Composition of the groups of participants

	Rambleros		Trepas	
	Women	*Men*	*Women*	*Men*
Speakers of Spanish	6	5	5	2
Speakers of Catalan	–	–	1	5

In my study, I adopted a post-structuralist conception of identity as constructed in discourse and in social interaction. I thus developed ideas from Bakhtin (1981, 1986), Fairclough (1992a), Foucault (1972) and Goffman (1967, 1974) in order to analyse face-to-face encounters in a way that stressed a sense of *process*. Traditional structuralist-based approaches have been *product*-centred, i.e. they have concentrated on purely formal features of language and identity, and their synchronic regularities and relations. One consequence of this latter approach has been the somewhat simplistic notion of *identity* that has been employed, usually as if it were merely a matter of group membership based on family background, level of income, sex, etc. This narrow view has, in turn, led many researchers to overlook the fact that meanings and identities are constructed and negotiated in social interactions through social processes that have a historical and political dimension (see Fairclough, 1992a; Pujolar, 1995; Johnson, chapter 1).

According to Goffman (1967), social actors in face-to-face encounters continually work to protect and develop particular forms of self-presentation, i.e. the features of their own characters which they choose to display to others. Individuals tend therefore to establish links with others, and participate in social events and activities which will facilitate their preferred forms of self-presentation. I thus chose to base my classification of gender forms on a detailed study of each person's participation in various types of social activities. The participants in my study were categorized according to the social events (games, forms of talk) which they got involved in, *and* according to *the way in which* they participated in those activities. But it is still important not to see the 'types' of events I describe as originating in ready-made models from which participants chose to draw (a common structuralist tenet). Such a static conception of the social situation can lead us to overlook the fact that actors work to *(re)define* or *negotiate* the meanings that are being constructed in a given context. My own reference to such activity types is therefore more of a descriptive device to understand the ways in which participants organized their various displays of identity, in this case, their *gender displays* (Goffman, 1976).

Masculine Identities amongst the Rambleros and Trepas

Gender Displays in Face-to-Face Interaction

On the basis of the following example, we can begin to explore the processes by which some of the Rambleros men produced their own particular displays of masculinity. In this episode, the men were walking along a street at night, and Andrés wanted to persuade the others to go for a sandwich:

Episode 1a

[Spanish in italics]

ANDRÉS: [fort] *eh vamos al bocata aquel* [?]
         [loud] Hey, let's go to that sandwich place?
LUIS: *mira (..) si quiereh comer (.) te puedes amorrar*
         entre mis patas sabes [?]
         Look, (..) if you wanna eat (.) you stick your
         snout between my legs, you know?

Andrés' initial proposal was taken as meaning that he wished to eat something. To this, Luis reacted by suggesting – indirectly – that Andrés could eat his genitalia instead. This is easily recognizable as a joke: in Goffman's (1974) terms, a *keyed* action where the speaker puts on a character which is not to be taken as 'real' or 'serious', but as engaged in a kind of play. In addition, the gibe about eating genitalia referred to a recurrent joke between the Rambleros men: *'cómeme la polla'* (eat my cock), which they frequently used as a playful but provocative sexual advance to women.

In this particular context, Luis' 'proposal' was also hinting at the possibility of Andrés' being homosexual, thus casting doubts on his heterosexual masculine credentials and, by implication, on the features of character which were the prerequisite for participation in talk of this kind. Furthermore, Luis' comment potentially constituted a rejection of Andrés' serious proposal to go to the sandwich bar. Andrés responded to both potential meanings of Luis' utterance as follows:

Episode 1b

ANDRÉS: *pues chico con esto no me llega pa nada*
         Well kid, with this I wouldn't really have enough.

After the other members of the group had insisted on offering their own genitalia to 'placate' Andrés' hunger, the latter affirmed that these too were inadequate. In doing so, he first defended his proposal to go to eat – which was again left open. Second, he cast doubts on the masculinity of his friends in return by suggesting that their genitalia were of inadequate size. The response to this was:

Episode 1c

RICARDO: *mira (.) te pongo yo la polla en la boca es*
           que no te cabe colega
           Look (.) I stick my cock into your mouth, and
           there won't be room enough for it, mate.

Here, apart from Ricardo's obvious intention to defend his position
and his own masculinity in this game, it is essential to draw attention
to the prosodic features of his utterance, which are lost in the transcription: first, the rising articulatory tension up to '*boca*' conveying a
sense of threat; second, the release of this tension suggesting that the
concluding remark was so obvious that it was beyond discussion;
and finally, the use of the term '*colega*', which conveyed a sense of
forgiving friendliness. Although the threatening tone was diminished
by his nearly bursting into laughter, Ricardo was playing the character of the street fighter who defends his face while simultaneously
offering a way out of the conflict. He was calling upon an image similar to the deeply rooted Spanish '*chulo*' (literally: a pimp), who treats
the streets as if they were a bull-fighting ring.

In the interviews with the Rambleros group, many considered the
kind of situation outlined above to be a common activity amongst the
men. In this particular episode, the men were asserting and defend-
ing a particular form of masculinity associated with heterosexuality,
physical strength and size, and a certain aggressiveness manifested in
verbal terms. This verbal duelling allowed them to claim these masculine features in theatrical form, and to display their own ability to
stand up to challenges.

Men and Displays of Intimacy

On the basis of step-by-step analyses of excerpts such as these, where
every intervention was examined in terms of its contribution to a particular definition of the situation and display of identity, I sought to
establish some common characteristics of the men's events. In order
to do this, I drew upon the work of Goffman on gender (1976, 1977),
and also on Bourdieu (1991), Goodwin (1990), Hewitt (1986), Thorne
(1993) and Willis (1977).

Goodwin (1990) and Thorne (1993) point to the fact that girls'
events are generally organized in a way in which participants can
display mutual interest, intimacy and sympathy. This can lead to the

(sometimes equivocal) impression that girls (or women) are more supportive and caring. What many studies fail to appreciate is that the conceptual opposite of this must not necessarily be 'aggressiveness' or 'hierarchy' on the part of boys or men (see Cameron, chapter 3, for a similar line of argument).

In my study, in contrast with the many all-female activities which provided opportunities for the participants to show a clear interest in each other, men's events were commonly organized to display interest in an element or fact which could be treated as *external* to the participants. This basic organizational principle constituted a common thread across remarkably varied displays of masculinity, of which strength, competitiveness and self-sufficiency were but one of the available options. Thus, the men were able to show personal interest in each other and nurture intimacy, but they appeared to do so less directly than the women, i.e. through coordinated engagement in what they treated as something else: a game, a hobby, and so on (see Johnson and Finlay, chapter 7, for a discussion of football talk in this light).

This realization helps to explain some of my early experiences with the Rambleros group. So, for example, I found that the women had no trouble in approaching me, asking me questions and chatting. Indeed, I soon learned much about their lives and vice versa. On the other hand, although they were kind and considerate, I did not manage to communicate with the men until *after* I had found out what they did, how they talked, and until I had found opportunities for participating in their games. It was probably more difficult for them to find a masculine way of accommodating a male stranger, as they were not used to displaying personal concern directly. A certain 'symbolic distance' seemed to be necessary (a point which Meinhof explores in chapter 12 in the context of very different data).

This contrast between masculine and feminine activities was analytically highly productive. It helped to explain, for instance, why activities related to music and drug-taking were much more important for men. It seemed that because their activities had to be ritually arranged around an external focus of interest, men were much more dependent on finding concrete reasons or excuses to get together. And it was often necessary for them to assert, enhance and recognize this common interest. Hence their common tendency to produce outrageous narratives of heavy drinking or drug-taking, or the need to sustain a sense of fun by telling good jokes.

Simplified Masculinity and Gender Crossing

The form of masculinity associated with the Rambleros was what I will call 'simplified masculinity'. This coincides with the stereotypical views of manliness which became apparent in Episode 1. In interactional terms, it frequently involves the exploitation of risk, either to face or to body. For many youth gangs, this means getting involved in fights, insults and heavy drug-taking.

However, these patterns appeared in a fairly 'diminished' mode amongst the Rambleros: drug-taking was (comparatively) moderate, and their fights and verbal displays of aggressiveness were playful. More importantly perhaps, such aggressive displays were always located within the group, where members were able to appreciate the limits and the significance of the actions so that serious confrontations would not occur. Furthermore, these displays of aggressiveness were often treated as potential displays to outsiders as well: one of the members pointed out how bystanders sometimes laughed at their games. The Rambleros men also took pleasure in getting close to the scenes of fights in the streets, and sometimes participated in the face-saving discussions that usually surrounded them. Other congruent features were their fondness for sport, especially football, and for heavy metal music, which relies heavily on the imagery and gesticulation of male bravado (see Breen, 1991).

'Simplified masculinity' thus provides a useful framework for analysing those activities which were considered appropriate for defining and displaying masculinity within the Rambleros group. But it is not to be expected that all men and women will be happy with the possibilities open (and closed) to their sex, as the types of activities available can be seen as undesirable or too restrictive by some people. Thorne (1993) therefore speaks of *gender crossing* when individuals seek to participate in some of the events normally associated with the other sex.

Gender crossing is a delicate matter because masculine or feminine events are often organized in order to produce displays of character which are deemed to be intrinsic or natural to a particular sex. However, such crossing appeared in both the Rambleros and the Trepas groups. So where my informants were concerned, if a man took pleasure in carefully choosing different styles of dress, in reading children's comics, or showed little readiness to get involved in aggressive acts, or no interest in heavy metal or football, he could easily be labelled 'queer' or, at least, 'special'.

Conversely, some women were keen to participate in men's activities and, correspondingly, shared an interest in 'their' music and football teams. If such women adopted features of what were considered to be typically masculine ways of talking, such as use of a particular accent, swearing, certain types of slang, or even verbal aggressiveness, they risked being teased as 'rough' or as talking 'like a miner'.

Amongst both the Rambleros and the Trepas, gender crossing cannot be construed as politically motivated in general terms. These 'crossers' were not really trying to challenge existing forms of gender display, but simply wished to participate in the activities associated with the other sex. They did not therefore constitute a class of their own with predictable patterns of participation and display. It was more a question of their presenting different ways of handling the delicate balance between the requirements and limitations of participation in markedly gendered events. This was often problematic if it was not accompanied by skilful tact.[2]

However, it was possible for crossing to acquire a political significance in some circumstances because there is always room for ambivalence in gendered activities. This was the case where crossing practices overlapped with those individuals or groups who displayed *politicized identities*.

Politicized Identities

The second group I studied, the Trepas, contained many members who were political activists of leftist, anti-military and/or feminist organizations. In this group, issues of identity were constantly being problematized. In the case of women, this involved the adoption of typically masculine forms of talk such as heavy swearing and use of argot, and also of styles of gesticulation, dressing and manners which can be best described as 'laid back'. At the same time, they preserved the basic features of feminine events, that is, mutual displays of intimacy and sympathy, though interestingly, it was often within the confines of their own relationships that they adopted aspects of typically 'masculine' identities.

In the case of the Trepas men, there were various possibilities where politicized identities were concerned. For example, one had performed a virtual gender 'switch' – though this should not be confused with homosexuality. This man was actually closer to the women than to the men, and spent most of his time in their company with no apparent difference in the way he participated in their events. Indeed, he was so well integrated in the women's group that he was allowed to sleep in their room on a holiday trip.

As far as the rest of the Trepas men were concerned, displays of masculinity differed significantly from those of the Rambleros. This became apparent from the very beginning of my fieldwork, when some of the men made a concerted effort to put me at ease within the group, for example by asking me to talk about my project or my life in England. These situations did not go as smoothly as with the women, but there was a significant contrast with the Rambleros men.

In addition, displays of aggressiveness or risk, either verbal or physical, were rare amongst the Trepas men. One of the members said he avoided rock concerts where one was likely to encounter violence; another told me that he had abandoned his previous clique some years earlier because they were taking heavy drugs, and he did not accept that drug-taking helped anyone to achieve a 'superior' status.

Rather than the exploitation of risk, the Trepas men seemed more concerned with displaying subversive or transgressive stances vis-à-vis mainstream standards of demeanour and appearance. Although the Rambleros also performed displays of transgression, for the Trepas, these tied with their leftist political views. In terms of appearance, they wore much 'rougher' clothing, had unconventional hairstyles, and adopted a very relaxed kind of gesticulation affecting constant laziness.

Where music was concerned, these men dismissed heavy metal on the grounds that its apparent rebelliousness was merely 'staged' as opposed to genuinely challenging the system. They preferred hardcore and punk-related styles, which have a contestatory political ethos, and which required of fans that they actively searched for groups and records that circulated outside the main commercial channels. Some of them had even created a band and performed concerts.

When they got together, drinking (often heavily) or smoking hashish (with the ritual of passing the joint) were important displays of transgression. Their talk commonly contained accounts of drunkenness or 'big highs' and their consequences, together with true or fictional stories of insubordination towards authority. Their music tastes and their fondness for drugs often separated them from the women, which in turn was a frequent source of unease and tension within the group.

Having examined the different types of gender displays within the Rambleros and the Trepas groups, I now turn to an exploration of the way in which these were linked to speech styles and language choice. I shall begin, however, by saying a little more about my theoretical approach.

Speech Styles, Language Choice and the Construction of Masculine Identities

Languages and Ideologies: a Dialogical Approach

In order to highlight the connections between particular forms of gender displays, on the one hand, and language use, on the other, it is necessary to bypass the structuralist assumption that linguistic diversity can be studied in terms of mere interactions between linguistic systems with some loose association with identity. Even the notion of communicative competence (Gumperz and Hymes, 1972; Hymes, 1964) can be misleading in this respect. This is because such competence is often treated as a static entity, and dealt with as though it could be reduced to a set of rules which exist in speakers' minds. Such an approach tends, therefore, to overlook the way in which historical and social processes underpin the acquisition of communicative competence in situated practices.

The key point in my study was *the role that linguistic varieties played in the construction of identities*, i.e. in the organization of social activities and the corresponding displays of self obtaining in them. In my analysis, I adopted the fundamental Bakhtinian premise which sees language as inherently 'dialogical': 'any utterance, in addition to its own theme, always responds [. . .] in one form or another to others' utterances that precede it' (Bakhtin, 1986, p. 94).

A dialogical conception of language is one that accepts the possibility of language only in as far as it enters into a dialogue. Language exists in social interaction (in the broadest sense), and any utterance can only be understood on the basis of its dialogical 'context', i.e. as a response to previous utterances which, at the same time, anticipate posterior responses. So for example, in the dialogue in Episode 1, all of the men's utterances were responding to the meanings produced, hinted at or expressed in the previous turns, and they were understood in those terms.

Nonetheless, this 'responsiveness' of the utterance is not restricted to the sequential dimension of spoken interaction, as some conversational analysts seem to imply. In responding to previous utterances, speakers always integrate (explicitly or implicitly) the words, voices and discourses of the wider cultural context (Bakhtin, 1981). The utterance is therefore the meeting point of a multiplicity of voices, which speakers re-work and transform according to their own expressive intention (see Talbot, chapter 10, for a discussion of this dialogic perspective with reference to the reading and writing of texts).

Because meaning is constantly produced in the situated processes of human communication, Bakhtin (1986) argues that each social group produces its own way of speaking in accordance with the particular expressive intentions of the situations obtaining in their social contexts. Utterances enter the social world in the form of *speech genres*. 'Speech genre' designates a unit of speech which inextricably integrates form and meaning by virtue of its social and situated character (Bakhtin, 1981). So for example, we can refer to 'verbal duelling' or 'gossip' as genres if we define their general features of form and meaning, but, at a lower level, the line 'eat my cock' can also be considered a genre.

This ongoing creation of genres is ultimately the source of 'heteroglossia', i.e. the social stratification of language, as different social groups produce their own forms of expression, repertoires and accents associated with particular activities, which in turn correspond to the groups' own ideologies and identities.

Masculinity, Speech Styles and the Claim to Simple Truths

In my analysis of the Rambleros, I was struck by the fact that the speech styles of the men and the women contrasted markedly in certain respects. All the men (plus women crossers) integrated in some way or other the southern Spanish Andalusian accent as typified by the aspiration of implosive /s/ or its deletion in word-final position (see Tusón, 1985), and particularly musical patterns of intonation. It appeared, therefore, that this Andalusian 'voice' – or at least the way it was appropriated in that particular context – bore some relation to the form of masculinity constructed by the Rambleros men.

In Catalonia, an Andalusian accent is usually associated with peasant or lower-working-class groups, and conveys a certain world view: that of the 'common people' who, in their simplicity, can claim authenticity and direct access to *simple* truths (an expressive resource usually exploited in theatre and comedy).[3]

This 'simplicity' was a key element in the way the Rambleros men organized their displays of self. For example, these men distanced themselves quite visibly from formal types of talk. In their group discussion, they teased members who spoke too elegantly, and took pleasure in integrating their own forms of (dirty) language, which subverted the supposed formality of the group discussion, causing considerable hilarity. This style of masculinity presented itself as spontaneous, unsophisticated, somehow self-sufficient – something which typified not only the form but also the content of their utterances. So, for example, the men tended to present their views and opinions as questions of taste or preference devoid of any underlying cause, elaborate intention or need for coherence. Their political beliefs, for instance, represented striking contradictions in terms of traditional categories such as combinations of racism and left-wing views.

Since many of the Rambleros women were committed to more 'well-mannered' and sophisticated forms of self-display, this 'simplified masculinity' often led to conflicts regarding the forms of identity which were being constructed within the group generally. The Rambleros women did not drop /s/, did not like heavy metal, excessive drinking or verbal aggressiveness, and only swore in narratives and exclamations, often using euphemized or clichéd terms. They engaged in teasing (a less offensive form of verbal aggressiveness) more often addressed to the men as a 'tit for tat'.

By dint of their aspirations to semi-skilled – usually clerical – jobs, the Rambleros women had a vested interest in presenting themselves as sophisticated, reasonably elegant and committed to good manners. In this context, the women did not experience men's verbal aggressiveness as playful, but as disgusting and contaminating. Moreover, on some occasions, it was clear that men used verbal aggressiveness and sexual taunting as a way of explicitly subverting the meanings and identities constructed by the women. This was also apparent in the way in which the women were teased for dressing too smartly, talking too much, or criticized for studying for too long and not confronting the 'real world' as the men had done after leaving school. It appeared that, through these verbal games and their own sense of fun, the men were imposing their notion of 'simple' truths.

This claim to 'simple truths' also appeared in some of the speech styles of the Trepas. But both the discursive resources drawn upon, and the meanings they implied, were very different from those of the Rambleros. Where the Trepas were concerned, the men, the politicized women and women 'crossers' used relatively standardized forms of both Catalan and Spanish, though with a considerable component of inner-city argot words.[4] This argot is very much associated with the lower classes, and often with the world of drugs, petty delinquents or lower-class Romany people. As such, argot originates in what are perceived to be predominantly masculine spaces.

But the Trepas reinterpreted this type of argot to construct quite a different ideological space as a reflection of their own political outlook, which was based on a Marxist view of society and saw the working class as the potentially liberating class. This became clear, for instance, in the way they appropriated terms such as *'la penya'*, the name given to Barcelona's young merry-making population, and to which the Trepas saw themselves as belonging. The term is frequently used to refer to young people in general or the audience of a concert, but it also connotes the penniless, the needy, drug addicts, and so on. Thus, where the Trepas were concerned, the views, reactions, voices and transgressions of '*la penya*' were accorded an authenticity that defied and exposed the flaws of the dominant 'truth'.

This commitment to a 'simple truth' was, however, restricted to those cases where it suited the political interests of the Trepas. In the group discussion, for example, the Trepas severely criticized the narrow-minded and sexist attitudes of many male manual workers who harassed their female colleagues. These 'ignorant' people were usually depicted or dramatized in the Trepas' talk as speaking in an Andalusian accent, and producing common speech genres of courting and verbal aggressiveness.

Clara, for instance, used an Andalusian accent to imitate the performance of a stupid disco womanizer who produced speech genres associated with cinema clichés (for instance '*háseme tuyo*' – literally: 'make me yours', 'take me'). In other examples, the Trepas men produced playful insults with this accent. Salva, for instance, shouted '*cabrone*' (bastards) with an Andalusian accent at fellow musicians when he was trying to get them to pay attention during a rehearsal. Through this dramatization, he diminished the potential face-threatening effect of an insult or of a command.

All in all, the Trepas used the Andalusian voice to express their rejection of aspects of 'simplified masculinity' typified by groups such as the Rambleros. But in addition to this appropriation of other voices and their use of argot, the Trepas had no real problem in adopting features of more formal styles of speaking. In their group discussion, they combined political discourses and the voices of argot in a similar way to many grass-roots political groups in Barcelona, which draw upon the meanings of '*la penya*' through their language and imagery.[5] One interesting consequence of this was the way in which arguments and reasonings were often presented as dramatized dialogues between different figures representing contrasting views, thus producing a remarkably 'multi-voiced' or 'polyphonic' style.

Unmasculine Catalan Voices

So far I have suggested that speakers integrate a multiplicity of voices into their talk, and that these are linked to particular identities, world views and activity types. In seeking to analyse this polyphonic character of speech, it is also useful to refer to Goffman's (1974) frame analysis of talk.

Goffman argues that any stretch of talk can be analysed as a narrative where different characters are impersonated (me serious, me ironic, me as narrator, me or others as protagonists, speakers), and a variety of scenic devices can be gathered (accents, gesticulation, gaze, even props). Furthermore, both Bakhtin and Goffman point out that what might appear to be direct quotations do not necessarily reproduce statements faithfully, but are subject to the expressive intention of the moment, such that they are often used to dramatize imaginary characters in fictitious situations.

Through these narrative impersonations we can investigate the ideological aspects of speech styles and languages. Thus, we construct our identities by the way in which we situate these different voices as spoken by characters closer to, or further from, our own self. For example, I illustrated in the previous section how the Trepas appropriated the Andalusian accent as a voice that was not their own in order to demonstrate their rejection of a particular set of sexist attitudes. This was the exact opposite of the Rambleros men, who adopted such an accent (and its associated speech genres) as their main voice.[6]

In the same way that the Andalusian accent was used by the two groups to dramatize particular voices, it became clear that the meanings constructed through the Catalan language could also be explored in terms of the characters and situations it was used to represent or evoke in the participants' talk. However, an analysis of code-switching between Catalan and Spanish could never be straightforward. Utterances point to a multiplicity of meaning potentials – ambiguities which the speakers may prefer to exploit rather than resolve. And one single language may contain a multiplicity of styles associated with different discourses and identities.

In the numerous instances of code-switching between Catalan and Spanish that I analysed, I found voices of teachers, comedians, television presenters, authority or official figures, stereotyped persons (peasants or nationalists, middle-aged women, boy scouts, and so on). In many cases, use of the two languages appeared to be interchangeable. For instance, I found both Catalan and Spanish voices impersonating teachers and other figures of authority.

But I also noted significant differences in the voices animated through the two languages. Moreover, these differences were linked in interesting ways to the meanings and identities constructed within the peer group, and particularly to the forms of masculinity I have

described. For instance, in the interviews with the Trepas, I noticed
that Catalan speakers would code-switch into Spanish much more
often than their Spanish-speaking friends would switch into Catalan.
This, and other examples, suggested that the world of the group and
of '*la penya*' was frequently represented in Spanish – and in the various styles of Spanish they identified with.

The following extract provides an example of the apparent symbolic asymmetry between the two languages.

Episode 2

[Spanish in italics, Catalan in bold type]

PEPE: *cogí una cogorza con esa mierda el otro día*
           tío
           Got drunk like hell with this shit the other
           day, lad.
MAURO: *ah es cerveza no [?].*
           Ah. It's beer, isn't it?
AYATS: **[veu] Ah (.) sí sí (.) et fots un parell i a (xx).**
           [voice] Ah! Yes Yes. Drink a couple and (xx).
Pepe: **[veu] sí nen (.) posa molt.**
           [voice] Yes boy. It really gets you.

Pepe was a Spanish-speaking member of the Trepas. He began by
narrating – in Spanish – a situation where he got drunk on a particular type of beer. Ayats was a Catalan speaker. The latter's intervention, performed in a stylized Catalan, was a playful dramatization
which Pepe then adopted, so that together the two speakers created a
pretend dialogue. The Catalan voices were uttered with a particular
vocal quality that conveyed ingenuous fictional characters, in this
case, non-experienced drinkers taken aback by the alcoholic level of
the beer. And this was humorous within the imaginary male world of
heavy drinking.

There were many other situations where Catalan was used to
impersonate innocent, teacher's-pet-like or simply silly fictitious
characters that did not share the transgressive, aggressive or subversive agendas of the participants in my study. This occurred both
amongst the Trepas and the Rambleros. On one occasion, Pepe
argued that the name of their hard-core band could not be translated
into Catalan because it would not sound tough enough, which he
illustrated by pronouncing the Catalan form with a silly voice. In
addition, the Barcelona working-class argot is associated with lower-

class gangs who express themselves in Spanish, and who were often dramatized by the Trepas as speaking in this language. This is why Catalan speakers borrow most of their argot and slang expressions from Spanish.[7]

On the other hand, there were also many *keyed* voices that were conveyed through code-switching from Catalan into Spanish. These were commonly used to express role distance, irony or exaggeration, and were central to the forms of talk and performance found within the peer groups, where ambivalence can be exploited to say things that could otherwise be construed as face-threatening.

Two points emerge, then, with respect to the identities conveyed by language choice and code-switching: first, Catalan was being used to invoke dry, serious voices, and was not considered amenable to the expression of ambivalence (a function accorded to Spanish); second, Catalan was used to convey what were clearly the voices of *others* – ingenuous, posh and *unmasculine*.

This contrast between Catalan and Spanish voices is reminiscent of the 'we–they' dichotomy (see Gumperz, 1982), but it should not be seen as a 'rule' merely operating at the level of interpretation or contextualization. It is the result of the particular experience of the groups concerned, who have had access to the Catalan language mainly through school and the media. They are processes that take place in situated practice, where voices are adopted, transformed and interpreted in terms of the characters and activities they evoke. Such meanings are *not* intrinsic to each variety. The voice of a teacher, for instance, may not mean the same thing for a person who has dropped his or her studies as for someone who is investing heavily, and successfully, in education.

Strategies of Language Choice

The process whereby Catalan acquired these particular connotations in this particular social context can be partly understood if we take into account the more general conventions of *language choice* in face-to-face interaction. Spanish speakers of this age are assumed to understand Catalan, but many feel awkward about speaking the language. Because in everyday conversation we are expected to attend to the face needs of our interlocutors, it is commonly expected that Catalan speakers of good manners will accommodate to the needs of Spanish speakers. The result of this was clearly the predominant use of Spanish, even amongst the Trepas, who had a significant number of Catalan speakers, most of them men. Spanish was, therefore, the language in which they did most of their day-to-day symbolic work, and this is probably why most young people in Barcelona generally shape their ways of speaking by drawing upon the resources of Spanish.

But there was a final and interesting facet to the relationship between gender identity and the patterns of language choice, which can be best explored by isolating four sub-groups amongst the participants.

First, from the quarters of simplified masculinity amongst the Rambleros men there was a strong resistance to the use of Catalan. In its most acute form, there was a self-confessed 'hate' for the language amongst some of these men, who complained that it had been 'imposed' on them by school. Sometimes, they would even chastise members of the group if they spoke Catalan in certain situations. More typically, though, they would actively seek to avoid using the language even when they declared positive feelings towards Catalan and Catalonia as a whole. In this latter type, we can also include some women crossers. One plausible explanation for this rejection of Catalan is that speaking a second language was perceived to be at odds with a form of masculinity based on displaying authenticity, spontaneity and self-sufficiency. This was especially so in cases where identities were being constructed within certain social events, such as verbal duelling, where vulnerabilities had to be masked. A second language – by its very nature – must forcibly convey ideologies and identities which are somehow different, and therefore pose a threat to the very single-sided construction of the self which typifies simplified masculinity.

The second sub-group I wish to discuss are the Rambleros women. In contrast to the men, they had a much more positive attitude towards Catalan, and actively sought opportunities to use it (although they were also sensitive to the danger of exposure, particularly within the group). This was in keeping with their aspiration to pursue studies or clerical jobs, trajectories for which the ability to speak and write Catalan were prerequisite. Such women said that they made use of the language in school or the workplace. When I gave the participants a bilingual first draft of analysis to read, one of the women went straight to one of the men who sometimes told off people for speaking Catalan, and defiantly told him that *she* had read the Catalan version.

Third, amongst the Trepas, the situation was different again. Catalan is the working language of most political groups in Catalonia, and the politicized Trepas had also participated in organizations where the use of Catalan was positively encouraged. They had therefore dealt with the question of speaking Catalan from its political dimension, and had rejected both Spanish chauvinistic attitudes and the views of the ruling Catalan conservative party. On the basis of their commitment to a 'respect for all cultures' and their support for Catalonia's self-determination, the politicized members of the group had decided at one point to try to overcome barriers to the use of Catalan. Such barriers included their own shyness where Spanish speakers were concerned, but also the resistance of many Catalan speakers to use Catalan with Spanish speakers. In addition, the Spanish-speaking Trepas had learned to reject the idea that the Catalan they spoke must be of the high standard set by schools or by many native Catalan speakers. One of the men said that he sought to speak Catalan with friends who would not pick on his correctness. Alternatively, one woman said that, whenever she felt she was at a loss for words, she just switched to Spanish.

Within the Trepas group, it is possible to isolate a fourth and final sub-group consisting of the politicized Catalan speakers. Here, there was a concerted effort to circumvent the norms of etiquette which restricted possibilities for using Catalan. One of the women indicated that she sought to establish precedents of speaking Catalan when she met new people. The 'gender-switching' man, who was a speaker of Catalan, had developed a bilingual or code-switched style of talking with Spanish speakers and campaigned for everybody to use 'their own language'. In doing so, he was questioning the general and highly pervasive assumption that conversations must be monolingual.

Thus, I hope to have demonstrated how the use of Catalan acquired very different meanings for the different individuals and sub-groups amongst the Rambleros and the Trepas. It appears that Catalan was constructed as conveying unspontaneous, inauthentic or 'unmasculine' voices – connotations which are all very much at odds with the forms of display of masculinity that the men of both groups preferred. But it is in the context of a political frame of thinking that some of the Trepas had found themselves willing to challenge and re-work the expectations and practices that had so far restricted their use of Catalan. Thus, even though Spanish predominated, and their use of Catalan was still limited, these men had been able to question, and were attempting to change, the discursive processes by which their displays of masculinity were produced through the two languages.

Conclusion

The findings of my study yield similar results to those of other researchers who have looked at issues of sexism and racism in working-class contexts. The evidence suggests that both sexism and resistance to Catalan were largely linked to simplified masculinity, i.e. the type of masculinity characteristic of the Rambleros men, and which is commonly associated with working-class gangs. Here emphasis is placed on a cult of the body (physical bulk, size, strength, heterosexuality and homophobia), the cultivation of transgression (through swearing, use of argot, drug-taking), and an entrenched defence of the self articulated through various games of verbal and physical aggressiveness.

In the case of the Rambleros, this form of simplified masculinity was discursively constructed through the appropriation of an Andalusian accent and its associated speech genres as well as via a rejection of Catalan. On the other hand, the political consciousness of the Trepas allowed them to perform significant transformations in a more egalitarian direction with regard to their patterns of gender display, relationships and conventions of language choice. This underpinned their attempts to use Catalan more often within the group, and overcome its connotations of an 'unmasculine' identity. Thus, like Kiesling in chapter 4, I have been able to show how groups of men draw upon both similar and different resources – in this case, argot, formal speech, an Andalusian accent, Spanish and Catalan – in order to construct their own very different displays of masculinity.

I would like to conclude by acknowledging that the kind of theoretical framework I have employed raises a number of questions that require a deeper conceptual grip of issues which cannot be dealt with in the space of this chapter. But if we are to make our research relevant to current political concerns regarding gender equality and multiculturality, we must be able to go beyond the local context, and pay attention to the social conditions that foster particular cultural forms.

In this chapter, I have provided evidence of people's ability to transform and re-interpret existing practices. However, in many cases, the flexibility I have described was severely inhibited by the limited resources (such as physical space and money) available in these working-class neighbourhoods. There are also signs which indicate that simplified masculinity is closely associated with school exclusion, and it is my own impression that some of the men I observed would willingly have changed their behaviour if, for example, they had seen genuine prospects of better jobs and housing. In this sense, I believe that an analytical framework centred on the processes whereby identities and meanings are constructed and developed in everyday life can simultaneously help us to explore not only linguistic phenomena, but also the sociopolitical issues that concern many people both inside and outside academia.

Transcription conventions

bold type   Catalan
italic type   Spanish
( )   Unclear stretches of dialogue enclosed within parentheses.
(xxx)   Inaudible stretches of dialogue enclosed within parentheses.
(...)   Indicates half-second pauses.
[?]   Indicates interrogative intonation.
[ ]   Author's comments and contextual information enclosed within square brackets.

Notes

This chapter is based on the results of research I carried out for my Ph.D. at Lancaster University (Pujolar, 1995). It was made possible thanks to the financial assistance of the Comissió Interdepartamental de Recerca i Innovació Tecnològica (CIRIT, the Catalan government research commission) and the Institut d'Estudis Catalans (IEC).

1   Catalonia lies in the north-east of the Iberian peninsula, and Barcelona is its capital city. The Catalan language is spoken, however, in other regions, including València, the Balearic Islands and the Rosselló in France. It is calculated that there are some seven million speakers of Catalan from a total of ten million inhabitants living in Catalan-speaking areas.
2   Rampton (1991) uses the term 'crossing' to refer to the adoption of voices from other ethnic groups in the activities of working-class adolescents. He points out that given the multiple meaning potentials of these practices, crossing does not necessarily involve the emergence of new paradigms of ethnic relations.
3   In British drama, similar voices are commonly expressed through speakers of northern dialects. An example is the famous concluding remark in the Monty Python film *Life of Brian*: 'you cum from nothin, you go to nothin; what've you lost? Nothin!'
4   I use the term 'argot' to refer to the jargon associated with a particular social group, particularly delinquents. I consider 'slang' to refer to more widespread forms of unconventional language. The Trepas, for instance, appropriated forms of argot extensively, while the Rambleros used only the more widespread forms of youth slang.

5   The most typical example of this is the pacifist slogan '*la mili no mola*', a
    slang expression which roughly translates as: 'the military service is a
    pain'.

6   It is worth pointing out that, amongst the Rambleros men, only two
    brothers had an Andalusian parent, so that their family backgrounds do
    not explain language use within the group.

7   Additionally, there existed a kind of stigmatization of Catalan vocal fea-
    tures, the most famous being the dark /l/, which is a common object of
    teasing, and which I felt many Catalan speakers sought at least to play
    down. Tusón (1985) also points out that some Catalan urban varieties
    adopt Spanish phonetic features. It was my impression that the particular
    type of Spanish spoken in working-class neighbourhoods articulated in
    the back of the mouth and the pharynx, a resource very much used in
    dramatizations of Andalusian speakers. Catalan was not articulated as far
    back, and it is significant that the Catalan voices were usually achieved
    by bringing forward the place of articulation or by a nasalization of the
    utterance. This is reminiscent of Bourdieu's remarks on *la gueule* (the
    throat) and *la bouche* (the mouth) as contrasting patterns of vocality
    between the working classes and the bourgeoisie, with their correspond-
    ing overtones of masculinity and femininity, respectively (1991, pp. 86–7).

6

One-at-a-Time: The Organization of Men's Talk

Jennifer Coates

Introduction

It's a strange paradox but, despite the androcentric tendencies of socio-linguistic research, we know very little about the informal talk of male speakers. This is in part a direct result of these androcentric tendencies: because male practices are accepted as the norm, with women's practices being viewed as deviant (see Cameron, 1992a; Coates, 1993, pp. 16–37; Graddol and Swann, 1989), then male speaking patterns are taken for granted, and are not seen as a salient topic for investigation. It is also probably true to say that the (less noticed and therefore arguably more pernicious) heterosocial tendencies of academic research have meant that sociolinguistic work has focused on speakers in mixed groups, so it is cross-sex talk (and cross-sex miscommunication) which has been analysed and discussed.

What we do know about the informal talk of male speakers is highly skewed to adolescents and to non-domestic contexts such as the street, the playground, the rugby changing room. We know, for example, about the linguistic behaviour of Black male adolescents in Harlem (Labov, 1972b); of young Black males in Philadelphia (Goodwin, 1990); of male rugby players in New Zealand (Kuiper, 1991); of 12-year-old schoolboys in Edinburgh (Reid, 1978); of adoles-cent boys in Reading (Cheshire, 1982a,b), while experimental data from same-sex friendship pairs is discussed in the volume edited by Bruce Dorval (1990).

None of this work focuses explicitly on those patterns of talk asso-ciated with the organization of conversation conventionally known as 'turn-taking'. This is what I want to examine in this chapter. In other words, I want to look at the ways in which a conversational floor is constructed in all-male conversation, and at the relationship between different speakers' contributions. I shall argue that, while women talking with women friends tend to adopt a collaborative floor, men talking with male friends stick to a one-at-a-time floor. I shall base this claim on an analysis of a corpus of conversations involving single-sex talk among friends.

The Corpus

Over the last twelve years I have been working on friends' talk, exploring the speaking practices of (white, middle-class) women and men with their friends, in pairs and in larger groups. In this chapter I shall draw on the recordings of conversations between boys and men in my corpus. These are all spontaneously occurring conversations, recorded with the agreement of participants in a variety of settings (chosen by participants themselves): in the pub, in the living room of one of the participants, in a study-bedroom, in a university office after hours, even in a garden shed in the case of one group of (dope-smoking) adolescent boys. (These choices contrast markedly with those of the girls and women in my sample, who all chose to record themselves in their own homes, apart from one group of adolescent girls, who recorded themselves in a room at the local youth club.)

Table 1 gives details of the corpus (further details and an account of the methodology employed can be found in Coates, 1996, ch. 1).[1]

Table 1   Details of corpus

Number of	Women	Men	Total
Conversations	20	20	40
Speakers	26	26	52
Hours of talk	19 hrs 45 mins	17 hrs 30 mins	37 hrs 15 mins

The Construction of a Conversational Floor

It has been assumed until recently that all conversation followed the one-at-a-time turn-taking model described in Sacks, Schegloff and Jefferson (1974, henceforth SSJ). More recently, some analysts have suggested that this model does not account for all conversational practice, and that speakers sometimes draw on another, more collaborative, model (Chafe, 1994, 1995; Coates, 1989, 1991, 1994; Edelsky, 1981; Falk, 1980).

The first detailed description of a more collaborative way of talking was given by Carole Edelsky in her ground-breaking paper 'Who's got the floor?' (1981). She suggested there that we need to distinguish between what she calls the single (or singly developed) floor and the collaborative (or collaboratively developed) floor. The main characteristic of the single floor is that one speaker speaks at a time, while the defining characteristic of the collaborative floor is that the floor is potentially open to all participants simultaneously. This means that the collaborative floor typically involves both the co-construction of utterances and overlapping speech, where several voices contribute to talk at the same time. As a result, some commentators use the term 'polyphonic' to refer to the kind of talk found in a collaborative floor where there are: 'separate voices articulating different melodies at once' (Chafe, 1995, p. 4).

Research carried out in English-speaking communities in Australia, North America and Britain on all-female talk, where the women involved are either close friends or sisters, shows that polyphonic talk is a significant feature of such talk (Coates, 1996; Coates and Jordan, in press; Scheibman, 1995). This more collaborative pattern of conversational organization has also been found in mixed groups (Bublitz, 1988; Edelsky, 1981) and in male–female pairs (Chafe, 1995; Falk, 1980; Johnson, 1990, 1996), so it is not the case that polyphonic talk is exclusively a feature of all-female talk. But whether or not it occurs in all-male talk is still unclear, and is the question to be addressed in this chapter.[2]

Men Friends Talking

Let's look at three brief (but typical) extracts from the all-male conversations.[3] (Transcription conventions are detailed at the end of the chapter, pp. 127–9.)

Extract 1

[Four friends, in their early forties, talk in a pub. Topic = the 1960s.]

BILL: that- that's what I ((can see from x)) from my- my view/ is

----

BILL: that- is that- . is that for instance   they made a hell of a
ALAN: %mhm%

```
------------------------------------------------------------------
BILL:    lot of mistakes ((by me))/ you look at these massive concrete
------------------------------------------------------------------
BILL:    council estates they wouldn't dream of building now/ .         but .
ALAN:                             mhm/               mhm/
BRIAN:                                                      mhm/
------------------------------------------------------------------
BILL:    at least they tried/ you know at least there was a Labour
------------------------------------------------------------------
BILL:    Government/ I mean I can remember a Labour Government/ but
------------------------------------------------------------------
BILL:    the students can't/ .          you know I'd- I'd just eligible to
JOHN:                        no/ it's true/
ALAN:                             mhm/
BRIAN:                  no/
------------------------------------------------------------------
BILL:    vote/ and Thatcher came to power/        and you- and you kind of
BRIAN:                                  mhm/
------------------------------------------------------------------
BILL:    think . just . does your head in really/
------------------------------------------------------------------
```

Extract 2

[Three friends, in their early twenties, talk about shared creative project in Alex's flat.]

```
------------------------------------------------------------------
TIM:    how long have you been thinking about it then?
SEB:                                              well I k- I thought
------------------------------------------------------------------
TIM:         ⌈ ((just))-                              =yeah=
SEB:    about ⌊ it       when I was living in Archway/ ((but it))=    =you
------------------------------------------------------------------
SEB:    know it's ready to be done/
ALEX:                              what? the Fantin-Latour portrait? sorry/
------------------------------------------------------------------
SEB:         ⌈ well yeah ((I mean)) it's not a Fantin-Latour/ because
ALEX:   ((what)) ⌊ ((xx))
------------------------------------------------------------------
SEB:    I- I think I'm- I'm better than Fantin-Latour=
ALEX:                                    =yeah yeah I know/
------------------------------------------------------------------
ALEX:   but I mean that sort of thing/
------------------------------------------------------------------
```

Extract 3

[Three friends, in their mid-thirties, talk at Mike's house about using a film projector.]

```
------------------------------------------------------------------
```

DICK: wh- which projector do you use? ((do they)) have one of

```
------------------------------------------------------------------
```

DICK: ((their own? ⌈ xx))
TONY: ⌊ two/ . we've got two projectors/
MIKE: that's important/

```
------------------------------------------------------------------
```

TONY: from school/ you know the ((x)) school/
MIKE: mhm/

```
------------------------------------------------------------------
```

DICK: what's the advantage of two Tony? it means you can switch

```
------------------------------------------------------------------
```

DICK: reels?
TONY: you can have two reels working/⌈you know/ two reels set up/
MIKE: ⌊mhm/

```
------------------------------------------------------------------
```

TONY: and switch from one to the other/

```
------------------------------------------------------------------
```

The SSJ model of turn-taking has as its central tenet that one speaker speaks at a time, and that participants in talk cooperate in the orderly transition of turns from current speaker to next speaker. The three extracts above are a good illustration of the model. In all three, we observe speakers orienting implicitly to the rules articulated by SSJ. The succinct summary of these rules – 'No gap, no overlap' (see, for example, Moerman and Sacks, 1971) – draws attention to the two main claims made by the model. 'No gap' refers to the claim that participants in conversation interpret syntactic, semantic and prosodic clues so accurately to predict the end of current speaker's turn that there is no perceptible gap between the end of one turn and the beginning of the next. The 'no overlap' claim complements this by asserting that participants in conversation predict the end of current speaker's turn so accurately that they start to speak just when current speaker stops and not before.

As predicted by the SSJ model, one of three things happens at points in talk where speaker-change is a possibility, that is, at Transition Relevance Places or TRPs, in SSJ's terminology (TRPs are marked with a double oblique (//) in these examples). Either current speaker nominates next speaker, as in Extract 3, where speaker Dick addresses Tony directly:

DICK: what's the advantage of two Tony?// it means you can switch
---
DICK: reels?//
TONY: you can have two reels working//
---

or next speaker self-selects, as Alex does in the following example from Extract 2:

SEB: it's ready to be done//
ALEX: what?// the Fantin-Latour portrait?//
---

or current speaker continues (the default option), as in Extract 1:

BILL: but . at least they tried you know// at least there was a Labour
---
BILL: Government// I mean I can remember a Labour Government// but the
---
BILL: students can't//

No Overlap

What is striking about the all-male conversations in my corpus, to anyone who is familiar with all-female talk, is the lack of overlap. The talk of women friends is characteristically all-in-together rather than one-at-a-time, and involves frequent simultaneous speech (see Coates, 1994, 1995b, 1996 for a detailed account of such talk). In this kind of talk, the group takes priority over the individual, and the women's voices combine to construct a shared text. A good metaphor for talking about this is a musical one: the talk of women friends is a kind of jam session. Here are three brief examples from conversations between female friends, to make the contrast clear. (In these examples, an extended square bracket indicates the start of overlap between utterances.)

In the first, Sue is telling a story about a couple she knows where the wife won't let the husband play his guitar:

SUE: she pushes him to [the abs-
ANNA: [he'll probably stab her with the

```
SUE:                              ⌈ she pushes him to the limit/    ⌈ yeah I
LIZ:                              ⌊ =yeah grrr <VICIOUS NOISE>      
ANNA:   bread knife one ⌊ day=                                     ⌊ she'll wake
```

```
SUE:    think he will/                    I think he'll rebel
LIZ:                  ='here you are Ginny'    <LAUGHS------->
ANNA:   up dead=                              <LAUGHS------->
```

The second comes from a discussion between two friends about the way history is taught at the local comprehensive school:

```
HELEN:   they ask them really to compare . their life now with the
```

```
HELEN:   nineteenth century/ it's very good sort of in ⌈ troduction
JEN:                                                   ⌊ yes/
```

```
HELEN:   ⌈ to history itself/              ⌈ yes very good/   and they
JEN:     ⌊ and they have newspapers and ⌊ stuff/         and ((it's))-
```

```
HELEN:   wen ⌈ t round the park/  and did all sorts of stuff/
JEN:         ⌊ and they use  ((list))   primary sources/  yes/
```

```
HELEN:   I was really impressed by that/
JEN:
```

The third is taken from a conversation involving four 14-year-olds, friends for many years. Here they are discussing backache associated with their periods:

```
BECKY:   ((well)) my back- my back is connected with my periods/
```

```
BECKY:   and I ⌈ ((xx))      yeah/
JESS:          ⌊ so's mine/      I get really bad back a-
```

```
BECKY:                                 ⌈ ((xxx))
JESS:    back ⌈ ache down there/
LORNA:        ⌊ ((so do I))     ⌊ I  get- ((get))  back aches/   I can't go like
```

```
BECKY:                                      ⌈ <QUIET LAUGH>     yeah/
LORNA:   that/ and I can't go like that/ and I just ⌊ ((xx)) a back rest/
```

```
----------------------------------------------------------------
HANNAH:                              ⌈ hot water bottles help me
BECKY:                               ⌊ hot water bottles help/
JESS:       but . ho- hot water bottles help/
----------------------------------------------------------------
HANNAH:     ⌈ as well/
LORNA:      ⌊ help so much/ yeah it's lovely . . .
----------------------------------------------------------------
```

All three examples demonstrate how easily speakers can speak and listen at the same time. Simultaneous talk of this kind does not threaten comprehension, but on the contrary permits a more multi-layered development of topics.

However, simultaneous talk of this kind is not evident in the all-male conversations I have collected. Overlap occurs only in the following circumstances:

(1)   Overlap occurs where a participant gives back-channel support with minimal responses such as 'mhm' and 'yeah':

```
----------------------------------------------------------------
BILL:      you look at these massive concrete council estates
----------------------------------------------------------------
BILL:      they wouldn't ⌈ dream of building now/
ALAN:                    ⌊ mhm/                      mhm/
----------------------------------------------------------------
```

(2)   Overlap occurs where two participants add minimal responses at the same time:

```
----------------------------------------------------------------
BILL: students can't/ .    ⌈ you know I'd- I'd just eligible to vote/
JOHN:                no/   | it's true/
ALAN:                      ⌊ mhm/
BRIAN:              no/
----------------------------------------------------------------
```

(3)   Overlap can occur when next speaker slightly over-anticipates a TRP:

```
----------------------------------------------------------------
TIM:       it's really strange that you don't drink  actually=
ALEX:                                                      =why?=
----------------------------------------------------------------
TIM:                        well ⌈ yeah/
ALEX:                            ⌊ ((do I?))/ yeah but only like
SEB:       =((he does drink a bit))/
----------------------------------------------------------------
```

ALEX: ⌈ ((a sip of beer))/
SEB: ⌊ I know- I know a few people who don't drink nowadays/

---

(4)   Overlap can occur where a potential next speaker mistimes the start of a turn (note that Tim does not continue but allows Seb to keep the floor):

TIM: ⌈ ((just)) -
SEB: I thought about ⌊ it   when I was living in Archway/

---

(5)   Overlap can arise from misunderstanding. In the following example Bill produces a series of rhetorical questions (still on the topic of the 1960s). Alan responds as if to a 'normal' question, which results in Bill and Alan's speaking at the same time until they manage to disentangle themselves:

BILL: d'you think if we were French we'd think 'All right that's it'?

BILL: er do you think if we were French we'd be very different?
ALAN: yes/

BILL: d'you think ⌈ because it's sixty-eight-   be different/
ALAN: ⌊ we- we- we- we- talk about- well what we've

ALAN: forgotten here . . .

Although overlap is infrequent in all-male talk, where it occurs, much of it is clearly supportive. The first three examples in this section, all involving back-channel support, illustrate this. We also find overlap where participants other than current speaker say something at the same time as the current speaker which is clearly a form of agreement, as illustrated in the next two examples:

[*Topic = revolution in the 1960s*]

ALAN: and there was Prague/ the Prague ⌈ spring/   and . . .
BILL: ⌊ spring/
JOHN: yeah/

[*Topic = joint creative project*]

```
--------------------------------------------------------------------
SEB:    there's some con ⌈ nection with that bit as well/
TIM:                     ⌊ connection/ yeah/
--------------------------------------------------------------------
```

These overlaps occur at points which are not TRPs, but in neither of them is a participant making a bid for the floor. These contributions are rather more elaborate than simple minimal responses, but fulfil the same function. The same phenomenon is illustrated in the next, more complex, example, where John's contribution 'Wenceslas Square', echoed by Bill, both supports Alan's utterance, and simultaneously adds to it. The proof that this is construed by Alan as supportive is shown by his incorporation of these words into his own turn.

[*Topic = Dubček making a political speech in Prague*]

```
--------------------------------------------------------------------
ALAN:   and you can see it on the video you know/
--------------------------------------------------------------------
ALAN:   on the- on the ch- an- an audience that filled . in this
--------------------------------------------------------------------
ALAN:   huge square every available square inch/      Wenceslas Square/
JOHN:             Wenceslas Square/
BILL:                      Wenceslas Square yeah/
--------------------------------------------------------------------
```

When male friends collaborate in the search for a word, overlap sometimes occurs, as in the following:

[*Topic = politics and Czechoslovakia*]

```
--------------------------------------------------------------------
ALAN:   the man of er Pra ⌈ gue himself/ what's his name?
JOHN:                     ⌊ ((Dubček))            Dub ⌈ ček/
BILL:                                                  ⌊ Dubček/
--------------------------------------------------------------------
ALAN:                        Dubček actually there in the middle of .
JOHN:   Alexander Dubček/
--------------------------------------------------------------------
ALAN:   Czechoslovakia/
--------------------------------------------------------------------
```

Note that these examples of overlap all involve repetition; in other words, the speakers use words already used by, or simultaneously used by, another speaker. This must defuse the potential for such turns to be interpreted as interruptions (see next section).

Overlap and Interruption

A key distinction between conversations involving a one-at-a-time floor and those involving a collaborative floor resides in the *meaning* attached to simultaneous talk. Where the floor is jointly owned by all participants, then overlapping speech is an inevitable consequence; in other words, simultaneous speech is a normal component of the conversational jam session. But where a one-at-a-time floor is operating, any overlap is potentially a violation of the current speaker's turn at talk, specifically of their right to speak. In other words, in a one-at-a-time floor, overlap will be construed as interruption unless it is of the minor kind described here. This means that in friendly talk using a one-at-a-time floor, between people who want to be considered as equals, overlap will be avoided. This is precisely what we find in the all-male conversations I've collected: they are characterized not only by lack of overlap, but also by lack of interruption. This is hardly surprising: dominance moves like interruption would be inappropriate in talk whose main goal is to maintain friendship.

The link between overlap and interruption for those who prefer a one-at-a-time floor was made explicit by one participant's reaction to a description of women's collaborative talk. He said: 'But how do women know how to do simultaneous talk? Why don't you [i.e. women] think you're being interrupted?'. Mary Talbot (1992b) analyses a conversation in which a husband misinterprets his wife's attempts to contribute to the story he is telling about their coming through customs. He labels them as 'interruption', rather than as contributions to a shared narrative. It seems that the conversational strategies which accomplish friendship among women may be construed as moves to seize the floor by speakers assuming a one-at-a-time floor.

Collaborative Talk

As I have already suggested, the collaborative floor involves more than just overlap. The fact that a collaborative floor is jointly occupied simultaneously by all participants has many linguistic consequences, of which overlap is only one (probably the most striking). In particular, the collaborative floor also involves the shared construction of utterances and the frequent occurrence of minimal responses and laughter. (Minimal responses and laughter signal that participants are present in the shared floor even if they are not saying anything substantive; this contrasts with the meaning they carry in a one-at-a-time floor, where they acknowledge current speaker's right to the floor – see Coates, 1996, for a detailed account of the collaborative floor.) The following extract from a conversation between five women friends demonstrates that, even where there is little overlap, talk involving a collaborative floor is significantly different from talk involving a one-at-a-time floor:

[Topic = apes and language]

| MARY: | I mean they can shuffle words around and ⌈ make a different meaning/ |
| BEA: | ⌊ draw up a conclusion/ |

BEA:	((xxx))-
JEN:	they put two words together to form a compound/
MEG:	yeah/

MARY:	⌈ that's right=
BEA:	⌈ =mhm /
JEN:	to mean something that they didn't have a ⌊ lexical item for/

MARY:	⌈ that's right/ for ⌈ a brazilnut/
BEA:	⌈ a stoneberry for a- ⌊ a brazilnut/
JEN:	⌊ which is-
HELEN:	right/

The most striking feature of this passage is the ease with which the speakers operate as a single voice (the main strand of talk is underlined to show this more clearly). Mary's utterance is continued by Jen, and then by Bea, with Mary joining in with Bea at the end. Meg and Helen say nothing substantive, but their minimal responses (as well as those of Bea and Mary) mark their continued presence in the shared floor. As this extract demonstrates, for women friends, who says what is not always important: the joint expression of shared ideas takes precedence over the individual voice.

There is evidence that women in these groups explicitly value this kind of talk. The following is an extract from an interview with two friends, Bea and Meg, who are struggling to describe what they call the 'shape' of women's talk (italics indicate key words and phrases).

BEA: Yes, I'm trying to remember now sort of talking with Geoffrey [her partner]. I'll- I'll tell him . something, then he'll often come back with something of his own, but it's- it's not quite- it's not quite the same. It's more *separate* somehow.

MEG: mhm

BEA: I can't really describe what it is but the- the things don't sort of *blesh in together*, it's sort of one *separate* thing and another *separate* thing [. . .]

JEN: And do you feel more or less satisfied with any of these shapes?

BEA: I think I prefer *the feminine shape* which- which IS more

MEG: mhm

BEA: *melding in together.*

Bea uses the verbs 'blesh' and 'meld' to describe the characteristic quality of talk with other women which differentiates it from what she calls the more 'separate' quality of talk with her male partner. Her assertion that women 'blesh in together' or 'meld in together' supports the claim that all-female talk is more polyphonic.

Men's Friendship, Men's Talk

Why would polyphonic talk be a common feature of all-female talk but not of all-male talk? I would like to look more closely at some key features of all-male talk before suggesting reasons.

Topic

There is considerable evidence that women and men tend to discuss different topics in same-sex groups (see, for example, Aries, 1976; Aries and Johnson, 1983; Haas, 1979; Pilkington, 1992; Seidler, 1989). It seems that, with each other, men avoid self-disclosure and prefer to talk about more impersonal topics such as current affairs, travel or sport. A man interviewed about his relationship with his best friend (reported in Davidson and Duberman, 1982) said, 'We are pretty open with each other, I guess. Mostly we talk about sex, horses, guns, and the army'. In one of the conversations in my sample, the men friends discuss the 1960s at some length, and this topic can be divided into sub-topics such as Bob Dylan; revolution and why it hasn't happened in Britain; Marxism; students today. By contrast, a conversation involving women of similar age and background has as its main topic sequence: taboo and mothers' funerals; child abuse; loyalty to husbands; the Yorkshire Ripper case; fear of men. The brief examples from all-male conversation given in this chapter have been chosen to illustrate turn-taking patterns, but nearly all of them involve impersonal topics: planning a joint creative project, using a film projector, the Prague spring. When talk does become more personal, it deals with matters such as drinking habits or personal achievements rather than feelings (see Johnson and Finlay, chapter 7; Meinhof, chapter 12; Pujolar, chapter 5, for further discussion of this point).

Topic is not a simple overlay category: topic choice has profound consequences for other linguistic choices. Epistemic modality, for example, is closely correlated with particular topics, those which deal with personal and/or sensitive matters (Coates, 1987, 1996). In terms of floor-holding patterns, non-personal topics encourage one-at-a-time floor-holding because these topics lend themselves to what I call 'expertism', which I shall describe in the next section.

Monologues and Playing the Expert

Monologues – that is, stretches of conversation where one speaker holds the floor for a considerable time – are characteristic of the talk of male friends. They seem to be associated with playing the expert. By 'playing the expert', I mean that conversational game where participants take it in turns to hold the floor, and to talk about a subject which they are an expert on. This is a game that seems to be played most commonly by male speakers; women, by contrast, avoid the role of expert in conversation (see Coates, 1996).

In the conversation from which Extract 2 is taken, for example, there are three main topics: home-made beer-making; hi-fi equipment; film projectors and the logistics of switching from one to the other. These three topics correlate with areas of expertise of the three friends who are spending an evening together, and means that each of them gets a turn at being the expert, and a turn at 'doing' a monologue. In the conversation from which Extract 1 is taken, the four friends discussing the 1960s all have an interest in the topic, and in this case there is some vying for the floor as their expertise overlaps. But in general they organize their talk as a series of monologues, with each of them having a turn to hold the floor. Extract 1 gave part of Bill's monologue; here is a longer extract with John's preceding monologue:

JOHN: I've got this tremendous ambivalence about the 60s/ ((cos

---

JOHN: I've got you know kind of)) on the one hand I see it as

---

JOHN: being this- . this potentially revolutionary era you know/

JOHN: and on the other hand .hh a- a bunch of middle-class

JOHN: creeps ⌈((xx))   ⌈growing growing their hair long/
BRIAN: ⌊oh I agree with ⌊John   ((xx))

JOHN: and sort of- and really nothing particularly happened/ .hh

---

BILL: well I wasn't middle class but I grew my hair long/ <LAUGHS>

BRIAN: ⌈so did I/ <LAUGHS>
JOHN: ⌊well I mean yes/ we di- I mean I did too/ but the-

JOHN: and I wear the- wore the- you know the bell bottom pants

---

JOHN: were de rigueur and all the rest of it/ but um . I er I I I do-

---

JOHN: I do think that there was a kind of a- it was a change/

JOHN: a k- a- a change/ . not revolutionary necessarily/ but

JOHN: it was a change/ . ((and))
BILL: I think it was hopeful from what I-

JOHN: ⌈yeah I think the change was hope/ ⌈that's what it is/ yeah/
BILL: ⌊I ((x))-   ⌊that- that's what I ((can see

JOHN: I'm glad you said that/
BILL: from x))- from my- my view/ is that- is that- . is that for instance
ALAN: %mhm%

BILL: they made a hell of a lot of mistakes ((by me))/

```
--------------------------------------------------------------
BILL:    you look at these massive concrete council estates
--------------------------------------------------------------
BILL:    they wouldn't dream of building now/          . but . at least they
ALAN:             mhm/                    mhm/
BRIAN:                                             mhm/
--------------------------------------------------------------
BILL:    tried/ you know at least there was a Labour Government/ . . .
--------------------------------------------------------------
```

Bill's monologue continues for some time: here is a brief extract, with minimal responses unattributed to save space:

```
--------------------------------------------------------------
BILL:    and I think that though they made lots of mistakes/ and I
         think again it's fusing that myth and reality/ (yeah) is that if you
         actually   historically . start writing about Wilson/ he was
         corrupt/(mhm) he was devious/ corporations still ((ran)) you know
         the record companies just as much as they do now/ (yeah) but
         whether or not it was the people believed (ah) that there was more
         amateurism about/ I think people genuinely believed (mhm) that
         the Beatles were amateurish/ . you know um but brilliant/ (mhm) .
         whereas now any group that's picked up is immediately run by the
         record company/ they're in it ((xx)) for money/ and the millions
         <LAUGHS> take over before that talent is squeezed out of them/
         (yeah)
--------------------------------------------------------------
```

I've quoted at some length from this conversation to make the point that speakers take it in turns to hold the floor, and that their monologues can be extensive. For most of the time, the speaker who is giving the monologue holds the floor with only occasional minimal responses from other participants. However, the preceding example demonstrates how the transition from one speaker to another may involve unusual and lengthy overlap:

```
--------------------------------------------------------------
JOHN:    it was a change/ . ((and))
BILL:                            I think it was hopeful from what I-
--------------------------------------------------------------
JOHN:    [ yeah I think the change was hope/[that's what it is/   yeah/
BILL:    L I ((x))-                          Lthat- that's what I ((can see
--------------------------------------------------------------
```

```
--------------------------------------------------------------------
JOHN:                    ⌈I'm glad you said that/
BILL:      from x))-     ⌊from my- my view/ is that- is that- . is that for instance
--------------------------------------------------------------------

BILL:      they made a hell of a lot of mistakes ...
--------------------------------------------------------------------
```

Bill interprets John's 'it was a change' as the final utterance of his monologue, and begins his own monologue with the claim 'I think it was hopeful'. John agrees with this interpretation: his agreement overlaps with Bill's continuing talk, and is clearly unsettling for Bill, whose talk at this point is full of repetition and false starts ('from ((x))- from my- my view is that- is that- is that'). But the evidence is that John intends his words to be supportive; he is not making a bid to regain the floor – having stated his agreement he relinquishes the floor to Bill, who develops his initial statement in his own monologue.

Questions

Questions occur with some regularity in conversations such as these which encourage speakers to play the expert, and they play a significant role in terms of turn-exchange. They are used primarily to seek information, as the extracts given at the beginning of this chapter illustrated. For example, in Extract 2, Tim asks Seb: 'How long have you been thinking about it then?' and, in Extract 3, Dick asks Tony: 'Which projector do you use? do they have one of their own?'. Both these examples illustrate how friends ask each other information-seeking questions which explicitly offer the floor to the addressee and, as in the second of these examples, invite them to play the expert. Here is another example of this kind of question from a discussion about speech synthesizers between two friends (in their thirties) in college (this example shows that addressees are not always able to take up the role of expert):

```
--------------------------------------------------------------------
PETER:     what else do they use it for apart from the deaf? or do they have
           other applications- I don't mean the deaf/ I mean the dumb/ do
           they have other applications?
ROB:       well they didn't develop it for the dumb/ I can't remember why
           they did develop it/ um — I don't know/
--------------------------------------------------------------------
```

At other times, questions are used as a way of introducing a new topic which the speaker can talk expertly about. In the following example, Peter's answer demonstrates that he interprets Rob's question not as a simple request for information but as having the pragmatic force of saying: 'If you don't know about this, I can talk about it at some length'.

ROB: do you know of the Pennsylvania experiment?

PETER: no/ tell me about it/ [Rob proceeds to talk]

Ownership of Ideas

In a one-at-a-time floor a speaker simultaneously has a turn and holds the floor. Turns are seen as individually owned – so a speaker can protest 'It's my turn' if another speaker attempts to talk. It is characteristic of men's friendly talk (and of much talk in the public domain) that the ideas expressed by individuals in those turns are also seen as individually owned. Participants in conversation typically make comments like 'Oh I agree with John' or 'I'm glad you said that', or refer to what has been said as 'your point' (all examples from my data). This careful attention to who owns which ideas is in complete contrast with the conversational practices of women friends, where the normal pattern is for ideas to be developed collaboratively, and seen as the property of the group (see apes and language example, p. 118, and Coates, 1996).

The Goals of Talk

These contrasting patterns need to be examined in relation to the goals of talk. All talk involves information exchange, but, in the talk of women friends, exchanging information is less important as a goal of talk than establishing and maintaining good social relations. In fact, it's generally assumed that the maintenance of good social relationships is the main goal of all informal talk between equals. 'It is not appropriate behaviour in situations of informal conversation to pack your speech with information and deliver it in formally complete sentences' (Brown, 1977, p. 117). However, it seems that the accomplishment of friendship for some men involves precisely this – the exchange of information.

This valuing of information, that is, of factual information, is clearly related to men's preference for impersonal topics, and for top-ics which coincide with areas of expertise. Where information exchange has high priority, monologues will be tolerated. (In women's friendly talk, by contrast, monologues are abnormal, except where someone tells a story – but narrators have privileged access to the floor in all kinds of talk.)

The talk we do with friends should, I contend, be viewed as a form of play. When adults are questioned about what they do with their friends, men emphasize shared activities such as playing football or pool, going to watch a match, going to the pub (Aries and Johnson, 1983; Johnson and Aries, 1983b; Miller, 1983; O'Connor, 1992; Pleck, 1975; Seidler, 1989). Women, by contrast, are more likely to deny that they 'do' anything. Here are two of the responses I received when I asked women what they did with their friends:

'We don't "DO" much of anything, we- we tend to TALK, I mean we- we- we talk.' (Bea)

'But for me just what I remember about the relationship is NOT like what we DID together, but just you know the amount of time we just spent sit-ting around and talking.' (Hannah)

The centrality of talk in women's friendships is well established (Gouldner and Strong, 1987; Hey, 1984; Johnson and Aries, 1983a; McCabe, 1981; Rubin, 1985; Wulff, 1988). It seems that, while women's 'play' centres on talk, men's 'play' is activity-oriented. As one man said about his best male friend (reported in Sherrod, 1987, p. 236): 'We don't act the same way my wife acts with her friends, but it doesn't mean we don't care – it's just different. We express a lot through racquetball'.

But talk is a vital component of all friendships. As I have argued elsewhere (Coates, 1995b; 1996), the fun of talk, for women friends, arises as much from *how* things are said as from *what* is said. But it seems that for men, *what* is talked about is very important, and play-ing with ideas, not to mention arguing about ideas, is what is con-strued as fun. 'Doing friendship', then, is a very different enterprise for women and for men, or at least for those women and men whose friendship patterns have been researched.

Conclusion

In this chapter I have demonstrated that men talking informally with their friends prefer to organize their conversation according to the one-at-a-time model outlined by SSJ. The one-at-a-time floor functions to keep speaker roles distinct, and to permit those with expert knowledge to hold forth, while at the same time guaranteeing the orderly exchange of turns. Conversation may then consist of serial monologues. Where all participants are more actively involved, talk is frequently structured by question–answer sequences, which also serve to demarcate speaker roles.

Friendship is a relationship of equals, but women and men draw on differential modes of conversational organization to 'do' same-sex friendship. Men, through scrupulous adherence to a one-at-a-time floor, avoiding overlap and thus avoiding interruption, maintain equality by respecting each other's right to the solo floor, and acknowledging the individual ownership of ideas. Women, by contrast, draw on a collaborative mode of conversational organization where their shared ownership of the floor symbolizes collective rather than individual values, solidarity rather than separateness.

It is currently de rigueur to argue, as Sally Johnson does in the opening chapter of this volume, that the similarities between the speaking practices of women and men are at least as important as the differences, and many of the researchers cited in my own chapter are concerned to make this claim. Marjorie Goodwin, for example, writes about the all-female and all-male groups of children she worked with as follows: 'It will be seen that as important as the differences between groups are the interactional structures they share' (Goodwin, 1990, p. 53). Indeed, the research evidence available suggests that men and women in English-speaking cultures have access to both a one-at-a-time mode of talking and a more collaborative mode (see, for example, Edelsky's original paper (1981), where she demonstrates that a mixed group of colleagues can shift between these two modes). But what is fascinating is that the research I have carried out focusing on single-sex friendship groups shows that all-female groups of friends typically choose to organize talk using a collaborative floor, while all-male groups typically choose a one-at-a-time floor. In other words, it is clear that women and men share linguistic and interactional resources, but that they choose to draw on these differentially.

While we need to avoid crude binary oppositions in our analysis of gender-related patterns of talk, we should also remember that we belong to societies where the hegemonic ideologies represent gender as binary. As Bronwyn Davies (1989, p. 234) puts it: 'Current understandings of what it means to be a person require individuals to take themselves up as distinctively male or female persons, these terms being meaningful only in relation to each other and understood as essentially oppositional terms'. We as actors actively engaged in the construction of our social worlds inevitably perform gender in our daily interactions as either 'being a woman' or 'being a man'. Even when we attempt to subvert the dominant patterns, our performance will usually be read in an either/or way, that is, as doing either masculinity or femininity, but not something other. And since one of the chief ways we do 'being a woman' or 'being a man' is through talk, then it would not be surprising to find that interactive practices differ.

The evidence drawn on in this chapter relates only to white, well-educated English speakers. Until we have evidence from a wide range of speakers and cultures, broad generalizations cannot be made. But given that conversational organization accomplishes far more than just the mechanics of turn-distribution, and has many important linguistic reflexes, if it can be shown that, in most social contexts, male speakers prefer a one-at-a-time conversational model, whereas women prefer a more polyphonic way of talking, then we will have demonstrated a very significant gender-related difference in conversational practice.

Transcription conventions

The transcription conventions used for the conversational data are as follows:

1   A slash (/) indicates the end of tone group or chunk of talk, e.g.:

she pushes him to the limit/

2   A question mark indicates the end of a chunk of talk which I am analysing as a question, e.g.:

what's the advantage of two Tony?

3   A hyphen indicates an incomplete word or utterance, e.g.:

wh- which projector do you use?

I- I think I'm- I'm better than Fantin-Latour/

4   Pauses are indicated by a full stop (short pause – less than 0.5 seconds) or a dash (long pause), e.g.:

> *in the middle of . Czechoslovakia/*

5   A broken line marks the beginning of a stave and indicates that the lines enclosed by these lines are to be read simultaneously (like a musical score), e.g.:

TIM: *it's really strange that you don't drink actually =*
ALEX: *= why?=*

----

6   An extended square bracket indicates the start of overlap between utterances, e.g.:

A: ⌈ *that's what it is/ yeah/*
B: ⌊ *that that's what I ((can see))*

----

7   An equals sign at the end of one speaker's utterance and at the start of the next utterance indicates the absence of a discernible gap, e.g.:

A: *I'm better than Fantin-Latour =*
B: *= yeah yeah I know/*

----

8   Double round parentheses indicate that there is doubt about the accuracy of the transcription:

> *((do they)) have one of ((their own?))*

9   Where material is impossible to make out, it is represented as follows: ((xx)), e.g.:

> *you're ((xx))- you're prejudiced/*

10   Angled brackets enclose additional information, e.g.:

> *I grew my hair long/* <LAUGHS>

They also give clarificatory information about underlined material, e.g.:

grrr/ <VICIOUS NOISE>

11 Capital letters are used for words/syllables uttered with emphasis:

the feminine shape which IS more melding in together/

12 The symbol % encloses words or phrases that are spoken very quietly, e.g.:

%mhm%

13 The symbol .hh indicates that the speaker takes a sharp intake of breath:

and on the other hand .hh a- a bunch of middle-class creeps/

14 The symbol [. . .] indicates that material has been omitted, e.g.:

it's sort of one separate thing and another separate thing [. . .]

Notes

1 I am very grateful to the following for making data available to me: Keith Brown, Noni Geleit, Janis Pringle, Andrew Rosta, John Wilson. I'm also grateful to Professor Sidney Greenbaum for allowing me to use an all-male conversation from the Survey of English Usage, University College, London.
2 There seems to be no published research focusing explicitly on the turn-taking practices of all-male groups. David Graddol and Margaret Keeton (personal communication), working on the talk of boys in the classroom, have found a great deal of simultaneous speech in their data, but it seems that these boys are experimenting with the possibility of multiple strands of talk in a way that is playful and individualistic rather than genuinely collaborative.
3 The names of all speakers have been changed.

7

Do Men Gossip? An Analysis of Football Talk on Television

Sally Johnson and Frank Finlay

Introduction

'Gossip' is defined in the *Collins English Dictionary* as 'casual, idle chat', 'light, easy communication' or 'conversation involving malicious chatter or rumours about other people'. It is probably because of the inherent connotations of gossip as discourse characterized by predominantly meaningless, yet frequently spiteful talk, perpetrated by those with little else to do, that the genre has often been associated with women. One rarely hears all-male interaction referred to as gossip.[1] In the light of this folklinguistic connection between a particular style of discourse, and women as its main perpetrators, it is no surprise that a number of feminist linguists should have sought to explore the nature and function of gossip (Coates, 1989; Jones, 1980). Gossip has been of interest to those keen to explore women's use of language because it is seemingly one of the few discourse genres engaged in more or less exclusively by women.

In a paper entitled 'Gossip: notes on women's oral culture', Deborah Jones presents the following definition: 'a way of talking between women in their roles as women, intimate in style, personal and domestic in topic and setting, a female cultural event which springs from and perpetuates the restrictions of the female role, but also gives the comfort of validation' (1980, p. 194). This quotation provides an apposite summary of two aspects of the theoretical approach she adopts to gossip as a female genre. On the one hand, there is the sense of a communicative act which constitutes a 'female cultural event'. That is to say, gossip is seen as an intrinsic part of the female subculture since women are speaking together in all-female groups, seemingly uninhibited by the presence of men. On the other hand, gossip is seen by Jones as an activity which derives from 'the restrictions of the female role' (p. 193), that is, from men's oppression of women, which forces women to seek solace in each other's company. Women come together in the private domain as a result of their exclusion from the public domain. Their talk then serves not only to provide comfort and mutual support within the group, it may also offer the opportunity to contest oppression. Overall, therefore, the characterization of gossip is one which is typical of women in both form and function.

In this chapter, it is not our aim to deny that gossip might constitute a particular discourse genre with certain meta-functions for women as a group. Rather, we wish to move away from the traditional assumption that gossip is a way of talking peculiar to women. Men, too, it will be argued, participate in gossip. The main difference is that the seemingly casual, superficial talk of men is rarely defined as such. It will be shown here how the formal and functional elements of gossip described by Jones in her analysis of all-female talk can equally be applied to the way in which some men talk about football.

Data

Our interest in men's talking about football stems originally from personal experience with friends, acquaintances and colleagues. In particular, we noted how football talk facilitated interaction between men in a variety of social and professional settings, irrespective of whether there was any history of friendship between the interlocutors: even perfect strangers were able to establish quickly a common ground for lengthy conversations in which they revealed relatively little about themselves beyond a shared interest in 'the beautiful game'.

In view of the fact that one of us remains an enthusiastic, albeit now more circumspect, exponent of such football talk, our casual observations soon gave rise to critical reflections on the nature of a discursive mechanism which so manifestly helped to establish and solidify relationships between certain groups of men. It is worth pointing out at this stage that we are well aware that not all men participate in such talk, and that there are many women who do ('gender crossers' perhaps as defined by Pujolar in chapter 5; see also Viner, 1993). But in our initial observations, this kind of football talk seemed to work remarkably well to exclude the non-initiated, almost invariably female bystander.

Given the informal nature of these observations, we embarked on a search for data and turned to the mass broadcast media as a potential source. In recent years there has been a proliferation of programmes that provide a forum for previewing and discussing sporting events. Initially conceived as a means of drawing attention to the actual screening of the event, such programmes have become popular in their own right. Typically, they bring together journalists and pundits, who are often active or retired professionals from the sporting field concerned. For our case study, we selected an example of one such programme: the popular Independent Television (ITV) series *Saint and Greavsie*, which used to be broadcast on Saturdays at 1 p. m. until transmission rights for live Premiere League football were won by global media tycoon Rupert Murdoch's competing Sky TV satellite channel (subsequently known as BSkyB).

New entrants to an increasingly unregulated television market, like Sky TV, have been quick to identify the large and loyal audiences which major sporting occasions can command as a crucial factor in establishing themselves in the face of fierce competition from public and commercial 'terrestrial' broadcasters of many years standing. Satellite and cable companies have been able to sell their hardware and multi-channel products not least by securing exclusive transmission rights for major sporting events, which are the cornerstone of the schedules on channels 'dedicated' to the coverage of every conceivable sport on a 'pay-to-view' basis. At the same time, and reciprocally, sporting bodies have been able to negotiate ever more lucrative broadcasting deals for their 'product', and the increased revenue from TV has enabled such bodies to expand their operations to new and otherwise unsustainable levels.

The programme under investigation in this chapter featured the well-established football pundits, Ian St John and Jimmy Greaves, and provided the usual weekly diet of football talk for fans of the game throughout the football season. The particular episode which serves as the basis for the analysis was shown on 14 June 1992. It was 45 minutes in duration, and was one of several special editions broadcast during the European Football Championships in Sweden. It contains a combination of dialogues and interviews on location in Sweden, featuring players and managers of not only the two teams who qualified for the tournament from the British Isles, England and Scotland, but also of other teams competing in the Championships. Interviews with fans on the streets of Stockholm are included, as are a number of clips from previous matches considered relevant to the tournament as a whole. The greater part of the programme, however, is devoted to an assessment of the British teams' chances in their forthcoming matches against France and Germany.

Methodology

On television programmes such as *Saint and Greavsie*, considerable effort is given over to making the atmosphere as informal as possible. This is achieved, for example, by the relaxation of dress codes and a convivial studio set for a cast of 'armchair experts'. The interlocutors give every impression of being good friends engaged in casual and spontaneous chat of the kind that might take place in the comfort and privacy of their own home or even the local pub. One simple and persuasive reason for the popularity of sporting programmes of this type (which their ubiquity in the schedules suggests) is that they really do succeed in their efforts to imitate and evoke patterns of discourse which viewers recognize as similar to their own. But there is an additional characteristic which it is important to emphasize at this juncture: for all the impression of informality and spontaneity, and for all the approximation of reality which they affect, these programmes are still clearly scripted and rehearsed.

According to Norman Fairclough (1989), one of the most important shifts in media reporting in recent years has been the way in which genres of talk traditionally associated with the private domain have increasingly been appropriated to the public sphere. This is a phenomenon which he refers to as 'synthetic personalization', and which is discussed by Neff (chapter 9) with respect to political discourse. In many respects, the *Saint and Greavsie* programme is an interesting case of such personalization. This is because the series represents an attempt by the programme makers to reproduce in the public domain the kind of talk which they believe to be typical of men in the private sphere.

In the light of Fairclough's notion of synthetic personalization, we decided that even an analysis of a very mediated version of 'football talk' might enable us to pursue the hypothesis that men indulge in gossip. Given that the programme is clearly an attempt to imitate men's talk in the private sphere, we felt that it was feasible to look at aspects of its discursive structure using Jones' framework for the analysis of women's gossip. In her paper, Jones proposes that 'the elements of gossip' can be examined in the context of the following five categories: setting, participants, topic, formal features and functions (1980, p. 194). In the following, Jones' analysis of the form and function of female gossip will be compared – and, in some cases, contrasted – with observations from the episode of *Saint and Greavsie* in question.

The Analysis

Setting

Jones uses the term 'setting' with reference to the time and place of interaction (1980, p. 194). Both, she argues, are characterized by restriction in the case of female gossip. Thus, the time available for such talk is brief in that it must be 'snatched from work time', that is, in the form of an interruption from domestic duties (ibid.). Similarly, the physical spaces available for all-female gossip are limited to domains traditionally associated with the female role, i.e. the home, the hairdressers or the supermarket. Gossip, therefore, is necessarily characterized by a 'serial nature'. Since it is liable to constant interruption, this kind of talk must be flexible in a way which allows it to be continued whenever and wherever brief periods of time become available.

Jennifer Coates points out that one of the main weaknesses of Jones' description is clearly the very restrictive image of women it presents, snatching time from their roles as wives or mothers (1989, p. 96). But if we are to adhere to notions of traditional gender roles for a short while, we can see that this concept of 'restriction' contrasts markedly with the parameters of time and space that typify football talk on television. Air-time for sports reporting such as the *Saint and Greavsie* programme is firmly located in a regular slot – 1 p.m. on Saturdays – on the same channel (ITV). It is not presumed that the audience will snatch time and space from other duties, but that it will make them in order to watch.

In their paper 'Images of men in sport media' (1992), Sabo and Jansen similarly explore the way in which sports reporting is characterized by guaranteed time and space for what is primarily masculine discourse. This guarantee is underpinned, they argue, by the 'symbiotic relationship' with the expanding sport industry whereby sport media are increasingly dependent on commercial sponsorship (p. 170).

A clear example of this relationship is the sponsorship of ITV's entire coverage of the European Football Championships by the software company Sega, one of the market leaders in computer games. Sega's commercial involvement is highlighted during the opening title sequence of *Saint and Greavsie*, which includes footage of goals being scored to the accompaniment of sound effects and superimposed messages from one of the company's own computer games. At the interface between these virtual reality products and sport, the viewer is reminded of what is more important when the following slogan appears on screen: 'Sega – The Greatest Game of All'! Prior to the commercial breaks, the Sega logo also accompanies a 'What happened next?' quiz, the answers to which are then provided by the presenters before they introduce the next section of the programme.

In addition, the commercials before, during and after the programme – which thereby provide it with an immediate context within which the football talk unfolds – feature advertisements for beer, aftershave, DIY products, cars and the ubiquitous Sega's own football game; goods targeted at a predominantly male audience. There is even a trailer for another ITV programme, a documentary on the side-effects on men of taking anabolic steroids to enhance physical appearance and performance.

None of this is to suggest that television viewing time is never specifically targeted at women. Many morning weekday programmes, for example, are aimed at women and concerned with what are perceived to be 'women's issues', and those broadcast on commercial channels similarly display a close relationship between audience composition and the products advertised. However, these are times when the male 'breadwinner' is assumed to be at work, and although Saturday lunchtime may not be considered prime-time television, 1 p.m. is a time when, in the traditional nuclear family, food is being prepared and served, presumably by the woman of the house. In addition, the lunchtime slot of *Saint and Greavsie* was timed to follow a similar BBC TV football magazine as well as to precede the afternoon visit to the local match at 3 p.m.

So whereas female gossip may be characterized by restrictions resulting from responsibilities in the private domain, the legitimacy of men's gossiping about sport would appear to be provided by programmes such as *Saint and Greavsie*. This legitimacy is, moreover, sanctioned by the commercial side of the sport industry. This is essential if the separation for men between work and leisure time is to be reinforced – a division not traditionally granted to women.

Participants

In terms of participation, the most obvious feature of female gossip is its status as a women-only activity (Jones, 1980). By implication, therefore, men are likely to define themselves as the only legitimate participants of men's gossip. Indeed, an analysis of the participants of the *Saint and Greavsie* programme illustrates how, when it comes to talking about football, women are deemed to have very little to say.

Throughout the programme, a number of interviews and discussions are shown. These are structured mainly around the studio presenters, St John and Greaves, who together participate in extended episodes of football talk. National and international players are profiled and, in several cases, interviewed personally. Both the subjects and objects of these discussions are, however, (almost) exclusively male. There is only one instance where a woman is featured in the programme – in this case, a young Swedish fan on the streets of Stockholm. Here, the football pundits content themselves with a passing reference to the woman's similarity to a well-known, Swedish-born, TV 'weather girl', and an enquiry as to the likely meteorological conditions for the big games ahead.

Jones describes gossip further as a 'language of intimacy', which arises 'from the solidarity and identity of women as members of a social group with a pool of common experience' (1980, p. 194). An important element of the apparent intimacy created between men by the football talk in the *Saint and Greavsie* programme is characterized by the relationship between the presenters themselves. The use of nicknames is significant here, underpinning the team-like camaraderie of the two, commencing with the programme title. St John is even elevated to celestial status with intermittent references to 'The Saint', and nicknames are similarly used for references to other participants – 'Trev', 'Big Ron' and 'Big Eric'. The long association of St John and Greaves as players extends to their presenting of the series, and is further underpinned by their physical closeness, illustrated most clearly during their time on the streets of Stockholm where the dialogue is accompanied by a number of paralinguistic features, for example back-slapping and affectionate jostling.

Similarly, the humorous banter between Greaves, the funny man, and St John, his straight man, creates an air of the special intimacy which can be shared by all friends, but is a way of talking particularly characteristic of men (see Easthope, 1986, p. 87). According to Easthope, banter has an important function for men insofar as the comic aspect allows certain things to be said that would not be permissible in routine interaction (p. 90). In this case, there is an element of playful antagonism between St John (the Scotsman) and Greaves (the Englishman), which is employed in order to legitimate racist and/or chauvinistic remarks. The two men's respective national affiliations are underlined by the 'England' and 'Scotland' commemorative T-shirts which they wear throughout the programme. When St John, for example, suggests that the Scottish fans ('the Jocks') will be going shopping in Stockholm, Greaves' rejoinder consists of a hackneyed allusion to their proverbial parsimony. When there is talk of England's impending encounter with France, historical references are made to the English monarch Henry V and his victory at the battle of Agincourt.

Through these dialogues we can observe what Easthope describes, on the one hand, as an outward assertion of the masculine ego underpinned by the aggressive emphasis placed upon national difference (p. 88). On the other hand, this aggression is offset by the tacit expression of personal understanding between the interlocutors – illustrated by their physical closeness. This simultaneous expression of difference and similarity is, Easthope suggests, a typically ambivalent strategy in the creation of in-group norms for men. It is a tactic which is furthermore founded upon the exclusion of women, used to assert the status of men as a group, and thus protect the male bond (p. 92).

If female gossip is a way of talking which solidifies relationships between women, then talking about football would appear to serve a very similar purpose for men. But whereas Jones sees women's gossip as a result of their exclusion by men from other forms of expression, men's football talk on TV can be interpreted as an active manifestation of that exclusion process. The close rapport between the two presenters as well as their relationship with the other male participants in the programme illustrate what Sabo and Jansen refer to as the social construction of hegemonic masculinity typically perpetuated through sporting activity and sports reporting (1992, p. 173). Thus, the physical and cultural superiority of the male is exemplified at least partly via the exclusion of the female. Though talking about football is not in itself a display of physical prowess, the right to participate in the discourse is very clearly portrayed in *Saint and Greavsie* as a men-only reserve.

Topic

In terms of topic of conversation, one of the main characteristics of female gossip, according to Jones, is its almost exclusive preoccupation with personal experience and the lives of other people (1980, p. 195). The meta-function of such communication is then one of comfort, catharsis and entertainment (p. 197). Women 'chat' and 'bitch' about others (including men), both reinforcing and contesting the limitations of the female role. In this way, Jones suggests that 'a

perspective on the world is created' whilst, at the same time, a framework for mutual support is established (p. 195).

At first glance, men's talking about football similarly appears to
reflect a concern with the lives of others. Throughout the *Saint and
Greavsie* programme we can observe an intense preoccupation with
the biographies of various footballing characters, past and present.
Extensive interviews take place with the French striker Jean-Pierre
Papin, Scottish captain Richard Gough and Aston Villa manager, 'Big
Ron' Atkinson. The relative merits of assorted footballing tactics,
along with psychological strategies for winning the next match, are
also discussed in detail. Similarly, frequent flashbacks, mainly to
goals scored during the Championships and other tournaments,
stress the shared history of the participants – and, by implication, the
viewers – in the form of a common heritage or footballing lore (players, goals, matches).

But if gossip is about the creation of a particular perspective on life,
then the way men talk about football on *Saint and Greavsie* reveals an
interesting dimension to their view of the world. Whereas women's
gossip arguably reflects an inherent concern with the personal lives of
individuals – be that of the narrator, the interlocutor or a third party –
men's talking about football provides a marked contrast. Whilst we can
observe a similar preoccupation with the lives of certain individual
characters, what we are dealing with are aspects of professional, not
personal, lives. The talk, it is important to note, delves no deeper into
the personal psyches of the participants than to express the relative
joys and disappointments accompanying a match won or lost.

Through football talk, the personal sphere of men's lives – outside the
world of the game – is marginalized. Ultimately, the apparent intimacy
of the active participants which alludes to personal knowledge emerges
as merely (scripted) artifice. As for the viewer, the talk is inevitably centred on a world external to their own lives, and yet it is one in which the
semblance of intimacy is maintained by a number of strategies such as
referring to the protagonists with the nicknames one would ordinarily
use only for one's friends. All of this compares with the function of gossip for women, for whom, according to Jones, the sharing of information relevant to speakers' own personal sphere is paramount.

Formal Features

Jones points out that little is known about the formal features of
female gossip. She outlines certain elements, however, which can be
compared with men's football talk on *Saint and Greavsie* (1980, p. 195).

The main characteristic of gossip, Jones suggests, is its 'allusive' nature (p. 196). Gossip is based on the sharing of knowledge accompanied by requests for additional information, as well as for further comments on the significance of what has been said. Of great importance for women, however, is the personal nature of the exchange. In this way, a meta-narrative emerges whereby form takes precedence over content. It is not so much a question of what is being said – of greater import is the way in which information adds to what is known about other people, and how the participants themselves feel about related matters. Thus, shared knowledge and values are reworked, but most significantly, intimacy – and solidarity – are nurtured.

As we saw in the previous section, in the case of men's talking about football, we are not dealing with exchanges based on direct personal experience in the way that Jones envisages as typical of women's gossip. However, the allusive nature of the discourse remains a central feature, as illustrated by the numerous anaphoric references to the shared body of knowledge that surrounds the game, for example: 'the big centre-back plays *like Alan Hansen used to play*' (our italics). When Greaves interviews Papin he is keen to emphasize that: 'the whole world knows' Papin and that 'we have something in common', namely Greaves' time as a player for AC Milan and the fact that Papin was about to join the Italian team. Similarly, the Sega 'What happened next?' quiz consists of a series of references to past events, which are an implicit invitation to reflect on a history of footballing trivia presumed to be shared by the participants and viewers.

But if it is the reciprocal nature of the information shared which forms the basis of gossip generally, this kind of programme highlights an important feature of men's gossip about football. On the one hand, the kind of talk in which *Saint and Greavsie* participate appears to rest on allusive references to a body of common knowledge and experience in the same way as Jones envisages as typical of female gossip. What is missing, however, is the element of personal revelation. It seems that we are dealing with a form of intimacy, but one which does not rest on direct personal revelation. As Lynn Spangler points out in her analysis of TV genres aimed at predominantly male or female audiences, where men are portrayed on TV, it is not so much the being together, but the *doing together* that counts (1992, p. 110 – our emphasis).

Spangler also notes how: 'Unlike feminine genres, such as soap operas, which show men as "caring, nurturing and verbal" [...], programs targeted toward men not only exclude women, but they reinforce a capitalist patriarchy by making men constantly prove their worth through work' (p. 94). In *Saint and Greavsie* it is this common experience of *professional* football which gains significance. Thus, gossip about football becomes a legitimate activity for men because, although it stresses the sense of shared history in a way that is characteristic of women's gossip, the focus is ultimately a public one. Such talk does not appear to be concerned with the *trivialities* of the private sphere. According to Deborah Tannen, talking about politics has a similar function for men: 'Exchanging details about public news rather than private news has the advantage that it does not make men personally vulnerable: The information they are bartering has nothing to do with them' (1990, p. 111). In this way, she suggests, men are able to preserve the 'sacred boundary between inside and outside', the private and public spheres (p. 109).

Functions

In her paper 'Gossip revisited: language in all-female groups', Coates refers to the androcentric bias of much early work on discourse, which assumed that the primary function of conversational interaction *per se* was the exchange of information (1989, p. 98). That this need not always be the case is now well-established from extensive work on discourse strategies. But a distinction has traditionally been made, Coates suggests, between private and public discourse, with women socialized into the former and men into the latter. Thus, she implies that, for men, the exchange of information normally associated with public discourse is central. For women, on the other hand, the basic function of conversation is 'the maintenance of good social relationships', achieved primarily through interaction in the private sphere (p. 98).

Many of the contributions to this volume make it clear that, as soon as we begin to study men's use of language, it becomes increasingly difficult (and undesirable) to generalize about structural aspects of the speech of either women or men as homogeneous groups, respectively. But by exploring the *Saint and Greavsie* programme as one instance of men's talking about football, we can add an interesting qualification to Coates' claim. Whilst this football talk may initially appear to be about the exchange and supplementation of information (scores, league tables, players and teams), it is actually much more. This is because this type of discourse also performs an important function where social relationships between men are concerned.

Through programmes such as these a discourse space is created in which men can interact without women and begin to perform masculinity (Brittan, 1989; see also Johnson, chapter 1). As with women's gossip, information is exchanged, and a pool of common experience becomes available which can be both relived and supplemented. A world of characters is accessed, whose lives and behaviour can be commented upon, criticized and sanctioned. Moreover, within the boundaries of what might be termed a 'game reserve', emotion can be shown – all the excitement and disappointment of goals scored and not scored, of matches won and lost.

Football, as depicted in *Saint and Greavsie*, represents a world which celebrates a past, present and future. It is thus able to offer a dimension of unity across not only time but also space (on a local, national and international level). Most important of all, however, is the way in which this world assumes a metaphorical status vis-à-vis the real world, hence the programme's motto and general footballing cliché: 'It's a funny old game' (read: it's a funny old world). In fact, the only difference between men's gossiping about this world, and women's gossiping about 'theirs', is that the world of football is not the real world of interpersonal exchanges, it is a second-order construct.

Through football talk, then, the subjective concerns of the private sphere are countered by the transferral of emotion to a reified world, in this case, the world of sport. There, a vicarious interest in, and personal response to, the lives of others can be expressed in the same way as 'real' world experience is alleged to form the basis for women's gossip. The crucial difference is that this alternative world of football is sanctioned by the consummate authority of that other 'real' world, namely the media and commercial sponsorship. Perhaps it is for this reason that the 'casual, idle chat' of men has rarely been defined as gossip.

Conclusion

The aim of this chapter has been to explore the concept of 'men's gossip' with reference to one episode of *Saint and Greavsie*. It is important to add that what has been said about men's talking about football lays no claim to universality. For the present purpose, the focus has been on what one particular television programme has to say about the construction of men's identities. Like Jones, we too have been concerned with 'mapp[ing] out a field for future and more specific study' (1980, p. 243).

Taking Jones' original definition of the social function of women's gossip as the maintenance of 'the unity, morals and values of women as a social group' (p. 193), we hope to have demonstrated that this can be applied equally to men's talk. Like Cameron (chapter 3), we have tried to move away from the notion of gossip as a 'female speech genre', and show how men also gossip in order to create solidarity within their own gender group. In doing so, it has become clear how men may use very similar discursive strategies to women's when doing 'identity work'.

But despite overriding similarities in the form and function of men's and women's gossip, there is one aspect of men's football talk that differs radically. Whereas the sphere of private and personal experience is thought to be the focus of women's gossip, men's talk about football would appear to marginalize precisely those issues. Even though there is the distinct appearance of concern for the lives of other people and a creation of intimacy in such talk, this is ultimately revealed as sham. It seems that, in this instance, the private and personal concerns that typify women's gossip are being transferred to a reified world located firmly within the public sphere – that of competitive sport.

In this respect, our conclusions are potentially similar to those of Meinhof in chapter 12. According to her analysis of written narratives, some men would appear to have difficulty finding clear forms of expression for issues of personal concern, sometimes going to considerable lengths to bypass or reject the invitation to narrate those experiences. Football talk, we propose, might constitute a further example of such a displacement of personal experience, possibly explaining why it is also used by men as a way of making conversation in situations where there is little else to say – an observation that we noted at the beginning of this chapter (see also Pujolar, chapter 5).

It must, of course, be emphasized that football talk is not a definitive element of every man's identity, nor can it be blamed for all the ills of patriarchy. Such talk is merely one of a gamut of devices which may serve to exclude women, and create a sense of in-group solidarity for some men. It is one example of 'doing masculinity'. Clearly, there are many men who take very little interest in football or sport of any kind, but this does not preclude an engagement in other types of discourse which are, as many of the contributions to this book have shown, potentially equally as exclusive.

Finally, one cannot ignore the simple fact that there are many women who display great enthusiasm for sports which, in their professional guises, are played only by men, and who derive pleasure from talking about them. Programmes such as *Saint and Greavsie*, however, do not appear keen to acknowledge this. Only future research will show whether these women are willing or unwitting accomplices in men's identity work, or whether something more subversive is at play.

Note

1 The widely held view that gossip is a discourse type engaged in by women is underpinned by the etymology of the word. 'Gossip' is derived from the Old English 'godsibb', meaning god-parent, which came to be applied to familiar friends generally, but especially to a woman's female friends present at the birth of a child.

8

The Role of Expletives in the Construction of Masculinity

Vivian de Klerk

Introduction

After a heady two decades in which women have formed the focus of
analysis in several fields of research, and have usually been problematized as a deviation from the (male) norm, there is now growing
recognition of the fact that men's behaviour is equally gendered, and
therefore worthy of analysis. The result – as with feminist work
focusing on women – is further critical exposure of the ideological
mystifications which obscure inequalities between the sexes, or present them as natural or immutable.

Masculinity does not exist in isolation from femininity – it will
always be an expression of the current image men have of themselves
in relation to women. At any given moment, gender identities will
reflect the material interests of those who have power, and those who
do not. Thus, relationships between men and women can be seen as
politically constructed. In this chapter, I wish to explore the way in
which one particular aspect of language usage can be regarded as
evidence of the process by which gender-linked roles are constructed:
expletive usage. On the basis of data gathered from six South African
schools, I aim to show how attitudes towards gender-related use of
expletives appear to be in transition, and that this, in turn, can be
interpreted as a reflection of changing power relations between the
sexes.

Theoretical Background

Power and Speech Styles

Research in the field of gender-linked conversational behaviour gives ample evidence of differences between the roles of the two sexes, and the use of different conventions in achieving conversational goals (see Graddol and Swann, 1989; Preisler, 1986, for reviews of this field of research).

Biology predisposes, but it does not predetermine. Men, born of women and nurtured by them, have to carve out some distinctiveness from them in order to assert their masculinity, and achieve identity as males. 'Be a man!' is a message heard in many societies, which nonetheless seem to lack the equivalent incitement to 'be a woman'. In most Western contexts, the tendency to categorize the male principle as one of strength, and the female as one of docility, has led to men having to choose between the hard and the soft, or some subtle combination of the two, both in trivial situations as well as in the basic course of life. Boys require a more extensive, arduous transition to manhood, somehow needing special prompting not to cry, but to compete, be a good sport, and win (Stearns, 1979).

Evidence suggests that this pressure on males extends into linguistic domains as well. In Western cultures, the stereotypical powerful speech style is portrayed by the assertion of dominance, interruption, challenging, disputing and being direct. Zahn (1989) describes stereotypical powerful language as 'high-intensity' language, which, by definition, subsumes usage of expletives. Stearns makes some telling remarks about this (from his own male perspective): 'Malely male gatherings confuse me a bit; they leave me feeling out of place. Gratuitous obscenities strike me as an unilluminating form of speech and I cannot hold my own in skirt-lifting stories. I have always, in sum, viewed manhood with a bit of perplexity' (Stearns, 1979, p. 8).

Although what is meant by powerful speech style is naturally culture-specific, it is generally accepted that, in Western society, it is males who exhibit the dominant speech styles described above (see Wetzel, 1988, p. 562 for a discussion of the Japanese; Keenan, 1974, for the Malagasy context; and Smith-Hefner, 1988, for the Javanese context). Differences in the behaviour of the sexes, while not necessarily leading directly to inequality, may serve the primary ideological role of marking gender as an important social division, and aiding the interpretation of subsequent behaviour according to these norms: 'When people talk to each other they are engaged in an important political activity, in which existing power relations dictate the way in which social reality is renegotiated amongst participants' (Graddol and Swann, 1989, p. 173).

What must be remembered is the fact that such linguistic styles are options, only meaningful within, and determined by, the given social circumstances. Critical linguists (e.g. Fairclough, 1989, 1992a, 1992b; Fowler et al. 1979) reject the idea that language systems are autonomous and independent of actual use; instead of viewing verbal interaction as harmonious and cooperative, they argue, one needs to link linguistic choices to wider social processes, relationships and power. Discourse is seen as reproducing and perpetuating existing social relations because people enter into social interaction with identities which are partly pre-formed, and which therefore influence people's linguistic practice. Language is seen as playing a role in reproducing and constructing ideologies, which may be oppressive to minority groups, and which are reinforced in daily spoken interaction.

The potential for change comes when groups with different discourse norms or conventions find themselves interacting (Kreckel, 1981), and this is the case when males and females come together and use language in accordance with slightly different pre-established norms. Their linguistic preferences can provide a microcosmic study of the power relations that exist in a given society, and their discourse can be seen as representing a social power struggle, which may often result in change, both in the mode of discourse, and of wider social and cultural domains (Fairclough, 1992a, pp. 28–9).

Social practice – that which is regarded as normal in the discourse – is representative of speakers' unconscious and internalized resources for interpreting discourse, based on and constrained by previous personal experience and social context. The ability to participate appropriately in discussions of any sort depends on mutual understanding and cooperation regarding 'norms', and such cooperation reinforces existing norms and power relations, ensuring their existence and durability (Tannen, 1984, p. 26), limiting the potential for change, because they appear automatic and natural. Indeed, the ideologies embedded in discursive practices are most effective when they are naturalized and achieve the status of 'common sense' (Weber, 1969, p. 152). We take for granted, and see as transparent, ways of talking which actually serve as powerful indicators of social view and group values.

The question this poses is whether the use of expletives can be regarded as indicators of power and masculinity, and to what extent the 'norms' with regard to their use are accepted by all the members of a particular linguistic community.

Expletives as Symbols of Masculinity and Power

From the point of view of the majority of at least (Western) members of middle and upper classes, swearwords and slang form a continuum of non-standard forms: expletives comprise the more shocking or taboo range of words, with slang coming closer to acceptability. Although cultures vary widely in the terms that serve as expletives, the focus is typically on sex and excretion (taboo subjects in most societies), and anything that has a sacred place in the belief systems of a community.

The functions of expletives in Western cultures are complex: as an extreme form of slang, they are typically used with the intention (depending on the context) to break norms, to shock, show disrespect for authority, or be witty or humorous. Another distinguishing characteristic is the fact that they are part of a shared linguistic code, reinforcing group membership, and indicative of shared knowledge and interests. Because a sense of belonging is important to the average 'insecure' teenager, one expects slang and expletives to abound among the young, who have a high degree of shared knowledge and interests. Apart from their overridingly emotive or expressive function, because expletives contravene social taboos and are often used to shock people, or indicate contempt, they have become associated with power and masculinity in Western cultures. We find taboo language 'strong' because it implies the violation of a code; every resort to it is an act of daring, however slight. In Western societies, the use of expletives has a covert attraction because of its connotations of strength, masculinity and confidence in defying linguistic or social convention. (See Keenan, 1974; Misra, 1980, with respect to non-Western societies.)

The cultural stereotype that men's speech is coarser and more direct than women's polite, conservative speech has been expressed for centuries, evident from the comment in *Gray's Inn Journal* (1754) that: 'a distinction might be made between a kind of sex in words according as they are appropriate to men or women, as for instance "D..n my Blood" [sic] is of male extraction, and "pshaw" and "fiddlesticks" I take to be female' (Tucker quoting Arthur Murphy, 1961, p. 86).

More serious linguists have reiterated this view over the years (Jespersen, 1922; Pickford, 1956; Wilson, 1956), and it is hardly surprising that a stereotype has evolved in which men do all the swearing, while tactful, sensitive and submissive females cower in the background. More recent investigations confirm this belief (Adler, 1978; Burgoon and Stewart, 1975; Flexner and Wentworth, 1975; Lakoff, 1973; Mulac et al., 1980, 1985). Thus:

[...] most American slang is created and used by males. Many types of slang words, including the taboo and strongly derogatory ones, those referring to sex, women, work, money, whisky, politics, transportation, sports and the like – refer primarily to male endeavour and interest. The majority of entries in this dictionary could be labelled 'primarily masculine use'. (Flexner and Wentworth, 1975, p. xii)

According to Burgoon et al. (1983), such habits are all a matter of careful socialization, with males in Western society learning habits of verbal aggression, thereby contributing to the perception that they are strong and powerful. While females avoid the use of expletives (Crosby and Nyquist, 1977; Holmes, 1984b; Key, 1975; McConnell-Ginet et al., 1980; Spender, 1980), males have a certain obligation to try them out, and conform to the expectations of society by using them.

While expletives are condoned in males, their use by females is generally condemned, seen as presumptuous and inappropriate. Thus, 'status may be judged differently from different perspectives and by different individuals within the same speech community' (Smith-Hefner, 1988, p. 552). As Burgoon and Stewart (1975) and Burgoon et al. (1983) note, adult males are expected to use highly intense language in persuasive attempts, and are most successful or effective when they choose such a strategy. Females, on the other hand, are seen as violating norm expectations when doing so.

But the situation is not static, nor does everyone conform to the rules. As early as 1943, Schlauch noted tendencies for females to encroach on this all-male precinct, and Hertzler (1965), and Maurer (1976) make the same point. It would appear that, with shifts in power, norms and habits of expletive usage are being challenged, and signs of change are revealed in recent studies by Oliver et al. (1975), Bailey and Timm (1976), and Staley (1978), all of which indicate a growing resistance by females to conformity to stereotyped norms regarding the use of expletives as symbols of masculinity.

The Pressure on Males to Conform to Masculine Behaviour

Adolescents form a subculture, and are known for their attempts to separate themselves from the larger community by various means, one of which is linguistic. If there is a general taboo against the use of expletives, and if we accept that in Western society expletive usage has a covert appeal as a typical example of so-called 'masculine' language, then we could expect that gender would be a significant factor in the use of expletives. With their more close-knit peer-group structures (Cheshire, 1984; Labov, 1966), and because of a pressure to exhibit confidence and assertiveness, male adolescents might be expected to know and use far more expletives than females. Indeed, most adolescent males would have very little choice: it takes considerable self-confidence to refuse to conform to the norms of the group as a whole.

Later in life, when social class and education outweigh age in indicating status, many males who have sufficient confidence in themselves for other reasons do not need additional linguistic evidence in the form of powerful language and expletives. In some cases, their masculine power will be displayed through status and material acquisitions. Indeed, one might go so far as to say that it is those successful males with social status who ultimately impose and uphold the taboos against the use of expletives; those with less social power, or those who lack alternative means of displaying power, appear to conform to the need to fit into local sub-communities by using the very expletives which those who have the power reject.

As Moreau (1984, p. 60) puts it, the concrete and verbal practices of the dominant seem to induce the dominated to adopt specific language practices; the use of expletives by adolescent males can be seen as a way of attempting to assert self, while at the same time it can be viewed as expected behaviour, which conforms to the definition imposed by the dominant.

Most literature on this topic emphasizes the pressure brought to bear on females in preventing them from using swearwords (Key, 1975, p. 102); the implication is that using expletives is somehow desirable to all, but that females are forbidden the pleasure of using them. But it is important to remember that the males in the community are similarly pressured to conform to their predefined roles, and that not all of them necessarily find the prospect of using expletives equally tempting.

The Study

The Data

In this study, 160 randomly selected adolescents from six schools in or nearby Grahamstown, South Africa, were requested to fill in an anonymous questionnaire on slang and expletives. The schools chosen were English-medium schools, and all were predominantly

white. The questionnaire examined two main issues: use and knowledge of current slang, and use and knowledge of expletives – only the
latter will be discussed here. In addition, attitudes regarding the
users of expletives were elicited. Informants were evenly distributed
in terms of sex, age/educational standard and type of school (single-
sex or coeducational). Pupils in standard six fell in the 12- to 14-year
age group, and those in standard nine in the 15- to 17-year age group.
All were English mother-tongue speakers.

Speaker variables under scrutiny were thus sex, educational standard and school type. Of these variables, sex and age were obviously
the primary foci, but the nature of the educational environment was
also seen as potentially important. Social class was not regarded as a
variable in the selection of informants. Grahamstown is a small
highly 'academic' environment with a disproportionately high number of academic institutions; the lack of industry to attract a 'working
class' would make it inaccurate to label any pupils in terms of class
(see Horvath, 1985, p. 64).

In order to assess informants' use, and knowledge, of expletives,
ten situations were sketched, each with four to six varying addressees
(e.g., alone, with friends, etc.). Informants were asked to imagine
themselves in each situation, and then to write down any expletive(s)
that they might use. The situations ranged from mild irritation to
extreme anger, from dismay to pain, shock, embarrassment and
delight, in an attempt to include as wide a variety of contexts as possible. These were deliberately presented in random order, to avoid
the possibility of an emotional build-up in the informants, who were
reminded that they could leave blank those contexts in which they
would not have responded with a swearword at all. Each informant
was asked to consider a total of 54 situations. Writing down an expletive was interpreted as evidence of some exposure to the word, its
meaning and association of some sort with its habitual users.

It is acknowledged that these data only really represents passive
rather than active use of expletives. All responses were therefore
interpreted as being representative of stereotypes and norms rather
than evidence of actual linguistic behaviour. At the end of the questionnaire, opinions about men, women, girls or boys who swear were
also elicited, as well as comments regarding the questionnaire as a
whole. It was hoped that an analysis of these might throw some light
on the existence of stereotyped views held by the sexes, and reveal
whether each gender group had similar views about each other's use
of expletives, or whether the standards of judgement differed
depending on the gender of the informant. Respondents filled in the
questionnaires alone, discussion being expressly avoided.

Expletive Rating Scale

Each response to the questions was assigned a numerical value in accordance with the scale presented in the appendix, and the numerical values of each individual informant's responses were tallied. The scale of values was devised in the following way: a list of all the words actually written by respondents was compiled and presented to a panel of twenty assessors, none of whom had taken part in the experiment as informants, but all of whom were aged between 13 and 18 years. The assessors were equally distributed between males and females in standards six and nine, and were asked to rate the words on a scale of one to ten, where one implied extreme mildness and inoffensiveness to the hearer, and ten indicated a high shock value and extreme disgust. Final scores for each word were achieved by rounding off the average rating of the twenty assessors in each case.

Inter-rater reliability was tested using the KR-21 formula proposed by Hatch and Farhady (1982, p. 246), according to which a resultant score of 0.87 indicates an acceptable degree of internal consistency among raters. The fact that words rarely encountered in 'respectable' literature were all given higher scores by assessors than those encountered more often, and that actual respondents with a declared aversion to swearing used words with very low ratings, tend to confirm the reliability of the scale, although it must be remembered that assessments are culture- and community-specific.

Responses were not gauged as a reflection of reality, but rather of stereotypes. It must also be acknowledged that people are often unreliable in reporting their own usage, and that females show a tendency to under-report, males to over-report (see Trudgill, 1974), and that this may have had the effect of inflating the scores somewhat in the direction of the stereotypes. Anonymity may lessen this tendency slightly, but it may also lead to frivolity, decreasing validity in such a way that the researcher cannot detect it. It is nevertheless interesting to note that three female respondents, despite anonymity, used asterisks or dashes (e.g., f**k) to avoid writing the word they said they would have used. (Such informants were given half the score assigned to the expletive in question.) No male used this avoidance technique.

Results

Sum of Responses

The mean scores of the groups under investigation are listed in table 1. Without exception, male scores were higher than female scores, and these differences were fairly large. They reveal a strikingly consistent trend whereby males generally used words which scored higher in terms of shock value. Males also offered a wider range of responses than females did, as table 1 indicates.

Table 1   Expletives: mean response values

Age	Coeducational		Single-sex	
	Boys	*Girls*	*Boys*	*Girls*
12–14 years	154.8	137.4	144.5	122.4
15–18 years	238.9	159.6	185.9	125.0

What is interesting is the very clear influence of gender, age/standard and school type as variables. An age by sex by coed status analysis of variance (ANOVA) was used to test the effects of the variables. It produced four significant main effects, and no interactions:

Sex:	$F(1.149) = 10.22$	$p < 0.01$
Age:	$F(1.149) = 7.14$	$p = 0.01$
Coed status:	$F(1.149) = 4.02$	$p = 0.05$

The lack of interactions between the variables reinforces the suggestion that each of the factors analysed can be regarded as important, and related to 'power' in some way. Results indicate that gender-linked behaviour is not clear-cut; scores show a more marked age-linked increase in scores for males than for females, suggesting that male adolescents are more keenly aware of the need to use expletives as a symbol of masculinity. The effect of the type of school (coeducational or single-sex) is particularly interesting: in single-sex schools, it would appear that there is not as much pressure on boys to use 'masculine' linguistic signals to reinforce gender identity – the comparatively low scores at single-sex schools suggest that gender is not in question in such environments (despite the expectation that there might be less linguistic inhibition in single-sex schools, and therefore higher scores for words which contravene taboos). In contrast, in a coeducational environment, the greater awareness of gender differences seems to increase the pressure on males to conform to gender stereotypes, and indicate maleness via linguistic bravado, as it were.

Effects of Situation and Addressee

Respondents reacted with striking consistency to the ten situations sketched in the questionnaire. The ranking, given in decreasing order of associated expletive elicitation, was: annoyance, shock, pain, horror, indignation, mild inconvenience and delight. All groupings concurred in their rankings of these situations, differing only in relation to the 'strength' of expletives overall, in accordance with their various 'claims to power'.

For each situation informants were asked to visualize differing addressees. These were grouped together, and analysis of scores revealed very clear conformity by respondents, all of whom were most relaxed (expletive-wise) with a friend of the same sex, and then became increasingly reticent when alone, with a friend of the opposite sex, with a (strange) adult, with father, with mother, and with a teacher. Males consistently selected more 'shocking' expletives than females.

Scores reveal that the taboo regarding the use of expletives is strongest with those who are higher in power than oneself, or with those who do not use them at all. One needs to remember that these informants were all adolescents, still subordinate to parental and other forms of social authority. This might explain the varying ratings of 'father', 'mother' and 'teacher': the latter two are not generally heard to use expletives by adolescents, while fathers often are.

Attitudes

Informants rated their attitudes to those who use expletives on a scale of one to five, a low score reflecting a low or negative rating, and a high score reflecting a very positive rating. Informants were asked to rate the appropriacy of expletive usage by junior school boys, junior school girls, senior school boys, senior school girls, adult males and adult females, respectively. It could be argued that responses would give a strong indication of current stereotyped views regarding acceptable behaviour by different gender and age groupings. The overall attitudes of female and male informants towards expletive usage by different groups are shown in table 2.

Results were remarkably consistent in sex-based groups: boys show a consistently more positive view about using expletives than girls, especially with regard to use by their own sex. Clearly, most of them have accepted a norm in which it is more appropriate for males to use expletives than females. The younger informants appeared to

Table 2   Attitudes to groups who use expletives

Group	Female	Male
Little boys	2.0	1.9
Adolescent boys	2.5	2.5
Adult men	1.3	1.3
Little girls	2.8	3.0
Adolescent girls	3.0	4.0
Adult women	1.7	1.7

be slightly more permissive regarding their *own* use than their older brothers and sisters were: in every case, the older students were less positive about younger students using expletives than the juniors were about their own use. Social attitudes appear to harden with age, or perhaps this is evidence of the older students trying to exert a little 'authority' over the younger ones with regard to maintaining taboos.

Without exception, male and female informants alike revealed greater tolerance for expletives from males than from females, with teenagers attracting the most support, sub-teens the second-most, and adults (especially women) the least. These linguistic views emerged as remarkably crisp and clear-cut, almost rule-governed phenomena, indicative of strong stereotyped beliefs: nice girls don't swear but nice boys can (and ought to?).

Discussion

Changing Perceptions of Expletives?

Moreau states that 'the school system expresses and strengthens power relationships between social classes [...] and between sex classes' (1984, p. 45); 'dissimilarities between language practices are meaningful only in the light of the social organisation' (p. 59).

The results of this study generally confirm the stereotype that girls know, and use, fewer expletives than boys, and that this is somehow right and proper. It is also noticeable that there is an undeniable relationship between sex and age, and the rate and level of expletive usage that is considered to be acceptable.

However, it is also apparent from the results of this survey that gender identification is not a simple matter of conformity to clear and unambiguous role models. Whilst most of these adolescents felt that expletives are more fitting for males than females, it is important to note that female scores are considerably higher than the stereotype might have led one to expect. Results do *not* indicate a clearly demarcated sexual division of roles and labour, along with harmonious conformity to a 'master stereotype'. There is ample evidence of deviance and opposition to the system of gender differences, and linguistic gender differentiation is neither smooth nor consensual – if it were, no girls would use any of the shocking words, and all boys would.

Not everyone has accepted the norms or feels comfortable following conventional rules, and the surprisingly high number of girls claiming to use expletives demonstrates this. However, in reporting on their attitudes, the females in the study revealed a small measure of guilt and self-condemnation: the average attitude score of girls about females was 1.9, and yet their actual usage of expletives in the questionnaire is much higher than one would expect. This can be interpreted as evidence that they themselves are not conforming to their stereotyped views of what is right and proper female behaviour. What is even more interesting than the trend among females to 'join the male bandwagon' in using shocking words is the number of males who (in the free comment section of the questionnaire) reported discomfort and a sense of obligation in using expletives. This occurs in spite of the fact that one might expect an enhanced sense of self-esteem and confidence in view of society's condonation (indeed, encouragement) of the male right to use them.

Expletives and the Social Construction of Masculinity

Among the various theories of gender, 'sex role theory' sees gender as a matter of self-attribution and self-perception; a subjective sense of being either masculine or feminine (see Connell, 1995, pp. 21–7 for discussion). According to this view, the foundations of gender identity are laid down at a time when the child is flexible and impressionable, and follows the lead of role models; people act out the generally accepted social definitions of what it is to be a man or a woman. From a linguistic perspective, this entails little boys copying the speech habits of other males, and girls using females as linguistic role models. Hence a man learns to sound like a man because he learns the required behaviour associated with the male gender role, and he comes to define himself as male from the perspective of those around him who treat him as such.

However, evidence from the preceding linguistic research suggests that the matter is far from clear-cut. Acquiring gender-appropriate linguistic characteristics is not necessarily smooth, harmonious or consensual, and not everyone feels comfortable following conventional, prescribed rules. Indeed, the 'invitation' to conform can be seen as coercive and deterministic in that the norm seems natural simply because the alternatives are suppressed. Furthermore, as such typical roles are challenged – by feminism, for example – not everyone is certain what the 'rules' are, and others may wish to challenge them more explicitly.

Some of the recent writing on masculinity argues that men's identities have become more problematic as a result of changes in society (mainly due to feminism), and that masculinity is therefore 'in crisis' (see Connell, 1995, for a discussion of such work). Whereas manhood was previously well defined and understood, the old certainties about the male role are no longer as clear, and increasingly there are challenges to typical models of sex roles. This is particularly true when it comes to acquiring gender-linked linguistic attributes, as this study has shown.

Connell (1995) proposes that a more useful alternative to the biographical and developmental view of gender is the 'social construction' model, with gender being seen as having no fixed forms, but being re-identified every time it is acted out:

> Like sex role research, this [social constructionist view] is concerned with public conventions about masculinity. But rather than treat these as pre-existing norms which are passively internalized and enacted, the new research explores the making and remaking of conventions in social practice itself. (Connell, 1995, p. 35)

Thus, one 'does' gender, not as automatic routine of replication and conformity, but as a part of a process whereby gender is repeatedly accomplished in social situations. Even though we may take our own gender identities for granted, and naturalize gender differences by giving them status as facts, we are nevertheless always in the business of putting together our sense of those identities. More importantly, within this constructionist view, gender roles are seen as flexible, and can be challenged as individuals and groups adapt the models on offer to them.

The research reported on here suggests that sex role theory cannot adequately account for the current use of expletives among males, and that the alternative approaches are more helpful in explaining the fluctuations and role challenges evident between the two gender groups. Each individual must go through the process of working out for him- or herself whether expletives suit his or her image. Traditionally, for young females, using expletives constituted a breaking of the rules, and thereby made a clear anti-authoritarian statement. For young males, *not* using expletives made a different kind of statement. However, the lack of conformity both within, and across, gender groups in this study suggests that expletives, instead of being regarded exclusively as signs of masculinity, are increasingly being seen as symbols of power more generally, equally available to both gender groups. Thus, as gender roles have been challenged, so too have the social and linguistic practices that have typically symbolized such roles. Usage of expletives (or at least perceptions thereof) no longer carry gendered meanings in quite the same way as was probably the case previously.

Conclusion

In this chapter, I have tried to show how the increasing female trend towards a contravention of linguistic taboos, and the concomitant unwillingness of some males to break such taboos, raises the question of whether expletives are still regarded as a necessary part of a masculine identity in the eyes of all of their users. It would appear that females have encroached on formerly sacrosanct male linguistic territory, and where perceptions of the use of both slang and expletives are concerned, the gap between the two gender groups is closing (Pujolar cites in chapter 5 further evidence of such a shift). It is possible therefore that expletives have been deprived of their gender-specific meanings, and that new ways of 'doing' masculinity are likely to be sought if the gender division is to be maintained.

Appendix: Numerical values assigned to swearwords

Value of 1: beggar, blinking, blooming, bother, brother, crikey, cripes, darn, dear, drat, flick, flip, fool, golly, gosh, grief, heck, hoender, jeepers, mother, Pete's sake, pluck off, rash, ruddy, schweppes, shaving cream, sherbet, shirt, shivers, shize, shoot, shot, shucks, sugar, wow.

Value of 2: ass, blast, bull, buzz off, can it, clot, cork up, cow, creep, damn, dog, doz, egghead, imbecile, gag it, GCM, geez, gits, heavens, holy mackerel, idiot, jis, jislaaik, jissus, jurrah, moron, shiff off, shut up, shut your trap, sow, tripe, twerp, twit, voetsek, vrek, wench.

Value of 3:   drop dead, 'f', faggot, Glory, God, hell, holy cow, holy mother, jerk, Lord, mess off, Mother Mary, scab.

Value of 4:   bastard, bitch, bloody, bulldust, donder, dosball, go suck, slut, stuff you, tit, up yours.

Value of 5:   bumface, Christ, crap, drol, dwat, dwax, fart, gwat, Jesus, kak, kaffir, shittoes, siffy.

Value of 6:   bulldung, bullshit, moer, shit, shithouse, son of a bitch, wank a plank, wanker.

Value of 7:   jerk yourself, piss off, screw yourself, wop.

Value of 8:   arse, arsehole, bugger, cock, dick, dickface, dickhead, dildohead, doos, dushbag, fucket, poephol, prick, shit-face, shittrap.

Value of 9:   cunt, cuntface, cuntsucker, fuck, fucker, fucking, poes.

Value of 10:   mother-fucking.

9

'Aceptarlo con hombría': Representations of Masculinity in Spanish Political Discourse

JoAnne Neff van Aertselaer

Introduction

While studies of female identity formation enjoy a history of at least two decades, the topic of masculinity (or masculinities) has only recently begun to be addressed (see Fejes, 1992). This concentration on portrayals of female sex roles and identity construction tends to support the notion that gender equality is, at least in the Western world, primarily a matter of changing our concept of women or femininities. Yet, if equality is to be achieved, we must also confront the way in which traditional masculine roles are constructed.

This chapter addresses the subject of representations of masculinity by analysing the interrelationship of political language and male identity formation, but I want to begin by offering some background information on the first part of its title: *'Aceptarlo con hombría'*. This phrase is a segment of a political statement made by Socialist Party (SP) leader and former President of Spain, Felipe González, as a suggestion to the leader of the Partido Popular (PP) upon the latter's defeat in the June 1993 national elections for parliamentary seats. Shortly after the Socialist victory, González declared to reporters, in reference to the PP members: 'Espero que sepan aceptarlo con hombría' ('I hope they know how to take it [the defeat] *like a man*'). In Spanish society, *hombría*[1] evokes male identity indicators pertaining to diverse areas: biological orientation (strength, versus weakness for women), societal orientation (power, control and dominance, as opposed to female submissiveness; men as leadership-centred, as opposed to relationship-centring for Spanish women), and rhetorical orientation (assertive speech acts versus passiveness on the part of women).

For me, the phrase also conjured up the symbols used in the Spanish advertising of the 1970s to mark off the boundaries of a closed male world. *Hombría* is slightly reminiscent of a Spanish television advertisement that featured the image of a black bull, still to be found as a billboard perched on Spanish hilltops, accompanied by a man's overvoice stating: 'Magno, cosas de HOMBRES' ('Magno, a matter for MEN'). What was lurking in González's mind, I was convinced, was the idea that 'La política es cosa de hombres' ('Politics is a matter for men'). Thus, González's metaphorical use of *hombría* as 'fair play' hinted at a fruitful area for investigation: forms of Spanish political discourse used as public manifestations of male identity construction.

In this chapter, I analyse some representations of masculine identity in Spanish political discourse – specifically that of the Spanish Socialist Party (SP), which was in control of the Spanish legislative and executive branches of government between 1982 and 1996. The particular advertising scheme I will describe – part of the social marketing strategy of the Spanish Socialist Party – is a component of a larger project I am carrying out on social advertising in Spain.[2] Here, however, I concentrate on the comic book: 'Por el futuro de todos' ('For the Future of All') used by the SP during the 1993 June elections as part of their campaign efforts to capture the attention of undecided voters. Using Fairclough's critical linguistics framework (1989, 1992a, 1992b), I give a brief description of the contents of the comic. Next, I discuss representations of masculinity in the comic as well as in other campaigns sponsored by the Socialist Party. Finally, I place gender issues within the wider sociopolitical context of Spain today. I examine the messages constructed by or about men as a way of investigating how institutional discursive practices shape the social subject, and how these messages might fit into larger patterns of discursive practices being carried out by Spanish social agents.

As a framework for the analysis of the masculinity myth, I have found useful the questions set out by Lance Strate (1992, p. 79) in his analysis of beer commercials. The principal question is: 'What does it mean to be a man?' Strate then breaks down this question into a more manageable subset: 'What kinds of things do men do? What kinds of settings do men prefer? How do boys become men? How do men relate to each other? How do men relate to women?' (p. 79).[3] I apply these questions to an analysis of male identity markers manifested in the public and private spheres, which appear in the comic book.

The main point of my analysis is the following: Socialist Party advertising appears to promote pluralistic political representation, regarding the citizen as a 'client', who freely exchanges tax revenues for good political management. For example, it claims to have attended to feminist demands, such as fulfilling the 25 per cent quota for women in political office, and especially through the politicization of activities traditionally excluded from the 'public sphere' (e.g., control of reproduction). However, the analysis of the SP comic shows that Socialist advertising reproduces patriarchal processes of identity construction by casting men in the role of 'principal economic actor' and 'citizen of the state', while interpellating women as 'working mothers' or 'supplemental earners'. In my interpretation, the verbal and non-verbal language of the comic denotes a gender sub-text in which male identity is constructed as the capacity to speak, to consent and to protect.

While the Socialist Party has been effective in changing gender-biased laws, it has been notably less successful in addressing problems of gender asymmetries in its own political discourse, primarily because the transformation of gender identities has entailed only the changing of women's self-perception, while maintaining patriarchal self-identification messages for men.

For the Future of All: Informing the Public

The Socialists explained their comic as an effort to inform the public of the positive changes effected by the Socialist administration in the ten years of their party's control of the Spanish government (1982–92).

The fifteen-page comic, which consists of forty-six frames, attempts to combine public and private world discourses. Each of the frames has an overall caption, supposedly emanating from Socialist government sources. For example, the caption in frame 1 states: 'On 28 October 1982, parliamentary elections were held in Spain. More than 27 million Spanish citizens participated in them'. But most of the frames also include private world discourse between the family members, or the family members and other members of the surrounding community. This discourse is set off in balloons typical of comic book style.

The comic was originally targeted towards the specific audience of the 'undecided voter' in the national elections, at first scheduled for the autumn of 1993, but then brought forward to June. The comic would be left at the home of a prospective voter; after, an SP worker would visit the voter and discuss government policy in an attempt to convince the voter that the Socialist Party had indeed promoted much-needed changes in Spanish society.

The Socialist Party focused on the following areas in its attempt to impress prospective voters:

(1)   Political

1.1   In 1982, the Socialist Party formed the first Socialist government in the history of Spain. Throughout its campaign the two most frequently used slogans were: (a) 'Cien Años de Honradez', '100 Years of Honesty', accompanied by a picture of Party founder Pablo Iglesias; and (b) 'Por el Cambio', 'The Party of Change' [frame 1 and all of page 1].

1.2   The role which the SP has played in the acceptance of Spain by the international political community, as opposed to the international ostracism associated with the Franco regime [frame 7; frames 43–6]. Especially salient are the references to Europe and the role that the Party President, Felipe González, has played in Spain's inclusion in the European Community [frames 26, 33].

1.3   The role played by the SP in validating Spain as a forum for international negotiations, such as the Israeli–Arab Peace Conference held in Madrid in 1992, or the 'Casa de América', the permanent forum for Iberoamerican affairs [frames 28, 36].

1.4   The SP's role in the establishment and transfer of power to the autonomous governments, such as Catalunya [frame 9].

1.5   The struggle against violence in its various forms, against Basque terrorism, racial intolerance and street crime [frames 19, 24].

1.6   The transformation of the armed forces from a coercive power into a professional organization which cooperates with civilian society [frames 29, 41].

(2)   Education

2.1   The creation of state-controlled schools and the extension of the school-leaving age to 16 (under the Franco regime, primary and secondary education was almost exclusively controlled by the Catholic Church) [frame 5].

2.2   The passage of the Law for Educational Rights (LODE), a top-down model for increasing student and parent participation in schools [frame 8].

2.3   Financing and promotion of research [frames 34, 39].

2.4   The promotion of student scholarship schemes [frame 6].

(3)   Cultural Policies
3.1   Support of museums through the Ministry of Culture [frame 25].
3.2   Support for exhibitions and cultural celebrations as well as for music, theatre and cinema [frames 16, 42–6].

(4)   Work
4.1   The reduction of the working week to forty hours and the extension of the annual vacation period to thirty days [frame 4].
4.2   Promotion of jobs for the young [frame 20].
4.3   Extending the coverage of unemployment and pension payments [frames 14, 27, 32].
4.4   Extension of maternity leave [frame 23].

(5)   Social Welfare and Equality
5.1   The construction of low-cost housing [frame 37].
5.2   The programme of 'social tourism' for the elderly [frames 13, 38]
5.3   Extension of health coverage through construction of hospitals or clinics [frames 12, 21] or various social assistance programs [frames 17, 18].
5.4   Establishment of the first Plan for Sexual Equality (for women) [frame 15].
5.5   Various schemes for social services, such as family planning centres [frame 22] and legislation in support of equality for women [frame 23].

(6)   Ecology
6.1   The proposal of new environmental laws such as the Law of Environmental Conservation [frame 31] and the Coastline Law [frame 35].
6.2   The establishment of wildlife parks [frame 30].

Interpreting the People's Needs: Representations of Public and Private Identities

The Socialist government claims that its social programs and its publicity constitute attempts to transform unequal power relations. Thus, analysis of the male and female roles in the SP comic should depict important changes in the way male (and correspondingly, female) gender identities are being constructed in both public and private spheres. Instead, the verbal and the non-verbal language of the comic work together to reinforce certain biased gender routines.

The cover of the comic features an 'ideal Socialist family' composed of a middle-aged mother and father, three children (two boys and one girl), and the grandmother and grandfather. In this setting, the two men have been placed near the centre of the group picture, but at its very heart is the mother, and rightfully so, since throughout the comic, she seems to be the person who holds the family together. The mother's body language, touching the daughter and looking lovingly at the grandfather, depicts her as 'care-taker', attending to the human relations of the group. The men, on the other hand, do not look at anyone. The grandfather's gaze is out into space, while the father, concerned with the 'public world', is reading a newspaper. He neither touches nor looks at anyone else, typical of body language with which he is portrayed throughout the comic. As Strate (1992, p. 91) perceptively points out, when more established relationships are illustrated in commercials: 'women are largely reduced to the role of admiring onlookers', watching men perform different activities. Throughout the SP comic, women are not always depicted as 'inactive'; however, when a man appears in the same frame, he is always made to be the centre of attention, either through the 'admiring gaze' or by comments made to or about him.

Appearing below this group portrait is the title of the comic, 'Por el futuro de todos' ('For the Future of All'). As it begins with 'for', the title presupposes for the reader a previous question such as: 'Why vote for the Socialists?' In this way, the prospective voter is reassured by the comic's title, which offers a worthy purpose or reason: 'So that all can have a more just future'. One other element of the title merits further mention before going on to the analysis of agency and gender roles. Because of the use of the definite article 'the' in the title, instead of the indefinite 'a', the presupposition set up for readers in 1993 was that Spanish citizens were in peril. Unless they voted for the Socialist Party, the Partido Popular would win: as a consequence, some people would have no future at all.

Throughout the comic, the public dimension of male agency is realized through political participation, debate and opinion formation. In fact, men are almost the exclusive agents when political questions (traditionally categorized) are discussed. For example, in frame 1, the ideal Socialist family is pictured waiting at the polls, where the two adult males of the family are about to fulfil their roles as 'persons of the public sphere' by voting. While exchanging self-satisfied looks, the men comment on the significance of their votes. The grandfather claims that they 'are going to ensure democracy', while the father elaborates on the manner in which this can be achieved: 'Yes, we are going to vote for the Socialists'. Apart from the implication that, without a Socialist victory in 1982, democracy would have been imperiled – as if the previous Centro Democrático Party had not played a major role in moving Spain toward the stable democratic transferral of power – the body language of the men, with their backs to both the mother and grandmother, implies that the connection between the public and private spheres is channelled through the citizens with decision-making capacity, i.e., the men. There is a strong implication that: 'la política es cosa de hombres'. The women, 'receivers' rather than 'senders' of messages, are again made to gaze toward 'the two wise men', it seems, in an attempt to partake of some of their political acumen. Women's participation is viewed as part of the environment, props for the male discourse.

Nevertheless, women are absolutely essential in their supportive role of providing regular assurance of men's primal position of public power. As one advances in the comic, masculinity's dependence on femininity for identity maintenance becomes ever more apparent. It is not that women cannot be political agents, rather that they can only do so if men allow them a political space. Thus, females are not entirely excluded from the political sphere. In one frame, the daughter has been elected as class representative [frame 8], and another depicts the mother as having been elected to a post, perhaps as trade union representative [frame 15]. These frames would seem to signal that men should be willing to share some forms of public power. However, the daughter's importance as class representative is subverted by the type of responsibility she will take on – hard work, but not much real power. And the mother's discourse undermines any facile assumptions women readers might have entertained about the effort required of female political contenders. The mother's utterance completely contradicts the political message in the box to the effect that women are 'equal', at least in the public sphere. She exclaims to a friend by telephone: 'They have elected me! I was afraid because there were a lot of men. But, I must get back to work. We'll have to celebrate this'. The effect of the election process has produced fear, not security and confidence after victory, while the causal conjunction 'because' links the fear with the causal agent: men. Here, the message for women is that many men will consider women's actions towards greater political and vocational ambitions as a threat to their control of the major institutions. This frame tells Spanish women that they can initiate a political career, but then they will be positioning themselves in direct competition with 'the opposite sex'.

There are other limited areas of public life in which, it seems, women are viewed as adequate participants. A female teacher is seen informing the class about the autonomous governments [frame 9], and the mother appears in a public consumers' agency, which, incidentally, is non-existent [frame 11], in order to make a complaint about a torn sofa!

In the context of this particular election (1993), the intended message for women, especially with regard to the wife's being elected as union representative, was that a victory of the right, i.e., the Partido Popular, would mean the disappearance of support programmes for women. The implication is that in the private sphere, women can act, to a certain extent, as decision makers, but outside of the home, women will need special protection. In any case, both in the private and the public spheres, the message for women is the same: men's ultimate control over women, a dialectic of the zero-sum game, of *power over*, not *power to*.

As in public life, men, when portrayed in the private sphere, are also seen as the principal agents in initiating topics pertaining to the public sphere. In frame 29, the husband initiates the topic of doing military service as a young man. The wife, on the other hand, is made to respond by attending to intimacy: 'John, do you remember your 20 months' stint in the Canary Islands? Oh, how many letters I sent to you!' Furthermore, the non-verbal message of the woman doing 'a wife's job' (hanging out the clothes) while the man merely watches, arms behind back, reinforces a married woman's traditional role as 'agent of communion' and a man's role as 'controller'.

Men are seen as valid conversants for topics such as the elections, government scholarship plans, roadway construction, pension plans, intellectual pursuits, while the marginal status of women can be noted in the topics for which women are seen as valid conversants: vacation, education, family planning, health care and pension plans, and culture. These coincide with the expected arenas of action for women: the home, relationships and community services. Women's private-realm practices help to sustain men's identity as 'controllers'.

There are two other frames which merit at least brief consideration in terms of agency in the private sphere. These are frames 22/23 and frame 29. In these, it is very clear that women's world is limited to certain spheres. The sphere of family planning and reproduction, seemingly a private concern, is, in reality, a profoundly political issue. In frames 22/23, family planning is seen to be a concern exclusive to women; no mention is made of men's part in procreation. The message I read from this frame is: 'Pregnancy is totally within the sphere of women'. The extended family planning systems supported by the SP might indicate to the reader that women have the right to terminate unwanted pregnancies, but it also implies that if a woman decides to have children, the responsibility will be all hers. This directly contradicts other Socialist social change advertising messages and political statements calling for responsible fatherhood; admittedly, this latter type of message emanates from the female-dominated Ministry of Social Affairs.

There is a mixing of perspectives in frame 22 as well. To the daughter's question of 'What are family planning centres?', the mother answers: 'It's about responsible maternity. Here, next door there is a centre that can inform YOU (fam.) about everything WE want to know'. The mother makes a very incongruent switch in pronoun reference in this utterance. The 'TE informa' presupposes that the daughter does not know how to prevent unwanted pregnancies. The fact that the mother did not include herself implies that SHE does. If this is so, why does the daughter have to go to the centre for information? The use of the pronoun NOS (us) in the last subordinate clause does include the mother in the group. Here the mother's discourse constructs *all* female subjects as wanting to know about 'responsible maternity'. As this is not the case (e.g., right-to-lifers, Opus Dei members, etc.), the mother is being used as a mouthpiece to present Socialist policies as common sense.

By analysing other non-verbal language throughout the comic, we discover how it supports the presupposition that men are agents of goal-oriented action, as opposed to emotion-oriented action on the part of women. In the two frames depicting the family in the car, the father drives. The mother accompanies the daughter in two frames, the two sons in two other frames, and the grandfather in another. All of the mother's activities are carried out on foot. Women are illustrated as looking at other people who are not usually returning their gaze [frames 1, 5, 12, 16, and in 41, 'the gaze of the admiring wife']. In contrast, the father accompanies only the elder son to the airport – of course, only the father can drive, it seems. The father makes eye contact only with the other male family members; in fact, the father never makes eye contact with the mother at all!

The setting for the male and female characters, in this case the objects surrounding the characters, further strengthens the presupposition that women are primarily concerned with social communion while men are concerned with agency. The mother appears in seventeen frames, while the father appears in only fourteen. But he is illustrated as reading a newspaper or book in three frames, as well as on the cover page of the comic; the mother also reads in one frame, noticeably a society rumour magazine, while she is at the hairdresser's.

In two juxtaposed frames, verbal and non-verbal messages reinforce the stereotyping of the sexes into two spheres: public-as-rational/private-as-emotional. In frame 39, the father discusses Spain's participation in the Hispasat communications programme with the younger son (complete with a picture of the satellite in orbit), whereas in the next frame, the mother declares herself to be incapable of learning how to use a computer. The language she is made to use ('This computer stuff – who can understand it?') leads one to wonder how this woman could ever have been elected as union representative. She is depicted as a 'pre-rational being', leaving space for the representation of male figures as 'logical'.

In frame 37, the verbal and non-verbal messages of the mother and father again maintain the private–public/emotional–rational divide. Here the father, whose body language denotes self-assurance and optimism, approves of the son's down-payment on a new flat, whereas the mother, whose body language indicates insecurity and apprehension, questions the wisdom of the son's decision with her question: 'But, son, flats are so expensive these days!' The son then answers her with a most annoying phrase, to which the Spanish reading public can easily attach the correct intonational pattern of vexation: 'But, Mum, it's under the Official Protection Plan'. Here we have the usual trepidation and weakness on the part of the mother, while the male figure is portrayed as the risk-taker and supervisor.

The women of the family, the mother and daughter, do take action, but it is action that affects the private sphere, i.e., the mother's informing the daughter about the family planning centre. The men of the family, in contrast, form a duo, which manifests a sub-text of the masculinity myth. They must seize opportunities and prove their ability. They must show mastery by controlling technology, their environment and, most of all, themselves. They can 'set their minds to work' to overcome any incapacitating fear, from which women must always be protected by men. In this way, the father, who is presented in images of confidence, success and control, initiates the son in men's role as 'protector'. The combined verbal and non-verbal actions of the father and son rest on the presupposition of men's capacity to protect and women's need of men's protection (see Fraser, 1989).

Private and Public Discourses

The most striking aspect of the comic is, I think, its attempt to create a Habermasian blend of private lifeworld and public lifeworld spheres by superimposing 'public discourse' onto the 'private discourse' world. That is, it tries to combine the discourse typical of interpersonal communication, represented by the speech of the family in the balloons, with discourse typical of public communication, realized by the political messages contained in the boxes located at the top or bottom of each frame.

This mixture of discourse types suggests what Fairclough sees as: 'current changes in societal orders of discourse' (1992a, p. 98). He outlines two such changes: (1) the democratization of discourse, defined as 'the reduction of overt markers of power asymmetry between people of unequal institutional power; and (2) synthetic personalization, defined as the simulation of private, face-to-face discourse in public mass-audience' such as print, radio or television. Fairclough proposes that both of these tendencies 'can be linked to a spread of conversational discourse from the private domain into institutional domains' (p. 98; see also Johnson and Finlay, chapter 7, for an exploration of this phenomenon on television programmes dealing with sport).

The question is: 'Why would the Socialist Party choose to articulate its political message in mixed discourse forms?' One of the criticisms directed at the SP during the winter of 1992 and the spring of 1993 before the national elections was that the party was increasingly alienating itself from the common person. The discourse strategy of the comic, then, would seem to be that of having the 'common person' give a testimonial. The familiar (*tu*) forms used by the family members obviate the use of overt power markers (such as the formal second person plural pronoun *Ustedes*). Rather than positioning the government as the sole source of political statements, thereby formulating rules for an 'unknowledgeable voter' cast in the position of 'coerced subject', the interpersonal textual structure of the comic attempts to construct the voter as a citizen who has a choice, thereby placing him or her in the ideological position of the 'interpreting subject'.

Conclusion: Unquestioned Orders of Hierarchy

Certainly, the former Socialist government should be credited for having been the first Spanish administration to bring about institutionally based changes in gender equality issues. Some of the changes were accomplished through specific laws (e.g. legislation on divorce in 1981 and abortion in 1989); others were instigated by the Ministry of Social Affairs, a branch of government created in 1988, with Social Agencies in Madrid, Murcia, Extremadura, Castilla-LaMancha,

Andalucía and Catalunya. As far as reconstituting gender relations, however, the analysis of the Socialist comic, and other social change advertising published before the 1993 national elections, suggests that such texts are merely instantiations of the then Socialist government's marketing strategy, i.e., voter enticement.

More recently, however, developments within the Socialist Party may corroborate the party's claims that it is trying to establish new rules for gender relations. During the thirty-third national Socialist Party Congress in March 1994, one of the most controversial national meetings ever held, two main areas of contention within the party came under public scrutiny: (1) public policies; and (2) the policy of democratization within the party itself. The second aspect is the most problematic among party members, since decisions promoting plurality will mean that some sectors of the party will have their power limited by the integration of other interest groups.

González's forces have insisted on such an opening up of the SP's structures, and González himself announced on a Madrid radio programme that 'the Executive Committee of the party must be highly representative'.[4] Supposedly, such representativity will include women as González has stated: 'I want there to be an important representation of women'. The majority of the SP Congress participants seem determined to incorporate into party structures this sector, which has traditionally been marginalized. The Congress has created an obligatory rule favouring the presence of women at all party levels by establishing the so-called '25 + 5 formula', which stipulates that there must be at least 25 per cent participation of women in all electoral lists and party structures, and for those which have already achieved a 25 per cent female affiliation, 5 per cent more must be added. Such actions seem to signal that Socialist women have been able to gain some political leverage to push for the achievement of the 25 per cent quota system they had presented in 1988, at the thirty-second Congress.

It was thought, however, that of the nine or ten women who might come onto the Executive Committee, they would be chosen to do so because of their links to political barons who control certain sectors of the SP.[5] That these statements have appeared in the media without the slightest qualification or justification presupposes that male political leaders accept male control of the political institutions to be a commonplace, and that women should, too.

The presupposition of male-dominated political structures points to an underlying conception of men's role as 'controllers'. Recent studies of masculine identity among Spanish males corroborate such an assumption. Studies of the answers of different generations of

Spanish men, when asked to define male attributes show, however, that there are some differences among men between 40 and 50, those over 50 and those between 25 and 40. For those between 40 and 50 (as are many of the men in power in the SP) 'the change [in the masculine role] has caught them off balance, and they have only carried out the essential readjustments' (de la Fuente, 1993, p. 8). Those over 50 are very set in their ways of thinking, and thus suffer little ideological conflict.

It would appear that the greatest identity crisis is taking place in men between 25 and 40 years old. Even though they have not yet achieved full political power, they still show the need to 'control and consent'. In a recent newspaper interview, Luis Bonino, of the Centre for the Male Condition in Madrid, pointed out how the need for control and consent surfaces in sexual relations (de la Fuente, 1993, p. 9). He explains that there is beginning to be a lack of sexual desire on the part of men, almost as a kind of resistance: 'Since there is no longer a need to conquer [a woman] and she is always willing, it is as if it has become uninteresting'. In the private realm, identity for many Spanish males, it seems, will continue to be constructed upon the capacity to speak, to consent and to protect, and not in the capacity to both give and take.

In the public realm, any hope that the governmental discourse displayed in the SP comic actually points to a dismantling of a masculinized hierarchy by state policies is thwarted by the Socialist Party's support of the politics of access. That is, it treats the division of labour as a problem that can be solved by the inclusion of more women in the workforce, but nowhere does it address change in *male* roles as fundamental to the radical changes in social interaction that must take place in both private and institutionalized contexts.

Notes

1 The María Moliner *Diccionario del uso del español* (1984) defines *'hombría'* as 'Conjunto de cualidades morales, tales como valor, voluntad, o energía, que ensalzan a un hombre' ('Set of moral qualities, such as courage, will-power or energy, which honour a man'). It is interesting to note that there is no corresponding term for women, i.e. *'mujería'* ('womanhood').

2 For a discussion of public communications strategies, see Kotler and Roberto, 1989; Meadow, 1989; Meyers, 1986.

3 I have also found useful three types of categories, adopted from Bate (1988): (1) Locations: where the non-verbal messages originate (voice,

face, body, environment); (2) Functions: how non-verbal messages relate to the verbal language used (reinforcement, qualification, replacement, contradiction); (3) Meanings: patterns of interpretation of non-verbal messages (agency, communion/purpose, dominance, liking, responsiveness, etc.).

4   'Los desayunos de Radio Uno' ('Breakfast with Radio One'), Friday, 18 March 1994.

5   F. Frenchoso writes in the *El Mundo* newspaper, Friday, 18 March 1994, p. 8: 'Al vicesecretario general del PSOE también le consta que González tiene intención de incorporar, al menos, a tres barones del guerrismo – Juan Carlos Rodríguez Ibarra, Francisco Vázquez, y Luis Martínez Noval – y a las mujeres vinculadas a su sector, dentro de nueve o diez que piensa integrar en la nueva dirección.' ('It is also clear to the Vice-Secretary-General of the SP that González intends to incorporate [into the Committee] at least three barons from the Guerrist sector – Juan Carlos Rodríguez Ibarra, Francisco Vázquez and Luis Martínez Noval – and the women linked to their sectors, amongst the nine or ten [women] that the Secretary-General [González] plans to integrate into the new Committee.')

10

'Randy Fish Boss Branded a Stinker': Coherence and the Construction of Masculinities in a British Tabloid Newspaper

Mary M. Talbot

Introduction

Hegemonic masculinity is under threat. Previously 'acceptable' expressions of dominant heterosexual masculinity, such as sexual harassment of working women, are now liable to prosecution. In this chapter, I want to examine a feature in *The Sun* newspaper[1] which reports an industrial tribunal's successful conviction of a male employer for sexual harassment of two female employees. The article is interesting because, superficially, it would appear to support the conviction of the employer for the unacceptable sexual advances made towards his employees. What I want to show, however, is that the text combines a number of rather contradictory messages about the challenge to hegemonic masculinity which is implied by sexual harassment cases such as the one reported. Thus, whilst the text seems to disapprove of the defendant's behaviour, it still manages to leave intact more traditional assumptions about masculinity and sexual relations between men and women.

In order to show how these contradictory messages are woven into the text, I will employ the concept of 'coherence'. I aim to demonstrate how, in order to read the text as coherent, readers must draw on a number of resources, some of which are contained in the text itself, but some of which must be taken from outside. I shall begin with a discussion of the main theoretical points that underpin this approach.

Theoretical Framework

Journalistic Discourse

The institutional order of journalistic discourse is structured into a range of practices, each of which has its own historical development and characteristic elements. These include the kinds of publication produced in the industry (broadsheets, tabloids, magazines, etc.), the genres reproduced in the pages of those various publications (hard news story, problem page, horoscope, etc.), and the genres used in putting them together (editorial board meetings, memos, interviews, etc.). Such practices also include the discourses drawn upon in production.

I am employing the term 'discourse' here in the sense used by Michel Foucault (1971, 1972), and developed in Critical Language Study (see especially Fairclough, 1989, 1992a, 1992b; Kress, 1985). The term refers to the discursive formation of knowledges and practices, and the positions of power which these bestow upon subjects. Medicine, for instance, is a body of knowledge, practices and social identities, with a long and chequered history. Medical discourse constructs those states which constitute health and sickness, as well as determining, via the social identities it bestows, those people who have the power to define such states. For Foucault, therefore, discourses are structures of possibility and constraint that define, delimit and control social subjects. In order to examine them, we need to consider questions such as:

> What are the modes of existence of this discourse? Where has it been used, how can it circulate, and who can appropriate it for himself [sic]? What are the places in it where there is room for possible subjects? Who can assume these various subject functions? (Foucault, in Rabinow, 1986, p. 120)

A body of knowledge and practice that is identified as a 'discourse' is generally associated with a particular social institution, or group of institutions. But there is also widespread use of the term to refer to kinds of knowledge and practice which seem to occur everywhere, e.g. racist and sexist discourses. Within journalism there is a particular conglomeration of such discourses that is characteristic of tabloids like *The Sun*. This '*Sun* discourse', as I shall refer to it, embodies sets of assumptions, values, prohibitions and so on, which are not normally openly asserted, but simply taken for granted – the newspaper's 'common-sense' view of the world. As Roger Fowler says:

> The [*Sun*] newspaper and its readers share a common 'discursive competence', know the permissible statements, permissions and prohibitions [. . .] (blondes are busty, work is a duty, play is a thrill, strikes are unpatriotic, and so on). (1991, p. 44)

In this chapter, I want to explore the conglomeration of discourses found in a single article in *The Sun*. I shall focus on the multiple voices that occur, and look at the way in which seemingly conflicting views of hegemonic masculinity are constructed by such voices. It would appear, for example, that somewhat contradictory discourses on gender and social class are being used in order to 'deflect' onto a scapegoat the threat to hegemonic masculinity which sexual harassment tribunals represent. To illustrate the manner in which this occurs, the analysis will look at those textual elements which require readers to draw upon such contradictory discourses in order to achieve coherence when reading the text.

Coherence and Intertextuality

In the act of reading, readers must construct coherence. We do this on the basis of (1) the cues manifested in the text, and (2) our own knowledge and expectations which we bring to that text (for a detailed examination, see Fairclough, 1989). Textual cues are a useful starting point when exploring the resources which a reader employs (Gough and Talbot, 1993; Talbot, 1990). These, in turn, provide a focus for attending to all the other resources a reader brings in, thus allowing us to look at the construction of social subjects in the act of reading.

Sometimes, however, coherence has to be constructed with very few textual cues indeed. To take just one example from a problem page study in Gough and Talbot (1993), there are no really explicit cues to the connection between the following two sentences, which form part of an agony aunt's response to a reader's letter:

> Many heterosexual men have a passing curiosity about homosexuality, and that isn't a bad thing. It compels you to make choices. (Gough and Talbot, 1993, p. 8)

In making a connection between these sentences, as a reader must, it is necessary to cast around for something to bridge the gap. The missing link, Gough and I suggested, is an assumption that homosexuality serves the useful function of confirming people's heterosexual identities. This assumption is of course highly contentious, but it is tacit, as opposed to explicitly stated. Nevertheless, the reader needs some such notion in order to make coherent sense of the two sentences. If it were stated, it would be more noticeable, and hence challengeable. As it stands, the assumption is unlikely to be contested by a reader, especially an unreflective heterosexual one, even though – or precisely because – he or she is complicit in its creation.

Coherence, then, provides a useful basis for exploring the way in which subjectivity is constituted in the act of reading. In the present study, however, I want to examine the constitution of subjectivity from a more explicitly dialogic, or intertextual, perspective.

When we read texts, we need to draw on a great deal more than our knowledge of the formal properties of language. The concept of intertextuality provides a view of the language user's relation to texts in which he or she is variously positioned as a social subject. This multiple positioning is what is known in the jargon of poststructuralism as the 'dispersion of the subject'. We are all of us positioned by the discourses in which we participate, actively or otherwise, and we may shift position from one moment to the next. Indeed, it is not uncommon for the positions we enter into in our lives to be highly inconsistent. For example, such contradictions may be all too familiar to women – one only has to consider the tensions and conflicting interests that are part of being both carer and wage earner, or both parent and child.

In terms of the intertextual view I present here, readers are involved in a 'textual dialogue' (Kristeva, 1970, p. 68). In reading a text, they are not encountering a single, seamless object. A text is never a unified thing; it always contains external elements. These elements may not be recognized by readers, but they are nevertheless needed in order to read a text *as though* it were a unified whole. In other words, they are essential for coherence to be possible at all. Reading a stretch of language as coherent requires the construction of intertextual connections (i.e. between different texts) as well as the establishment of linear, intratextual coherence (i.e. within the same text). These *inter*textual connections draw in an indeterminate collection of 'voices' from outside (a phenomenon I have attempted to explore elsewhere by identifying a text's 'population' of voices; see Talbot, 1990, 1992a, 1995a). Through 'intertextual coherence', then, the very process of interpretation constructs the language user's subjectivity (see Pujolar, chapter 5, for an application of this dialogic perspective to spoken language).

The Analysis

The 'Fish Boss' Feature

The following is a study of a single news item, which is reproduced in figure 1. Featured as a *'Sun* News Special' on 'Page Three' (19 April 1989), the item appeared alongside the customary nude pin-up, the 'Page Three Girl', which is approximately three times its size. The article reports the conviction of an employer, Mike Alway, for sexual harassment of two employees, Lisa Loveless (!) and Marnie Stinson.

Figure 1   The 'fish boss' feature

(1) **£6,000 BILL PUTS RANDY FISH BOSS IN HIS PLAICE!**
(2) Sex harassment rap
(3) By SUN REPORTER
(4) A RANDY fish company boss who tried netting two pretty young employees was branded a stinker by an industrial tribunal yesterday – and landed with a £6,000 bill.

[photo]
(5) *Marnie told Alway no way*

(6) Persistent 53-year-old Mike Alway tried every way to go all the way with lovely Lisa Loveless and attractive Marnie Stinson.
(7) He offered to INCREASE Marnie's salary, help BUY her a flat, and TAKE her to Gibraltar.
(8) And Lisa claimed she LOST her job after refusing his advances.
(9) *But the bearded, balding boss's chat-up lines really did leave a lot to be desired.*
(10) The tribunal heard how the old romantic told Marnie: 'You make things happen in my trousers,' and 'I like your skirt – it shows off your backside'.
(11) His attempts at seducing buxom 24-year-old Lisa were even worse.
(12) 'My thing throbs when I see you,' he said, and described her bosoms as 'big juicy boobs'.
(13) Experiences
(14) Marnie said that shortly after she started to work for Mr Alway he took her out to dinner.
(15) She told the tribunal: 'He told me details about his experiences at wife swapping parties'.
(16) Then on the way home he stopped his car and stroked her leg.
(17) Marnie, 22, of Scarborough, Yorks, yesterday said she was harassed out of her job as a linguist with his L'Amiral seafood firm.
(18) She told the Exeter tribunal: 'He would not pay me my proper salary of £8,000 a year unless I went to bed with him'.
(19) Lisa, of Plymouth, Devon, claimed she was fired as operations manager for Mr Alway's Flow International food distribution company after refusing his advances.
(20) Hope
(21) Tribunal chairman Brian Walton said Mr Alway was guilty of 'galloping carnality'.
(22) He awarded Lisa £2,600 in damages and back pay for sexual harassment.
(23) Marnie received £2,000.
(24) Mr Alway was ordered to pay £1,250 costs.

In making sense of this news story, a reader must, as I have already proposed, draw upon a range of resources from outside the text itself. In this analysis, the reader resources I intend to concentrate on are discourse types and prior texts. Cues to these resources are reportage, verbal play and naming practices.

Reportage

In news genres, there is one form of intertexuality which is particularly important, namely 'prior-text intertextuality' (Talbot, 1990, 1995a). This refers to the 'embedding' of an earlier text in a current one. Quotations and reports – the reportage of the previously uttered words of other people – are obvious manifestations of embedded prior texts. They generally involve explicit marking of the 'join' between texts with reporting verbs, and often with quotation marks too, as in (10):

(10) . . . the old romantic told Marnie: 'You make things happen in my trousers'

Prior-text intertextuality in news genres can be highly complex. In the 'fish boss' feature, there is a good deal of quotation (seven extracts are marked off with quotation marks), and report. It is important to note, however, that quotations and reports are also central to the giving of evidence in legal discourse. In the news story, what we allegedly encounter are quotations from statements uttered at the tribunal, which are themselves quotations of the defendant's incriminating utterances. In reality, the voices from the tribunal itself are likely to be highly mediated. Only once is an individual tribunal official identified, and supposedly quoted, and this is in order to rearticulate the absurd verdict that he allegedly pronounced:

(21) Tribunal chairman Brian Walton said Mr Alway was guilty of 'galloping carnality'.

The other prior texts selected for quotation are the defendant's 'chat-up lines' (as in sentence 10, quoted above), and selected statements from the two women pressing charges.

   In most cases, the prior texts in the 'fish boss' feature have probably been translated into a version of 'vernacular speech' favoured by *The Sun*. We can only say 'probably' here, since to be certain we would need the actual transcripts of the tribunal's proceedings.[2]

Apparent translation from one variety to another (from legal discourse to *The Sun*'s 'vernacular') is particularly evident in the first paragraph:

(4) A RANDY fish company boss [. . .] was branded a stinker by an industrial tribunal yesterday

The distinctive reporting verb 'branded' almost invariably accompanies accusations and convictions in the tabloids. It seems to be signalling the voice of *The Sun* even as it reports the judgement of the industrial tribunal. The members of the tribunal are, of course, highly unlikely to have called the defendant a 'stinker'; this is a kind of name-calling, which is not a feature of legal discourse. But it is certainly characteristic of '*Sun* discourse'. For example, an article in *The Sun* once ridiculed 'the Silly Burghers of Sowerby Bridge' for banning the newspaper from their libraries.[3] A less humorously intended example was in the headline 'the Bastards of Baghdad' during the 1991 Gulf War.

It is clear, then, that the 'fish boss' feature is not univocal. Voices other than that of the anonymous *Sun* reporter are present, though in heavily mediated form.

Verbal Play

The insult in the 'fish boss' feature (i.e. 'stinker') has been selected, of course, in order to continue the punning word play initiated in the headline:

(1) £6,000 BILL PUTS RANDY FISH BOSS IN HIS PLAICE!

'Verbal play' is another very familiar characteristic of newspaper reporting. Of particular interest in this respect is journalists' preoccupation with the (broadly speaking) poetic function of language. Mixing verbal play with information-giving can also be seen in elite, broadsheet newspapers, of course, but it is in the tabloids that it occurs with the greatest frequency and intensity. The 'fish boss' feature is no exception. It abounds with alliteration, assonance, and other forms of parallelism (e.g. (6) 'Mike Alway tried every way to go all the way'), dreadful puns (on the theme of fish), and other elements, which might also be considered literary, such as irony ((10) 'the old romantic'). As Roger Fowler observes:

> *The Sun* indulges in 'poetic' structures in places where it is being at its most outrageous about politics or sex [. . .] even a critical reader can be disarmed by pleasure in the awfulness of the discourse. (1991, p. 45)

These 'poetic' devices are crammed into the attention-getting segments of the article (the headline/abstract and orientation). Such intense focus on playfulness, however, combined with the framing of the whole news item (not least its placement next to the topless 'Page Three Girl'), strongly cues an interpretation of the information content as non-serious, and undermines the legal discourse articulated by the tribunal. A kind of producer–audience relationship is set up, which is unlike that of a 'straight' news story in the tabloids or elsewhere. In this way, the coverage of the harassment case is portrayed as a source of entertainment, with the verbal play and the dominating image of the nude pin-up contributing to its overall trivialization.

Naming Practices

A brief examination of the naming practices in the 'fish boss' feature draws attention to a number of interesting points on the discourses of class and gender that are articulated, and about which I shall say more in the next section. Of particular importance are the noun phrase elements used in identifying, classifying, or otherwise labelling the protagonists, namely the defendant and the two women pressing charges (see table 1). The categories used are taken from Theo van Leeuwen's quantitative study of grammatical differences between two British newspapers, *The Times*, a quality broadsheet, and *The Sun* (van Leeuwen, 1994). *Appraisement* involves the use of evaluative terms to refer to people. *Relational identification* occurs where people are identified in terms of their relationships with others; in this case, it is work relations that are at issue. Further labelling devices are the use of honorifics (*Honorification*), last-naming and first-naming (*Formalization* and *Informalization*, respectively), and identification using both first and last name (*Semi-formalization*).

As we can see from table 1, the two women pressing charges against their former employer are identified most often by physical attributes, and referred to by their first names. The defendant himself is repeatedly appraised, identified as a 'boss', and referred to by honorific and last name. This formality of reference is untypical of *The Sun*, however, and in stark contrast with the more customary 'egalitarianism' of naming (van Leeuwen, 1994). The naming devices seem, therefore, to be placing the employer at a distance. Indeed, the label

Table 1   Noun phrase elements used to label the protagonists in the 'fish boss' feature

The defendant

Appraisement	*Relational identification*	*Honorification Formalization + Semi-formalization*	*Physical identification*
randy (× 2)	boss (× 3)	Mr Alway (× 4)	bearded
a stinker		Mike Alway	balding
persistent			
the old romantic			

The complainants

	Relational identification	*Informalization + Semi-formalization*	*Physical identification*
	employees	Lisa (× 4)	pretty young
		Marnie (× 6)	lovely
		Lisa Loveless	attractive
		Marnie Stinson	buxom

of 'boss' probably contributes significantly to this distancing, since the targeted readership of the newspaper is working class, a point which I shall now explore further.

Discussion

Discourses of Class and Gender

I think we can safely say that *The Sun* embodies a consensual (as opposed to conflict-based) view of society. In the 'fish boss' feature, it is this view of social class that presumably underlies the lexicalization of the identities of capital owner and waged labour as 'boss' and 'employee'. So, for example, the term 'boss' is in lexical opposition with 'employee', not 'worker'. This is because the relationship between bosses and employees is considered to be one of mutual benefit (whereas bosses and *workers* are engaged in class struggle). With the exception of this particular example, the consensual view of class is not strongly articulated in the article itself, though it is manifestly present elsewhere in the newspaper. For instance, it is apparent in what is deemed newsworthy, such as the assumption that the behaviour of elites is inherently interesting (members of the British royal family and pop stars, in particular). However, in the article's ridicule, vilification even, of the 'fish boss', we have something rather different. The article seems to be giving expression to a form of working-class antagonism. As a boss, Mike Alway is at a distance from the target audience, and bosses, who are presumably middle class, are generally present as villains in *The Sun*.

As far as gender is concerned, it comes as no real surprise to find in the 'fish boss' feature the dominant, sexist discourse that traditionally permeates 'Page Three'. The two women are physically identified several times (one of them, Marnie, is also visually represented in a passport-like photograph that accompanies the news item). The defendant's appearance is mentioned as well, but only once, and for a specific purpose. In this dominant discourse on gender, women enter into the subject position of visible objects for men's perusal and assessment. For women, the cultivation of an attractive appearance is of paramount importance.[4] Men, on the other hand, are observers, assessors and natural predators on women, an aspect of the dominant discourse on gender which has been referred to as 'male sex-drive discourse' (Hollway, 1984).

However, this position as an object in male sex-drive discourse does not construct women exclusively as victims. Being attractive to men also places them in a position of power. In fact, it is women's goal to attract men. This view is very much in evidence in the account of sexual harassment in the 'fish boss' feature, especially in the frequent alleged quotations from what the copywriter calls the defendant's 'chat-up lines'. Of course, male sex-drive discourse is itself grounded in a biological discourse, according to which sexuality constitutes a natural male instinct, and is, therefore, uncontrollable. This is most clearly illustrated by the fragment of the tribunal's verdict selected for quotation: 'galloping carnality'.

The dominant discourse on gender is also behind common-sense notions in the article about the way in which romantic relationships are, or should be, conducted:

(7) He offered to INCREASE Marnie's salary, help BUY her a flat, and TAKE her to Gibraltar.

(8) And Lisa claimed she LOST her job after refusing his advances.

And we especially need to draw upon such notions in order to account for the disjunctive 'but' in the following example:

(9) *But the bearded, balding boss's chat-up lines really did leave a lot to be desired.* (original emphasis)

In other words, the boss offered to increase his employee's salary, and so on, because her power to attract him was so strong. But *even though* he did all these things, his attempts to strike up sexual relationships with his employees were unsuccessful because he was ineffectual in other ways. Despite his evident economic prowess, he did not make the grade as a sexual predator. Presumably, he wasn't smooth-tongued enough, and was unable to find the most effective phrasing for his 'chat-up lines'. Moreover, as a 'bearded, balding boss', he clearly wasn't good-looking enough, either.

The dominant sexist discourse on gender is, of course, what one would expect to find on 'Page Three' in *The Sun*. It is perhaps more surprising, however, to be confronted – in addition – with a kind of feminist counter-discourse in the 'fish boss' feature. So, for example, the term 'sexual harassment' occurs in the sub-heading, in the slightly abbreviated form of 'sex harassment'. This is a term which was originally a feminist coinage and, like 'sexism' itself, was employed in order to fill a lexical gap (Farley, 1978; Spender, 1980). Nowadays, sexual harassment is legally established as a form of discrimination, and legislation against workplace harassment has redefined – as public – practices which had previously been construed as private (as has also been the case with rape and battering). In the 'fish boss' feature, the legislation against workplace harassment is not being ridiculed, as it was initially by the press (trade union guidelines published in Britain in 1983, for example, were widely mocked as legislation against human nature; see Stanko, 1985, p. 139). Nor is the coinage being contested, as has also been the case (see Ehrlich and King, 1994). On the face of it, then, the article is reporting a successful conviction of a sexual harasser with wholehearted approval.

Masculinity meets Feminism

I find it fascinating that a feature appearing on *The Sun*'s 'Page Three' appears to be both articulating class antagonism, on the one hand, and using a feminist counter-discourse on gender taken up by an industrial tribunal, on the other. The tabloid press is the last place I would have looked for coverage of a prosecution for sexual harassment in the workplace. It did not fit in with my previous expectations about the kinds of agenda, positions on gender issues, and so on, that one would be likely to find in the pages of *The Sun*.

Simultaneously, however, the article provides more of the same old thing. The sexual objectification of women is retained, and the selective quotations from the tribunal proceedings have presumably been

incorporated for the purposes of titillation. Moreover, sexual harassment is unproblematically paralleled with 'normal' interaction
between women and men, via naturalized assumptions from 'male
sex-drive discourse' about male and female sexuality. In other words,
despite the presence of feminist discourse, the dominant sexist discourse on gender is still intact.

Yet to me, the feature is especially interesting because it is clearly
responding to social changes brought about by feminism. In a social
world in which feminism has gained some institutional power in the
legal system to bring to bear on perpetrators of sexist practices, hegemonic masculinity is having to make some adjustments. For one
thing, it is no longer invisible; that is, hidden from view as the
unproblematic norm, or accounted for as 'just human nature'.
Feminist research and activism has brought hegemonic masculinity,
especially white heterosexual masculinity, out into the open, where it
is vulnerable, to some degree, to the kind of scrutiny and criticism
previously reserved for the gender identities of straight women, lesbians and gay men. This new-found problematization of masculinity
has had a real impact. Thus, men whose gender identities depend on
oppressive forms of masculinity no longer have the easy justification
of appealing to naturalized conventions. At the same time, legislation
against such oppressive practices as sexual harassment and child
abuse undermines men's previous positions of dominance in the
institutions of the workplace and the family (albeit with very variable
effectiveness). As Jonathan Rutherford observes:

> Like the Invisible Man of H. G. Wells, whose death is signified by his
> return to visibility, the weakening of particular masculine identities has
> pushed them into the spotlight of greater public scrutiny. The reality of
> men's heterosexual identities is that their endurance is contingent upon an
> array of structures and institutions. When these shift or weaken, men's
> dominant positions are threatened. (1988, p. 23)

Threatened, however, is not tantamount to undermined. Until the
structures and institutions that shore up hegemonic masculine identities are transformed (whenever and however that might be), oppressive forms of masculinity are unlikely to be replaced.

Heterosexual Masculinity, Sexual Harassment and the Sun Reader

I should like to draw this discussion to a close with some direct
observations about the construction of a '*Sun*-reader' type of

masculinity in the light of the problems facing hegemonic masculinity. I believe that the 'fish boss' feature provides the male reader with the opportunity to deflect the potential threat to his hegemonic status in two distinct ways.

The first relates to the nature of the reader's contact with the oppositional, but now legitimized, feminist discourse that has found its way into the newspaper. In focusing on the multi-voicedness of reader resources, I was drawing attention to a particular constellation of discourse types, which I have informally labelled '*Sun* discourse'. This would appear to be undermining both the legal discourse of the industrial tribunal, and the counter-discourse on gender that the tribunal is serving to articulate on this occasion. As we saw in the section on prior-text intertextuality, both of these are heavily mediated and channelled through '*Sun* discourse', such that the reader does not meet them head on.

The second way in which the potential threat to hegemonic masculinity is being deflected involves a scapegoat. The reader is thus given the opportunity to lay the blame for sexist practices on an outsider. It was some work within stylistics that provided me with a clue to this deflecting strategy. In a study of reportage of sexual assault in *The Sun*, Kate Clark (1990) observes that the men who commit sexual assaults are frequently represented as fiends, alien others, and therefore distanced from the average *Sun* reader: 'The intense hyperbole of fiend-naming focuses a self-righteous fury on stranger attacks, which are actually a very small area of male/female violence' (p. 224).

What would appear to be happening in the 'fish boss' feature is that the sexual harasser is being constructed as a randy, but ineffectual boss, certainly not the average male *Sun* reader. As I pointed out in the section on naming practices, his social class sets him apart from the working-class target readership of the newspaper. At the same time, his ineffectuality as a sexual being sets him up as a figure of fun. Thus, his physical shortcomings (as 'bearded' and 'balding'), coupled with his middle-class status (as a boss), mean that he doesn't quite make it in the working-class masculinity stakes. In this way, the blameworthy practice of sexual harassment is deflected onto a sexually ineffectual, middle-class scapegoat, providing male readers with an easy solution to the dilemma facing their masculinity: Mike Alway is clearly 'not one of us'. All of this means that male readers can condemn Alway's behaviour, but without having to go through the uncomfortable business of actually changing their own ways. Of course, it is ironical that this deflecting strategy should take place on 'Page Three', right next to the nude pin-up. The male *Sun* reader is provided with a cosy distance from the villain of the piece, despite the obvious parallels that can be drawn between sexual harassment and 'normal' male behaviour, such as ogling the pin-ups on 'Page Three'.

In terms of reader-construction, my main focus of attention has been men. But, of course, a large proportion of *Sun* readers are women (over half, in fact). While the crisis facing dominant hetero-sexual expressions of masculinity is primarily a problem for men, it also has a great deal of significance for women, particularly women who engage, or want to engage, in heterosexual relationships. Although it is true that the '*Sun* discourse' in the 'fish boss' feature undermines the legal discourse of the industrial tribunal, and the counter-discourse on gender that the tribunal is serving to articulate, it does not necessarily alienate women readers. It does not, after all, challenge the verdict of the industrial tribunal, nor does it take issue with the identification of the practice of sexual harassment in the workplace. On the contrary, it appears to approve wholeheartedly. For female readers, therefore, the offer of a middle-class scapegoat may provide a certain reassurance: that their man is not like that, that the men they have relationships with are not potential harassers.

Conclusion

In conclusion, I would argue that, whilst the legitimacy of its domi-nant forms may be under threat, the stability of hegemonic masculin-ity might well lie in its very flexibility. I hope to have shown how the 'fish boss' feature appears to have assimilated elements of the opposi-tional discourse of feminism, yet simultaneously left intact more tra-ditional assumptions about sexual relations between men and women. This has been achieved partly by drawing upon a kind of class antagonism in order to deflect the accusation of sexual harass-ment in question onto a (middle-class) outsider. Significantly, how-ever, these contradictory discourses have been combined in a way which produces a text that can be read as coherent. Tentatively, I would propose that it is precisely the capacity to blend such seem-ingly contradictory discourses that might enable hegemonic mas-culinity to withstand the risk of larger, more disruptive structural changes.

Notes

1 *The Sun* is a national, politically conservative newspaper targeted at a working-class readership in Britain. 'Page Three' is the daily location of its customary topless pin-up, known as the 'Page Three Girl', whose image occupies over half the page.
2 See Fairclough (1992a, pp. 105–9) for inspection of discourse representation in *The Sun*, which also refers to the original: that is, to the document being reported.
3 'Burghers' is a pun on 'buggers', which is a term of abuse.
4 In an alternative account of women's subject positioning as visual objects, women are constructing their feminine identities for their own benefit, not primarily as sex objects for the male gaze. For this complementary view of women's active participation, and investment, in constructing their identities as feminine, see Smith (1988) and Talbot (1995b).

11

'The Object of Desire is the Object of Contempt': Representations of Masculinity in *Straight to Hell* Magazine

John Heywood

Introduction

Masculinity is notoriously difficult to pin down. Its recent pluralization in academic discourse reflects the growing awareness that significant differences in ideology and practice are disguised and subsumed in the singular abstract noun. Over the last thirty years, since feminist and gay theorists began to explore the construction of patriarchal ideology, the status of masculinity as a relational term has become clear. According to Antony Easthope, in popular culture it is put forward 'as a pure essence defined against what is wholly other than it: femininity as a pure essence. Men and women, male and female, masculine and feminine are to be compartmentalized, sorted into opposed categories, and assigned to separate places' (1986, p. 111). The inevitable consequence of this basic opposition is the stigmatization of homosexuality, conceived in a particular way. Thus, Connell notes that: 'In homophobic ideology the boundary between straight and gay is blurred with the boundary between masculine and feminine, gay men being imagined as feminized men and lesbians as masculinized women' (1995, p. 40).

How the stereotype of gay men is constructed within a range of cultures, ideologies, and specific discourses, has been well examined (see also Cameron, chapter 3, for a discussion of the way heterosexuals construct both gay men, and themselves, through their talk). This chapter sets out to survey the boundary from the other side; to explore the language of straightness and masculinity through a particular set of gay or queer perspectives.[1]

The Texts and Aims of the Analysis

The texts to be analysed are taken from a magazine called *Straight to Hell* (henceforth *STH*), which flourished in the United States during the 1970s and early 1980s, and which, from a current perspective, can be seen to preserve the attitudes of the period between the beginning of Gay Liberation and the onset of AIDS. The publication belongs to what might be described as a sub-genre of gay pornography, consisting mainly of narratives that also claim to be first-person accounts of 'real-life experiences'.

In its original A5 pamphlet format, initiated and edited by Boyd McDonald, *STH* rapidly became an underground cult classic.[2] It is currently on the market in the form of anthologies, whose pithy one-word titles such as *Meat, Flesh, Sex, Cum* and *Juice* unambiguously declare their primary pornographic function. Since being anthologized, *STH* has become big business, with an evidently huge readership, some volumes selling in excess of 50,000 copies. But it began as a small, counter-cultural operation. When he died in September 1993, McDonald was still living in a single room in the Riverside Hotel on the West Side in Manhattan. His last interview gives, perhaps, the root of his motivation: 'It's an obsession for me. It's a monomania' (*The Guide*, November 1993, p. 22).

Pornography is usually dismissed as a locus of falsity. The single asymmetrical act of communication between the writer and a body of text consumers – through the apparatus of text production – lends itself to being analysed as an example of not just the construction, but the inculcation of an ideology. But in *STH*, this act of communication is more complex, because the consumers of its texts are also drawn in to become writers. Thus, any sense of an overall ideology that begins to emerge from these multiple and sometimes conflicting voices can be seen as a co-production between the readers-as-writers and the editor. Of course, this particular sub-genre of gay pornography is also suspect, as the border between it and fictional pornography is blurred. Some rival collections of 'first-person accounts' read with a suspicious evenness of style, as if the editor has either extensively rewritten the pieces or is in fact the inventor of the material.[3] But where the editorial process in those versions is rendered invisible, the variety of style in *STH* is impressive and the relationship between the editor and his writers is prominently displayed.

The sheer size of the corpus undeniably presents difficulties of conceptualization and selection. *Sex* alone, from which most of my examples are drawn, contains 129 separate texts (110 narratives, eight editorial articles, and eleven interviews), any one of which would yield much to close attention. Taken as a whole, the texts offer a range of representations of masculinity embedded in claims about personal experience gained in the social arena of sexual encounters between men. They may therefore provide some insight into the interplay between the identities of their writers and hegemonic masculinity, an insight more valuable for not being the conscious focus of the writing.

But it is the editor's power to select and process the narratives that is clearly the principal factor in establishing the particular nature of the discourse. This chapter therefore focuses on what, in my reading as a gay man, are the outstanding features of the 'macro-text' that emerges from the relationship between the discourse frame set up by the editor and the narratives. Through a close examination of both this frame and the narratives, I aim to show how many of the traditional oppositions employed in the construction of gender identities (straight/gay, masculine/feminine, active/passive) are thrown into question. But this subversion acts only on the construction of masculinity at the level of popular ideology. I hope to demonstrate that at the deeper level from which these texts appear to be composed, masculinity survives this subversion. The overall message of these texts emerges as a paradox.

In what follows, references to the anthologies will be by date and page number, and to original copies of *STH* by the number of the issue – exact details of these primary sources are given at the end of the chapter.

The Discourse Frame

Eliciting and Establishing a Pornography of Truth

The discourse frame consists of several different text-types. The narratives are given headlines and, occasionally, editorial postscripts are added in italics, which comment on them drily. Interspersed with the narratives are interviews, conducted mainly through postal questionnaires, collections of genuine news items about incidents involving homosexuality, and short expository pieces – witty, assertive and bitingly satirical – in which McDonald makes his own position clear. The discourse frame thus circumscribes a particular space within the whole range of narratives that might have been elicited. In conjunction with the textual traces of the interaction between editor and writers, it serves to legitimate the narratives, providing a contextual frame that makes *STH* into something more than just a collection of erotic tales – a 'theory' of homosexuality and of sex between men for which the reader-writers supply the evidence.

McDonald set out to create a grass-roots pornography. In this respect, he was particularly proud of the increasing number of letters he got from Black men and older writers (1992, p. 9), at a time when members of both groups felt excluded from the sense of gay identity then developing in the burgeoning institutions of the post-Stonewall gay scene.[4] In a piece reprinted as the editorial postscript to *Filth*, he makes explicit the sort of writing he is inviting from his readers: 'I welcome letters for anonymous publication from all men, young and old. I want only actual experiences, rather than fiction. I like them written in a plain style – just the facts, the sight, taste, touch and smell of sex. How men look, act, dress, undress, and talk. What happened, in A-B-C, 1-2-3 order' (1987, p. 192).

The request for 'actual experiences, rather than fiction' is central to the project. By showing men as they are, the claim to truth is at the core of *STH*'s resistance to the dominant ideology. The opposition of truth to fantasy runs through many of McDonald's own editorial contributions and statements, for example: 'The truth cannot be pornographic. It has a purity of its own and a right to be told' (1981, p. 9). But while pornography as fiction is condemned, the greater pornographic power of the real is celebrated. 'The truth is the biggest turn-on. Knowing that it not only can but did happen' (ibid.). The contributors similarly refer explicitly to the stories' pornographic power, and assert the truth of their own accounts. The comment of one writer, 'Reality can really put fantasy to shame' (1982, p. 107), echoes throughout the texts. Another, agreeing that only the apparently authentic carries a genuine erotic charge, distinguishes *STH* from a similar kind of publication on precisely that basis: 'You made one comment in your letter which I must agree with. You said "The simple truth is more pornographic than pornography, which lacks credibility". You are so right. A good example of this is the magazine *First Hand* (when edited by Brandon Judell). It became more pornographic until the magazine lost all appeal' (1986, p. 61).

But despite the mass of assertions from both editor and writers, and of incidental internal evidence in the texts, the credibility of the accounts in *STH* has still been questioned, suggesting that *STH* is a site where the meaning of being homosexual is being contested. The authenticity of the texts cannot be resolved here, and is, in any case, irrelevant to their power – as discourse – to enter into their readers' construction of experience. Their credibility rests with their readers, as does their power to arouse. Relating acts of sexual communication, the narratives serve as vehicles for exploring paradoxes of identity, of both the writers and their objects of desire. The peculiar combination of qualities that *STH* exhibits is summed up by one reader: 'Who would ever dream that fantastic jerk-off material & consciousness raising stuff could be found in the same rag. Right on and keep on turning on. My neighbors & I are all creaming over it' (1981, p. 189).

'Straightness' Assaulted

The central element of the discourse is signalled by the pun in its title. *Straight to Hell* explicitly sets out to collect stories of transgressive sexual acts that would indeed traditionally have sent a person 'straight to hell'. But McDonald was not interested in the whole range of possible desires or acts that might be classed as homosexual. The pun declares his intention to elicit stories of encounters and acts with supposedly 'straight' men, thus implicating them in this metaphorical descent. Derived from a curse, the title expresses defiance. As Charley Shively points out in the introduction to *Meat*: 'STH does not address itself to the needs and sensibilities of straight people: they can go to hell, straight to hell' (1981, p. 6).[5]

In its original magazine format, *Straight To Hell* appeared with a fluctuating range of subtitles, the most constant of which became *The Manhattan Review of Unnatural Acts*. Others it employed from time to time included the *U.S. Chronicle of Crimes Against Nature*, *The American Journal of Cocksucking and Current Events*, *Archives of the American Academy of Homosexual Research* and the *American Journal of Debauchery: Revenge Therapy*. The titles thus subvert the values of the larger society through ironically appropriating and parodying its styles of inquiry and discourse. The irony extends into the headings assigned to the narratives, which, in turn, parody newspaper headline style. The following, all drawn from *Sex*, frequently focus on the incongruity between the participants' public social identities and the acts in which they engage: 'Professor Sold as Slave' (p. 157) or 'Mississippi Man, 26, Asks Doctor To Beat Him' (p. 19). With an eye for the absurd, they highlight the 'facts' of the event: 'Toilet Star

Wears (A) Levis (B) Jock Strap, (C) Scumbag' (p. 153), sometimes through awful puns: 'Hunky Black, 8½" Meats Youth, 11"' (p. 22), or through quoting lines from the text: '"A Huge One [...] I Thought I Would Choke"' (p. 42). Frequently, they play on the associations between geographical location, racial or ethnic identity, and masculine stereotypes: 'South Dakota Sailor Fucks Boston Boy in Mouth' (p. 18). Alternatively, they point up some political or social irony in the story: 'Conservatives in South Dakota Call Youth "Faggot" Whilst Raping Him' (p. 105).

The headings delight in the outrageousness of the material they introduce, suggesting that sex is an arena in which social boundaries dissolve. Despite their satirical tone, the headings retain, however, their crucial function of announcing the presence of 'fact'. In this respect, McDonald had a serious underlying empirical intent: 'My books tell what the soldier and sailor *do*' (*The Guide*, November 1993, p. 21). The 'plain style' McDonald requested for the narratives is, indeed, close to the 'masculine' style of journalistic discourse, as described by Easthope (1986, pp. 79–85). *STH* is to function as an informal catalogue of male/male sexual practices transacted across the 'border' between 'straight' and 'gay'. But instead of being produced from a superior expert perspective, as if by a Krafft-Ebing or a Kinsey, it is to be written by the participants themselves. Their point of origin is indicated in capitals at the beginning, e.g. CONNECTI-CUT, creating the sense of a widely scattered community of strangers, although, significantly, location gives way to occupation when the writer holds a position of status within the hierarchies of power in society, e.g. FROM A PROFESSOR, FROM A PRIEST.

Simply by collecting stories of encounters between 'gay' and 'straight' men, *STH* subverts and undermines the notion of an unproblematic heterosexual identity. But McDonald takes this process a step further. In the series of short expository pieces interspersed throughout the magazines, he carves out a space for the narratives to exist by launching explicit attacks on the notion of 'straightness' as expressed in the dominant ideology. Several of these pieces explore paradoxes in the use of the word 'straight', exposing its use as code for those who collude with the corruption of the system: 'Charles Colson, a lawyer and the hoodiest of Nixon's hoods, was recommending a guy to carry out one of the White House's crimes. Colson called him "straight"' (1981, p. 20). McDonald thus neatly lobs the accusation of moral inversion back onto the other side. The attack on 'straight' men in a piece entitled 'America's True Perverts' reduces them to mere sexual playthings, and re-appropriates courage on behalf of homosexuals:

Some are fun in bed, but only because their membership in the powerful sexual majority gives them a certain ease which is called 'masculinity'. But under their surface show of virility they are ipso facto, by being 'straight', too timid to be of any real interest or value. Only men with balls dare to be different – to be homosexual for example, or refuse to kill innocent Asians. The frightened ones do what Nixon or the church or somebody tells them to do. Historically, this has been, 'Make war and money, but don't make love.' Thus they are America's true perverts. Killing is the ultimate perversion and America has become history's greatest killer. To value people by the value of their bank accounts is another perversion. To use sex to express hate rather than love is another. (1982, p. 5)

Crucially, for the purposes of his project, McDonald detaches the concept of perversion from sex, and re-assigns it to violence, materialism and hatred. In positioning *STH* in opposition to what he sees as the values of hegemonic masculinity, he then offers sex as both a point of resistance and as an alternative source of value. And not sex according to its privileged definition as the meaningful expression of the depth of a relationship, but largely anonymous, spontaneous, casual sex. He is thus dealing with sex both as the revelation of some inner truth of identity in desire, but also as sequences of events that may be entirely sealed off from any consequences on the participants' sense of identity.

STH *and the Gay Liberation Movement*

These attacks on the dominant ideology read like gay liberation manifestos. Yet, although, in order to produce the anthologies, McDonald linked up with the cultural sector of the gay press (the first to be able to negotiate some immunity from state repression), the sexual values he championed led to an ambivalent relationship with certain sections of the Gay Liberation Movement. McDonald thought the advent of an open gay identity had involved the denial of actual sexual identity: 'My work is an alternative to the gay liberation movement and to the gay press. The gay press has to be sexless because they are public. And in order to be publicly gay they have to be closet homosexuals' (*The Guide*, November 1993, p. 19). In a further inversion of conventional values, he attacks the gay cultural establishment: 'Any gay publications that do not deal with the elemental discussion of gay sexual desire are not serious – they are frivolous [...] shallow publications. They have nothing to do with basic homosexuality' (1993, p. 199).

On the other hand, McDonald knew that his work was being seen as uncomfortably close to the stereotype of the homosexual in the dominant ideology: 'The leaders of the gay liberation movements [...] say that my books help confirm what Jesse Helms and Pat Robertson and the worst people in America say about homosexuals' (*The Guide*, November 1993, p. 20). But in a piece entitled 'Wax Fruit', written to accompany a cartoon caricaturing a 'piss-elegant'[6] polo-necked queen, both 'straight' and gay establishments are assimilated into a single enemy identified with middle-class values:

> I write for the lower and upper classes, not the Rising Middle Class. S.T.H. is always coarse, never common; the middle class are endlessly vulgar, with no redeeming obscenity. [...] They have little interest in what's real, and do not respond, on their way to be entertained by packaged, plotted, performed pieces in theatres, to the real spontaneity and grace of boys and men, which is on the streets of New York. [...] To this day they love lovely things. They are themselves lovely things, things more than people, robots like the 'straights', performing as programmed by the 'straight' world and, in their case, the Gay Liberation Movement. They are the sort of 'gays' their mothers always wanted, but no one else does; they are the true undesirables, the undesiring. (*STH*, No. 48)

Thus, the goodness of desire emerges as the central tenet of McDonald's beliefs. The magazine functions as a repository of desires, a confessional space, but one in which the notion of sin is abolished. Obscenity becomes 'redeeming'. McDonald ironically signalled his position as 'high priest' by acquiring a mail order divinity degree during the 1970s. From then on he relished calling himself the 'Reverend Boyd McDonald'. The precision of his request for 'just the facts, the sight, taste, touch and smell of sex' parodies the scrutiny of the confessional. In the detail of sexual practice, desire – the 'essential' truth of the self – is to be revealed.

The Narratives

Straightness Dissolved/Masculinity Affirmed

The discourse frame sets the presumption of 'straightness' so firmly that the majority of the narratives make no explicit reference to the sexual identities of either their writers or their objects of desire. The location of the 'original event' is rarely defined unambiguously as a 'gay space'. More often, however, the setting is clearly marked as liminal: a street *outside* a set of gay bars, a cruising ground in a park, or a bath-house – a space on which the two 'categories' can converge.

In *Sex*, the word 'straight' itself only occurs in sixteen out of the 122 accounts and interviews. Whereas in the headings the word is always subverted by inverted commas, e.g. '"Straight" Youth wants Asshole Licked, But Writer Finds It Too Dirty (At First)' (1982, p. 31), in half of the instances in the narratives the term is used without any sense of irony. Either way, the social stereotype in which 'straight' unproblematically entails heterosexual behaviour is effectively undermined. One writer declares: 'I love to hear a straight telling me what he wants and that I am making him happy. I've had spells of Ivy Leaguers, Navy uniforms, truck drivers, in fact every type except queens & faggots' (1982, p. 64).

In rigorously excluding effeminate or self-identified gay men from the field of his desire, this writer is one of the purer exponents of McDonald's 'theory'. Later in this narrative, he generalizes from his experiences in the Appalachians: 'The amazing part was all these hill-billies were straight and when sex was over, they treated me as a straight friend' (1982, p. 65). The feature these objects of desire appear to share is the willingness to engage in homosexual acts without displaying or adopting signs of a homosexual identity. Yet the majority of the writers are clearly still signifying a distinct category of man. Thus, as the category of 'straightness' dissolves, the notion of masculinity is explored and affirmed.

What matters to many of the writers, in the first place, is whether the object of desire bears the signs of 'authentic masculinity'. The perception of the masculinity of the other, often a matter of non-verbal classification achieved in a split-second of recognition, leaves traces in the texts. The writers use a range of well-known terms such as *hunk* and *macho*, but others, which derive from gay discourse, such as *butch* and *trade*,[7] work through the assumption of shared knowledge. Initially, this knowledge relates to physical attributes, and in their concentration on size, muscle and length of penis, many of the narratives display the same tendencies towards fragmenting and measuring the object of desire that has often been remarked on in fictional pornography involving women. The length of a penis, of course, can stand metonymically not just for the organ itself, but for the entire man. In the texts, penises are represented not only as objects that possess length and width, but, through converting the word 'cock' into an uncountable noun, as a substance possessing weight.

But physical attributes are often inextricably entangled with, and sometimes less significant than, the eroticized signs and symbols of occupation, class and ethnic identity. One narrative entitled 'Rude

Italian Sits Bareass on Reader's Face' is set in a celebrated and long-established Manhattan bath-house that was finally closed by the AIDS epidemic. The sequence of assumptions this writer records are entirely based on appearance, and are not confirmed in the subsequent, largely non-verbal encounter:

> One night in Everard Baths, I opened the door on a couple of men rooming together, second floor. I'd seen them come in and watched them go to and from the showers. Probably truck drivers, I figured. Their first visitor left, and that was when I opened the door and went in. Both men were in bed on separate cots; the shorter, younger man, probably Mexican, had been taken care of by the first visitor and was on his way out. The other man, obviously Italian and a real hunk of macho, in his early 30s, had been watching [...] I was very hot because straights of his calibre weren't all that common even in the Everard. (1982, p. 181)

In several of the stories about ethnic others, written by white men, racial difference alone is enough to support the assumption of authentic masculinity. In stories which recall sex with police officers, priests, soldiers, sailors and fathers, the assumption of straightness belongs to the social role rather than to the individual. The rubric of exploring straightness therefore disguises a range of criteria for inclusion, and the subversive impact is such that the more bizarre the story, the more its value increases. Indeed, as the anthologies progress, the focus on the 'straight' man weakens, and the proportion of stories that read simply as encounters between gay men goes up. However, the most important criterion, as I will show in the next section, is undoubtedly the *embodiment* of masculinity.

Defining the Essential Masculine

What was meant by the request for 'just the facts, the sight, taste, touch and smell of sex. How men look, act, dress, undress, and talk' is brought out by the questions McDonald asks in his interviews. His style of questioning is obsessive, its function to concretize as far as possible the experience being recounted, and the sexual behaviour of both interviewees and their partners gets minutely explored along every channel of the senses. Through openly displaying his own obsessions: 'Was his underwear ever soiled or, worse, didn't he wear any?' (1982, p. 36), McDonald releases his writers from inhibitions and proscriptions around discussing the nature of their sexual desires and actions, and the ways in which their sexuality involves attitudes towards 'body dirt'. For many of the writers, real masculinity is therefore apprehended as much through touch, taste and smell as through sight.

The headline 'The Love That Dare Not Speak Its Name: Armpit-sniffing' (1982, p. 6) wittily suggests that homosexuality, as such, is no longer contentious. What is still beyond the pale, however, are the details of actual sexual practice. Where some writers extol the cleanliness of their partners, others prefer them unwashed. The headline 'Airman's Ass Sweat Has "Macho" Taste', for example, singles out the writer's perception that the essence of masculinity is inherent in the fluids and odours exuded by the body: 'The sweat was strong, salty, musty and tasted like raw Irish potatoes, so macho I could hardly keep my dick from popping out of my shorts' (1982, p. 82). In 'I Slept With My Nose Up His Ass', no money is exchanged between the man and his 'hustler', but the man gives him 'a new pair of socks. I wasn't going to let his beautiful pair get away' (1981, p. 44). The value placed on unwashed socks or jock-straps by various writers is not mere metonymical displacement: the objects in question are imbued with the sweat and smell of the objects of desire.

Several of the writers construe their acceptance of 'body dirt' in a way that dovetails neatly with McDonald's rejection of the fastidious, middle-class, effeminate gay, described earlier. The friend in the following extract is lampooned for adopting aspects of feminine identity, which is associated both with erasing bodily presence with perfume, and with understanding sex as the expression of love: 'I have a black homosexual friend [. . .] He's paunchy, prissy, phoney, drowns himself in cologne, deodorant soaps and sprays. He foolishly believes that sex means love. He is baffled that my friends constantly come back for sex and his don't. He has excessive pride. I explained to him that men want a dirty, low-down cocksucker, not someone acting like a woman in the bed. He can't comprehend your magazine' (1982, p. 57).

The word 'cocksucker', as in the above example, is in fact used by *STH* writers far more frequently as a sign of their identity than the word 'gay'. Indeed, the focus of the magazine on the pursuit of the masculine through *sexual acts* has a fundamental constitutive effect on the narratives as a body of texts.

Sexual Roles and Social Power

Defining active and passive sexual roles on the basis of who penetrates or gets penetrated, four-fifths of the accounts in *Sex* are written from the point of view of people taking 'passive' roles, evidence that the distinction remains at the core of the concept of masculinity. But, in terms of agency, the words 'active' and 'passive' often misconceptualize what is going on. The acts – principally cocksucking, anal intercourse and rimming[8] – can be performed with different meanings. In lexicalizing their experience of oral sex, for example, the writers distinguish the 'face-fuck', where the 'active' partner performs the action, from the 'blow job', where the man in the 'passive' role does all the work. 'Active' writers make a similar distinction in describing anal intercourse: 'After awhile all I had to do was brace myself against the bench and he did all the rest. He rode my dick like a champion cowboy' (1982, p. 23).

Accounts of the construction of masculinity in ideology which are influenced by psychoanalysis argue that 'Success in the world as a man depends on the sublimation of anality, that is the privatization of the anus' (Simpson, 1994, p. 81). Yet, the title of 'Rude Italian Sits Bareass on Reader's Face' points to a common feature of this and other stories, the reversal of their writers' expectations. In their pursuit of the phallus, they frequently end up discovering the role of the anus as a site of masculine pleasure. The whole set of accounts reveals that the act of rimming holds no intrinsic meaning in itself, as in it, the active/passive distinction breaks down. It can be either a vehicle through which dominance is expressed – ironically, through being penetrated – or one through which dominance can potentially be reversed.

According to Easthope, 'The dominant version of masculinity treats masculinity as undivided' (1986, p. 111). At this end of the scale, where all the elements of masculinity appear to coincide in their objects of desire, some of the 'passive' writers seem to revel in their willing surrender of control. A kind of pride shines through their accounts of enduring rough treatment and sexual 'violence': 'You've heard of "too little, too late". Well this was too much, too big, too fast. The moans and screams I heard were coming from me. But I never tried to get him off me. I guess the truth is that I wouldn't have missed it for anything' (*The Guide*, November 1993, p. 115).

These narratives, although reading like accounts of rape, often reveal their writers' power of choice to stay with, or curtail, the experience. Sex is frequently constructed as an act of service, of worship, or of submission to the masculine will, by authors writing from both passive and active perspectives. Indeed, an assumption emerges in several of the narratives that, far from being modelled on heterosexual connections, only the homosexual, in offering an encounter freed of the need to show respect, is able to permit and accept the full expression of masculinity in sexual behaviour.

Space does not allow a full exploration of the whole range displayed by the narratives, from the expression of untrammelled masculinity, through its collaborative construction, to its performance as play. While the set of messages about the dynamics of power in sex between men serves to problematize the notion of masculinity, their focus on the experience of the bodies of others acts in the opposite direction to confirm it. Insisting on masculinity as something that can be physically experienced as embodied in the self or others, they make it clear that the set of 'elements' that are commonly qualified as 'masculine' – appearance, attitude, behaviour, and desire – do not necessarily entail each other.

The active/passive distinction, in fact, intersects with the operation of power and control, and the sources of power themselves are plural. Power issues not only from the body, but also from desire, from the will, and from those social roles in which it is invested by society. The narratives eroticize both those invested with power by the system, and those whose only power is that inherent in their bodies. The writer of 'In Fast and Out Slow', who makes no statement regarding his own identity, describes a Transport Authority policeman bursting in on a subway toilet: 'Man did we move fast but I think he knew something was up. [...] He went back outside & got a sign saying closed, then came back & told me to drop my pants' (1982, p. 121). The description of the policeman's penis, as 'nice hard cop cock', invests it with the power of his role. The implication of the story – that all categories of authority can be subverted through seduction – may appear to be at the cutting edge of the social order, moments when social roles are revealed as sham. But the TA cop retains his power throughout, as its ending shows: 'I asked him when he got outside if he would call or pass me on to any other cops, TA, city of Nassau or Suffolk. He said no & advised me to keep the story to myself' (1982, p. 121).

Placed against the following story, the message that emerges overall is that asymmetries of power in sex in turn give sex the power not only to reinforce social hierarchies, but also to invert them:

For the duration of the act he showed me no tenderness, neither holding nor stroking my head or shoulders as I worked on him. Despite his coldness, I serviced him with the greatest skill and deference that I could. Perhaps it was the bleeding heart in me, but I felt acutely aware of the inequity of our social situations – that I was a white, middle-class, upscale professional, and he was a poor black youth. In this interaction, I wanted him to be the winner, the boss, the Man. It made me feel good to trade off my social superiority to him, if only for a few minutes. (1992, p. 61)

This Black youth's physical embodiment of masculinity allows him a brief moment of being on top. But it is transient. The instant these moments are over, curtailed by detumescence, the social order reasserts itself. Apart from impinging on the subjectivity of their participants, the acts change nothing. The subversion lies not so much in the sex as in the act of public retelling.

The Paradox between the Narratives and the Frame

Hodge and Kress point out that 'the ideological content of texts is typically characterized by contradiction and inconsistency' (1988, p. 266). The outstanding contradiction in *STH* is the way in which texts that celebrate masculinity are framed by texts attacking it. Whereas the narratives reify, almost deify, heterosexual masculinity – including those of its qualities which have most come under critique in sexual politics, selfishness, arrogance and the need for control, the editorial position is explicitly subversive.

To the extent that the dominance of male heterosexuality is the cornerstone of a whole social order, McDonald's attacks not only invert that gender hierarchy, but subvert its ramifications throughout the system of values it supports. In a piece entitled 'No Such Thing as "Born Straight"', McDonald extends the parody of newspaper style, presenting himself in the third person as 'a leading lay analyst', and paradoxically increasing his authority by explicitly denying any legitimation from the system:

> Pure heterosexuality as a sexual category does not exist, while pure homosexuality does, according to a leading lay analyst. The analyst – editor of *Straight To Hell* – does not hold a degree in psychology, but he holds a jaundiced eye on the hypocrises, poses, sex substitutes, sex additives and defenses of the straight and narrow world. There are such things as 100% heterosexuals, he says, but they are that not instinctively but merely as a conscious choice of a way of life. Most of them have sex for the same reason they do everything else – to win society's respect. The Editor does not view society's respect as worth having. Thus, being a 'strict heterosexual' is like living on the East Side. It's not necessarily something you were born to do, merely something you do for status. Heterosexuality is not primarily sexual at all, but mainly social, and therefore unnatural. It is no accident that weddings are reported as 'social' news, whereas homosexual couplings are sexual, natural, and forbidden by society. (1982, p. 111)

By naturalizing homosexuality and problematizing male heterosexuality in this way, McDonald neatly inverts the traditional position in which homosexuality was the deviation from the natural that had to be explained. Homosexuality becomes the stable, natural term, the essential form of male sexuality, and heterosexuality the unstable, socially nurtured, artificial construction that has to erect defences against the pull of the underlying instinctual force of homosexual desire. His inversions deftly reverse the conventional references of a whole series of paired terms, challenging the attempts of hegemonic masculinity to structure social reality by ordering phenomena into sets of opposing categories. They force open the boundary between private and public, making it possible for the 'unspeakable' to be spoken. The experience of being excluded, of being positioned on the margins, creates the ability to see through the dominant ideology. As signalled by one of its subtitles, *STH* performs *Revenge Therapy*. The object of desire is also the object of contempt:

> 'Straight' males can be used for fun in bed but they are not worth talking to, their writing is not worth reading, their films not worth seeing, their attempts to give leadership in religion or psychiatry or any field are not to be followed, and they should not be allowed power in business or government because they have proved they cannot handle it. In their craving to express virility – in war, greed, violence, hate, corruption – they have ruined the most promising nation and made America a nation you can't trust. Inadequate use of their pricks has turned America into a nation of pricks. (1982, p. 5)[9]

Women, of course, are notably absent from *STH*. In a theory that posits homosexuality as the 'true' form of male sexuality, and represents heterosexuality as inauthentic, women have no place: 'The S.T.H. books are written by the only real authorities on sex: the men who have it. They are the only real histories of sex in our time' (1987, p. 192). But, socially and politically, McDonald sees women as possessing all the qualities that 'straight' men so sadly lack. In a final inversion, women become the rational sex, the guardians of sanity:

> Most American women are decent. We wish them power. But it is a man's country – America is 'he', not 'she' – and the men have ruined it. [...] The growing importance of women, and the corresponding growing impotence of men, offers some hope for the future. Someone – women, blacks, homosexuals – someone who's out of the competitive virility rat race – should take over. The men have bombed. (1982, p. 5)

This last piece brings into sharp focus the exact point where the respective messages of the narratives and the (messages of McDonald's) frame most conflict. The aspect of masculinity that

McDonald places at the root of his diagnosis of the political evils of male power – virility – is precisely the quality the *STH* writers most celebrate in themselves, or pursue in their objects of desire. But for McDonald, *desire* is the irresistible given of human existence. It is in this respect that he is able to separate his overall condemnation of the system, on the one hand, from his acceptance of the futility of resisting the way hegemonic masculinity structures desire, on the other: the power of desire, it seems, is ultimately greater than the power of contempt.

It is at this point that the frame and the narratives concur. In projecting their desires, the *STH* writers objectify, and the frame reflects this back to them. In Issue 48, a photograph of a smiling male model advertises the publication of *Meat*. His image appears to relish its juxtaposition with its speech bubble, which merrily inverts the logic of the central feminist critique of male sexuality: 'I'm not just a human being. I'm a piece of meat.'

Conclusion

Charley Shively argues that: 'STH and *Meat* do not just invert middle-class values, they enunciate cocksucker values' (1981, p. 6). And these do not ultimately challenge the basic opposition between masculinity and femininity, which is at the core of hegemonic values (see Talbot, chapter 10, for a similar conclusion on the basis of very different texts). On the contrary, the rejection of identification with the feminine, the concomitant emphasis on hardness, endurance and sexual skill, along with the conversion of the masculine subject into a sex object, all suggest that *STH* writers are very much a part of the system of hegemonic masculinity that they appear to be expelled from. Indeed, *STH* can be seen as part of the trend towards the remasculinization of homosexuality that has developed post-Stonewall. The value of their accounts partly lies in the opportunity they offer, embedded in their style, of catching a glimpse of masculinity perceiving itself. Thus, it is interesting to note, for example, that whereas hegemonic masculinity can only construe sex between men in terms of playing masculine and feminine roles, the accounts I have analysed suggest that, for many of the contributors to *STH*, what is being expressed and achieved through playing 'passive' no less than through playing 'active' sexual roles, is indisputably masculinity.

STH does not attempt to resolve the paradox of its simultaneous vilification and vindication of the heterosexual male. Asked in an interview how he reconciles 'all the accounts of wild sex with seem-ingly "straight" men [with his] constant editorial put-downs of het-erosexuals', McDonald agrees that this is a 'common homosexual ambivalence':

> It's so difficult that all I usually do is cover it with a slogan. "Love and hate for the American straight." I think it's that, for men like me, men are no good for anything except sex; they certainly shouldn't be entrusted with governing. Women should do that. But it's hard to get men to have sex because in this culture they are supposed to express their masculinity in sports and war, not sex. (1982, p. 52)

If the paradox remains unresolved, McDonald does succeed in eras-ing the contempt for the homosexual that underpins hegemonic mas-culinity by turning it against the hypocrisy of its originators.

Postscript: *STH*, AIDS and Censorship

In the later anthologies of *STH*, writers begin to refer to the changes the awareness of AIDS had made to their sexual practices. The corpus of earlier texts suddenly became the history McDonald claimed they represented. With the emergence of AIDS, however, the level of anxi-ety about McDonald's narratives became acute. The stories were by then being syndicated in the gay press, published individually in a column.

In *Policing Desire*, Simon Watney quotes a letter to the *New York Native* (Issue 137, 2–9 December, 1985) from the kind of gay activist who takes it upon himself to speak on behalf of others in a way which is profoundly unrealistic: 'It is editorially inconsistent and morally irresponsible to follow fifty pages of AIDS reportage with the kind of pornography Boyd McDonald serves up [. . .] Let's have a cre-ative pornography constructed along lines other than power and the exchange of body fluids' (1987, p. 75). Watney, however, goes on to argue the value of a pornography that speaks to 'real' desires in achieving the changes in sexual practice AIDS has made necessary: 'Such materials remain the only means by which recalcitrant desire can be worked upon, at the level of fantasy itself, in order to encour-age changes in sexual behaviour which are our only defence against the virus' (p. 14). He also outlines the disastrous impact of official state attitudes to morality on developing an effective response to this crisis in public health in Britain, and describes, for example, how, in the 1985 'Operation Tiger' customs raid on London's Gay's The Word bookshop, a medical book on AIDS was seized alongside *Straight To Hell* anthologies. Watney then argues quite clearly that: 'What matters in such instances is that we defend the latter as vigorously as the former, and do not collude with a censorship system which evidently regards all references to homosexuality as such to be intrinsically indecent and/or obscene' (p. 13).

In the following year, in which all charges against Gay's The Word were dropped, Watney records how this system of censorship still led to the absurd situation whereby the chief medical officer of the Department of Health in Britain had to have copies of the gay papers *The Advocate* and *The New York Native* 'quite literally smuggled into England in diplomatic bags, in order to avoid seizure by British customs officials' (ibid.). Both papers were at that time essential sources of up-to-date information on the AIDS crisis needed in drawing up the British government's public information campaign on AIDS. Ironically, in 1986, that campaign led to the sudden eruption into the public media of a frank and somewhat less judgemental discourse about sexual practice – something that Boyd McDonald had, in a sense, pioneered.

Notes

1   Since around 1990, many gay activists and theorists have re-appropriated the term 'queer' to describe themselves. 'Gay', originally chosen as a positive term to counteract the negative insult 'queer', came to imply a unitary 'gay subject', privileging sexual object-choice as the basis of sexual identity, and a 'gay community' based on an 'ethnic framing of same-sex desire'. But Seidman, for example, argues that: 'Queers are not united by any unitary identity but only their opposition to disciplining, normalizing social forces' (1993, p. 133).

2   From 1980 onwards, *STH* was also edited by Victor Weaver and others, although McDonald continued to write editorial pieces, and be involved in the production of the anthologies until his death.

3   Vast quantities of commercial gay pornography are produced, especially recorded monologues on phone lines, which purport to be 'true-life' experiences. Darnton (1994) points out how the fiction of autobiography is one of the basic forms pornography has taken historically.

4   'Stonewall' refers to the riots that sparked off the Gay Liberation Movement, following the police raid on the Stonewall Tavern, a drag bar in Christopher Street, Greenwich Village, New York on 27 June 1969.

5   The pun may extend into the name McDonald gave to their original format – *Chap-books* – a term which the *Shorter Oxford English Dictionary*

dates to 1824: 'small pamphlets of popular tales, ballads and tracts, as hawked by chapmen'. This aptly sums up the combination in STH of 'popular tales' with 'tracts' – the editorial articles Boyd wrote. 'Chap' itself derives from old English *ceap*, barter or dealing, which is also the root of *cheap*.

6   Gay slang for 'fastidious dresser'.

7   'Trade' traditionally signified a man with whom one has casual sexual contact which does not compromise his masculine identity. The sexual transaction is asymmetrical. A piece of trade is not expected to reciprocate physically. Nor does it imply payment. One of McDonald's interviewees implies the boundary: 'Colombian was mutual sex – others trade only' (1982, p. 168).

8   'Rimming' = anilingus. McDonald's rejection of euphemism gives rise to a stylistic dilemma. Academic terms for describing sexual acts look foolish against the frankness of the texts discussed. His mockery of Dennis Altman's use of the term 'anus' as opposed to 'asshole' (1985, p. 29) points up the way in which lexical choices invoke discourses, in this case, the discourse of the dominant ideology.

9   If one substitutes 'women' for 'straight males', and makes the other lexical changes entailed, the language of this attack reads like the discourse of sexism. 'Revenge' thus purports to be achieved through turning sexist discourse back on its originators.

Primary sources

Original issues of *Straight to Hell*

Straight to Hell, 1980, No. 47.
Straight to Hell (undated), Nos 48 and 49.

Anthologies

McDonald, Boyd (ed.) 1981: *Meat. How Men Look Act Walk Talk Dress Undress Taste & Smell. True Homosexual Experiences from STH Volume 1*. San Francisco: Gay Sunshine Press.

McDonald, Boyd and Leyland, Winston (eds) 1982: *Sex. True Homosexual Experiences from STH Writers Volume 3*. San Francisco: Gay Sunshine Press.

McDonald, Boyd (ed.) 1985: *Wads. True Homosexual Experiences from STH Writers Volume 6*. San Francisco: Gay Sunshine Press.

McDonald, Boyd (ed.) 1986: *Cream. True Homosexual Experiences from STH Writers Volume 7*. San Francisco: Leyland Publications.

McDonald, The Reverend Boyd (ed.) 1987: *Filth. An STH Chap-book*. New York: The Gay Presses of New York.

McDonald, Boyd (ed.) 1992: *Lewd. True Homosexual Experiences. An STH Chap-book Volume 12*. Boston: Fidelity Publishing.

McDonald, Boyd (ed.) 1993: *Scum. True Homosexual Experiences.* An STH
    Chap-book Volume 13. Boston: Fidelity Publishing.
The Guide. Gay Travel, Entertainment, Politics, & Sex, November 1993 issue.
    Boston: Fidelity Publishing.

12

'The Most Important Event of My Life!' A Comparison of Male and Female Written Narratives

Ulrike Hanna Meinhof

Introduction

This chapter analyses and contrasts texts by male and female students and academics in response to a single question: 'Tell us the most important event of your life, and describe it on half a page'. Whereas all texts exhibited the same tripartite pattern of recurring discourse units, they differed in the extent to which the 'most important event' chosen by the informants was narrated, hidden or displaced in the writing. Detailed linguistic analysis of the wording of the texts, and the frequently contradictory relationship between the language of each of the three discourse units within them, reveals a marked gender difference amongst the academics, though not amongst the student informants.

It is important to begin by stating that the study presented here does not attempt to categorize male as opposed to female verbal behaviour in any essentialist form. This is not only because the sample of data was much too small for quantitative conclusions, but also because the difference between the discourses of male students and male academics cut across gender divisions. Instead, the texts are to be seen as highly suggestive instances of the kinds of discursive practices which different groups of men and women engage in when writing about themselves, and as an exploration in the analysis of written narratives about the self in more general terms.

Theoretical Framework and Data Sample

Since the publication, translation and international reception of Sigmund Freud's work, especially his *Introductory Lectures on Psycho-Analysis* (1922 [1916–17]) and the earlier *Psychopathology of Everyday Life* (*Zur Psychopathologie des Alltagslebens*, 1901), it has been acknowledged that the language we use to narrate ourselves is itself worthy of analysis. How we describe our experiences, our dreams, our anxieties and pleasures, can be analysed and interpreted not only for what the language expresses in its wording, but also for what it hides, and thereby reveals. Psychoanalytic approaches in the Freudian tradition are thus concerned with re-interpreting discourse, focusing, for example, on slips of the tongue, repressions or mispronunciations of names, and displacements in dream narratives in order to allow hidden meanings to emerge.[1] In contrast, the more specific text-linguistic studies of psychoanalytic or therapeutic discourse such as, most notably, the work by Labov and Fanshel (1977) in the US, and Wodak in Austria (1980), are concerned with the systematic patterning of the surface structures of the text.

The research underpinning the analysis of my text corpus in this chapter owes much to both of these traditions. It draws on Labov and Fanshel's work in its emphasis on the discursive patterns and text-linguistic features that can be found in the narratives.[2] But at the same time, the relationship within, and between, the discourse units, and clashes between other structural properties of the texts, are taken as indicative of possible underlying tensions in the writers' life experiences. The text corpus itself consists of short autobiographical written narratives, collected anonymously from a group of male and female British university teachers and students. All narratives were elicited by a single written question: 'Tell us the most important event of your life and describe it on half a page'. In addition, informants were asked to indicate their age, sex and status (academic/student/other).

The study was originally set up to complement an earlier project by the German sociolinguist Hartig and his team at the University of Paderborn (Hartig, 1984). Hartig's research showed that informants' selection of a single event, and the required condensation of the narrative onto less than a page, had created a recursive discourse pattern in most responses. This pattern was marked by three distinct units, which were defined as follows:

Unit 1: Selection of event, and relativization of selection.
Unit 2: Description of event and complication.
Unit 3: Evaluation: ascribing of meaning.

All but a few texts could be analysed in terms of these three blocks. Tensions and contradictions appeared in the discourse within and between the units, and were, in Hartig's case, most often interpreted as signals for unresolved parent–child and partner conflicts. Most importantly, he found in many instances a striking discrepancy between the explicit description of the external features of a situation, and the more implicit and disguised references to important conflict-ual moments in the chosen event. Hartig did not control, however, for professional status or educational background, only for age and gender.

My follow-up study was motivated by three observations or questions:

First, the assumption behind eliciting such data is that control over one's biography implies control over its linguistic representation and reconstruction. Thus, the ability – or inability – to narrate oneself is taken as an indication for the control over one's biography, or lack of it. Tensions and fissures in the discourse patterns and in the language of these narratives are taken as possible signals for unresolved conflicts in the informants' lives. In my work, I was trying to establish whether the same tensions would still be evident if the narratives were written by academics. Academics, by training and profession, must be in possession of an elaborate meta-language. Professionally, they are used to creating a critical distance between themselves and their writing. In answering such a highly personal question, albeit anonymously, would they not edit out of their writing any of those clues which the discourse analyst could later use for establishing the contradictions and tensions? To supplement – and possibly contrast – the narratives of academics, I also sent out questionnaires to students.

The second interest in eliciting these texts was the one most rele-vant for the context of this book. Given that two decades of research into language and gender have suggested that there are considerable differences in the behaviour of women and men with reference to spoken discourse (see, for example, Coates, 1986; and, for an overview, Johnson, chapter 1), would there also be a gender-related difference in my written autobiographical narratives? Although Hartig had asked for gender to be declared on his forms, there was no discussion in his evaluation of the German data of whether gender had any role to play in the type of answers that were produced. My research, by balancing the number of questionnaires sent out accord-ing to gender and profession, was to provide the opportunity to observe potential similarities or differences in the responses, accord-ing to the gender of the informants.

The third question related to the different linguistic and cultural background of my sample group. My informants came from British institutions and wrote in English, whereas Hartig's were from the Federal Republic of Germany and had written in German. Would there be sufficient differences in the use of language so as to necessitate an alternative model of analysis, or would similarities in the organization of the narratives suggest more generalizable discursive principles beyond the language-specific structures?

The responses to my questionnaires by academics and students proved highly suggestive in all three respects, though no claims of a quantitative nature can, or will, be made. For one, the sample was too small, and no attempt was made to render it numerically more representative. Of 160 questionnaires sent out (forty to each group), fifty-four were returned overall, slightly more from the female informants in each group (sixteen academics/fourteen students) than the male (eleven academics/thirteen students). More importantly perhaps, my main interest was in an in-depth analysis of each narrative, and not in any statistical survey. In this respect, it owes more to the qualitative methods familiar from conversation and ethnographically based discourse analysis. But since the question asked was of such a highly personal nature, no further ethnographic work could be conducted with the writers, who remained anonymous. Any generalizations of the kind I will suggest in my analysis will, therefore, have to be treated with the utmost caution, and can only be taken as a starting point for further work in this direction; as contributing to the debate about male and female, and other social group-related narratives rather than any hard and fast conclusion. To this extent, it corresponds to the exploratory intention behind all the contributions to this volume.

With these qualifications in mind, and supported by a detailed discourse analysis of all the texts, examples of which will be given below, I will now suggest the following preliminary generalizations:

First, interculturally, between German and British informants there was no difference as far as the success of the analytical methods was concerned. In all but two cases, the three discourse units emerged clearly, though there was a great deal of variation in the amount of text in each unit. The two cases (one male, one female student) where the texts did not exhibit these features were both broken off in mid-sentence: both described traumatic events.

Second, all the texts returned from academics were well written, often poetic in style, and impressive in their narrative technique. Some, as can be seen from the examples below, were also very moving. Those from the students were more comparable to Hartig's examples in that their style was much more straightforward. My assumption that academics would exhibit a great deal of control over their writing thus turned out to be justified. In spite of this, however, texts by students and academics alike signalled tensions and paradoxes through the language used, and through the differences within, and between, the discourse units. The detailed analyses below will show the method of analysis used, and highlight the kinds of features which were taken to be an indicator of such tensions. Intriguingly, then, the recourse to an elaborated meta-language in the case of the academics, and the often self-conscious, self-reflexive style of narrating, did not in most cases suppress the revelation of unresolved tensions in the discourse (for one exception, see the text: 'Telling Lies').

Third, the differences between the social groupings proved fascinating. The professional categories of academics and students contrasted as follows: within the students' narratives gender difference did not lead to variation in either the choice of event or the way in which it was narrated. Male and female students wrote similar kinds of texts. But amongst the academic responses, gender proved to be a marked dividing line. As will become clear, the writing of academic women differed markedly from that of academic men, though both as a group differed from the students.

The Texts

Below are transcripts of a selection of texts from the corpus, four by women and five by men, followed by an account of the discourse analytical methods that were used in their evaluation. Since the difference in gender was marked only in the writing of the academics, and not the students, only one typical student text from the sample will be included. This will allow me to concentrate on the narratives from academic men and women, where gender did play a part. To facilitate the discussion, I will reproduce the texts first as direct transcripts, and then again with emphasis on those features which were the main focus of the analysis. In a few instances I have made minor changes, such as using different place names, in order to preserve the anonymity of the writers. As far as possible, however, I have preserved the layout of the texts as they were written down.

Lincoln Football Club

(Male student, 22 years)

The afternoon that Lincoln City got promoted back to the football league from the GM Vauxhall Conference at the first attempt. With my father being heavily involved with fund raising at the club and a particularly dedicated supporter, family honour was at stake. Especially since the end of the 86/87 season relegation coincided with the death of his father creating a real bad atmosphere for months. Thus, promotion was seen as a goal to which he should aim for to work his grief out of his system. The atmosphere at the match was extremely tense as the whole of Lincoln was there desperate for a good Saturday afternoon's entertainment. Once the first goal had been scored everyone relaxed at [*sic*: and] the atmosphere was fantastic. The pitch invasion at and the end was definitely not to be missed even if I did lose my voice. I could then go off and take my finals in peace in Manchester.

The Moment of my Conception

(Female academic, 45 years, 6 months)

The most important event in my life must have occurred, I suppose, at the moment of my conception. That mysterious process, whatever it is, that sometimes ordains the splitting of an ovum duly occurred, and determined that I should come into the world eight, not nine, months later and not singly, but preceded by my twin. "What is it like, being a twin?" I am still asked, and I still feebly reply "How can I say, having known nothing else?" My sister, my twin, – in my infancy we were so much part of each other that I can remember not really knowing where I ended and she began – is now both my mirror – same size, same shape, same voice, same tastes and caste of mind, same set of abilities and competencies – and totally other. The person that she is and the person that I am, now both complete and freestanding, have both been shaped and fashioned out of the long struggle to be ourselves, not that composite figure and composite personality that answered to the appellation "twin". So the most important event of my life has to be the accident of nature that has given me an extra dimension – my "other half".

The Birth of my Daughter

(Female academic, 39 years)

I had been intensely ambivalent about the prospect of becoming a mother, indeed very inclined not to do so. I feared a loss of identity and my hard-earned professional status; was dismal about the prospect of an endless round of domesticity and confinement. I loathed the doctor and nurses at the pre-natal clinics when they called me "Mum" and implied that it was time to "grow up" and abandon my penis-envying intellectual ambitions. I'd thought so hard about the disadvantages I couldn't conceive of the pleasures: my self was at stake. The conflicts were more than anything I'd suffered during a tortured, anorexic adolescence. So when A. was born I was unprepared for the joy, not of childbirth which hurt, but of her. She was like a plump fruit. She smelled good and was intelligent, and endlessly lovely. She looked at me, and was other. I was still me, but enriched by a passion and terror I could scarcely cope with. Every morning was full of the exhilaration I'd felt as a child on X-mas day, full of anticipation and a warmth which was physical and could be felt from toes upwards. It got better and better, and my second child was just as good. Both daughters were always and continue to be, my greatest joys and greatest vulnerabilities in life.

The Birth of my Son

(Female academic, 44 years)

The most important event of my life was the birth of my son. It was and has remained, the only experience in my life which was unmarred by any taint of disappointment or compromise. Far from the usual mismatch between expectation and reality, the fulfilment I experienced was beyond my most ardent imaginings. Looking back, I am amazed at the strength of my compulsion throughout my teenage years to have a son. It clouded my judgement. I married one of my lecturers. My perception of him as lovable – distorted, alas, by my subconscious drive to find a husband able to provide the financial support I needed to devote myself full-time to having and raising my son – was remorselessly eroded by his unloveable reality, and I came to despise him. But despite the prolonged pain of an unhappy marriage, the birth of the son of that marriage remains the supreme experience of my life.

My Father's Suicide

(Female professional, 39 years)

My father's suicide.

the shock – that I had lived for 23 and a half years with this waiting to happen to me and not known

the horror – that the man I loved the most, who'd given me life, could take it away from himself

the freedom, that the man who had dominated my life was no longer there

Leaving me able to discover myself professionally, and to relate to men, trying not to compare them with him.

Having Children

(Male academic, 44 years)

1) HAVING CHILDREN
2) FOR MY WIFE AND I, BOTH WITH CAREERS, THE DECISION TO HAVE (OR NOT TO HAVE) CHILDREN WAS ONE OF THE MOST DIFFICULT WE EVER FACED. IN PROSPECT, ONE CAN SEE ALL THE DISADVANTAGES AND ONLY A HANDFUL OF BENEFITS. IN RETROSPECT IT ANCHORS ONE'S WHOLE LIFE. ABOVE ALL IT IS, AS SO OFTEN STATED, ONE'S PLACE IN ETERNITY. BUT NO WORDS OF WHICH I AM CAPABLE CAN EXPRESS THE EMOTIONS UNLEASHED BY THE MOMENT OF BIRTH, EVEN IF THE MALE'S PERSONAL PHYSICAL CONTRIBUTION WAS SO LIMITED.

The Anti-Climax

(Male academic, 60 years)

Most important? That would mean birth or death, both difficult to describe on half a page. But plain 'important': I can think of several and to my surprise find myself thinking of internal rather than external dramas. What follows is not different in kind from certain others, only earlier – and, being earlier, perhaps of greater importance.

A town boy, aged perhaps four, I am in a wood. The sun is shining and it's a warm day: the wood is dark and cool by contrast, excitingly so. It fills me with a sense of drama, not as of danger but as of something interesting to come. I wander on, directionless and temporarily separate from friends and family. Something in the distance beckons secretly: light, a shining something, and I respond to it as to a promise of happiness. My heart beats: I run towards the brightness, the need to get there becoming more urgent as I run. I get closer and closer, I arrive. It is a road cut through the wood, ordinary, newish, metalled, straight; nothing paradisiacal about it. And soon my companions reach it too. An anti-climax but I don't mind it too much because the sense of the marvellous outlasts the mean fact, and lingers still.

Change of Orientation

(Male academic, 44 years)

The problem is obviously: important to what? I could easily decide to outline my relationship with my family or aspects of my school life. Accidents of my birth (English, liberal/left middle-class parents etc.) might logically take precedence. I will however pick as an important event in my life a visit to Algeria to take part in a relief project after the Algerian War when I was about 18 or 19. A number of features of my 5 months there led to a major depression and a break-up with my first love. These experiences fundamentally changed my orientation to life. I came to depend much less on intuition and beliefs and to accept the importance of more formal knowledge. This led to my decision to do 'A' levels and go to University etc.

Telling Lies

(Male academic, 31 years)

> The most important event in my life can make no immodest claim to being unique, but does make the immodest claim to being the most important event in anybody's life: the repeated telling of that life in a story. Mother-supervised discovery, in a derelict air shelter cool and rank in its suburban garden, of a toad in my pre-loathing childhood, first exposures to atheism, music, sex, injustice and anxiety only ever could proclaim priority or idiosyncrasy in the tellings they already called for and must have had before this time. Importance slips into what can't be told about those tellings, and makes the event escape again in ways that make irrelevant the indubitable fact that I've spent most of my life telling lies.

The Analysis

What is very striking about all of the texts, especially those by the academics, is how well written they are. Clearly, the experience of organizing one's ideas in written form had enabled all the academics to produce well-patterned mini-stories, whereas many of the students' texts (not reproduced here) lacked this cohesion. Indeed, two of the most disturbing student texts – one about the divorce of his parents, and one about her leaving home for the first time – finished abruptly, and contained several syntactic errors. To this extent, the student texts were much more like those produced by Hartig's sample. None of the academic texts, however, showed any such disturbance: they were all clearly structured and written with obvious care.

The requisite condensation of the narratives onto less than a page produced highly concentrated texts. All of them, as can be seen below, were clearly divisible into the three discourse units that marked the German texts collected by Hartig. I will now reproduce each of the nine texts in turn, highlighting the three discourse units and any striking linguistic features, before proceeding with the analysis of each individual text.

Lincoln Football Club

(Male student, 22 years)

Selection/Relativization

> The afternoon that Lincoln City got promoted back to the football league from the GM Vauxhall Conference at the first attempt. *With my father* being heavily involved with fund raising at the club and a particularly dedicated supporter, *family honour was at stake.* Especially since the end of the 86/87 season relegation coincided with the *death of his father* creating a *real bad atmosphere* for months. Thus, promotion was seen as a *goal* to which he should aim for to work *his grief out of his system.*

Description/Complication

> The *atmosphere* at the match was *extremely tense* as the whole of Lincoln was there *desperate for a good Saturday afternoon's entertainment.* Once the *first goal* had been scored *everyone relaxed* at [sic: and] *the atmosphere was fantastic.* The pitch invasion at the end was definitely not to be missed even if I did lose my voice.

Evaluation

> *I could then go off and take my finals in peace in Manchester.*

This text by a male student is better written than most of the other student texts, but it is typical in that the majority include some kind of reference to leaving home and going to university. A particularly noticeable feature of most of the student texts is the relationship between what is selected as the most important event (see Unit 1), and what is actually described (see Unit 2). Selected events in Units 1 typically read: 'The day I was selected for X-University', 'The day I came down to X-University with my parents' etc. Units 2 then comprise descriptions of uncertainty about impending disorder, express fear of being left on one's own for the first time, or the opposite: exhilaration regarding a kind of new-found independence. The choice of the day is a barely disguised metaphor for this rite of passage. The above text is particularly striking in its displacement between the choice of an essentially trivial event – a football match – and the huge significance of breaking free from a depressing home environment.

The choice of the event, the success of a football team, is only referred to in the first line, and later on, in the descriptive part, the invasion of the pitch and the loss of his voice. Everything else in the text is re-signified around the father and the family honour:

> With *my father* being heavily involved with fund raising at the club and a particularly dedicated supporter, *family honour was at stake.*

The father's involvement with the football team is itself described as displacement, in that the father's grief about the death of his own father is set in parallel to the football team's losing its place in the football league. The parallels between those areas of signification, football and family, appear as linguistic juxtapositions of key words and phrases: 'atmosphere' – *real bad atmosphere* in the house v. *extremely tense atmosphere at the match* v. *fantastic atmosphere* after the first goal; 'goal' – the (father's) *goal* to work his grief out of his system v. the first *goal* scored by Lincoln; the father's *grief and tension* v. the whole of Lincoln, which is said to be *desperate for entertainment* until *everyone relaxed.*

These are very striking oppositions and parallels between two sets of events which the writer sees as deeply connected. But the real significance of the event for the student's own life is not revealed until the final and important climax in Unit 3, which is not referred to anywhere else in the text: the young man leaving home, being able to go his own way – in this case being able to take his finals at the University of X. Unit 3 suddenly and surprisingly reveals what a more self-conscious writer might have prioritized in the text to start with. The chosen event (football) and the displaced event (breaking free from home) are both present in the text, but not consciously brought together by the writer. Only by means of an innocuous event – a football match – can the father's pressure on the family, and the son's relief to escape this and live his own life, be brought together in the same narrative. This lack of self-consciousness differentiates all the students' texts, male or female, from those of the academics. The latter, as the analysis below will show, use different, and gendered, strategies in their writing.

The Women's Texts

The Moment of my Conception

(Female academic, 45 years, 6 months)

Selection/Relativization

> The most important event in my life *must have* occurred, *I suppose*, at the moment of my conception. That *mysterious process, whatever it is*, that sometimes *ordains* the splitting of an ovum duly *occurred*, and *determined* that I should come into the world eight, not nine, months later and not singly, but preceded by my twin.

Description/Complication

> "What is it like, being a twin?" I am still asked, and I still *feebly* reply "How can I say, having known nothing else?" My sister, my twin, – in my infancy we were so much *part of each other* that I can remember *not really knowing where I ended and she began* – is now both *my mirror* – same size, same shape, same voice, same tastes and caste of mind, same set of abilities and competencies – *and totally other*. The person that *she is* and the person that *I am, now both complete and freestanding*, have both been *shaped and fashioned* out of the long *struggle to be ourselves*, not that *composite figure and composite personality* that answered to the appellation "twin".

Evaluation

> So the most important event of my life *has to be the accident of nature* that has given me an extra dimension – my *"other half"*.

The text above is written in an elaborated literary style. It is strongly self-reflexive and evaluative. It shows control even to the point of including literary conventions such as the embedded question–answer sequence with an imaginary interlocutor:

> "What is it like, being a twin?"
> I [. . .] *feebly* reply

The selection of the event in Unit 1 immediately raises a paradox. As the most important event of her life, she quotes the moment of fertilization in *her mother's* body, that is, a moment prior to her own life. It is a moment of *mystery*, outside the woman's control. This recourse to the mysterious is repeated in Unit 3, which again stresses the accidental, *the accident of nature*. In both units, it is the determination of the self by some force other than the self which is centralized. This uncertainty about the self is emphasized by linguistic forms such as *I suppose, whatever it is, has to be*, modifying expressions of insecurity and doubt.

Against the determination of the self from the outside stands the struggle for her own separate self in Unit 2. Here the text is marked by a series of oppositions:

> *where I ended* [. . .] *she began* [. . .] *my mirror – same size, same shape, same voice, same tastes and caste of mind, same set of abilities and competencies* [. . .] *totally other* [. . .] *The person that she is* [. . .] *the person that I am* [. . .]

Unit 2 ends with an assertion of selfhood and independence – *complete and freestanding* – yet the moment of assertion is described in a passive clause: *have both been shaped and fashioned out of the* [. . .] *struggle to be ourselves.*

There is thus a tension inside Unit 2 between the form and the content of the language, a tension that finds expression in the recourse to outside determination in Units 1 and 3. The finding of the self in Unit 2 is again undermined by the return to the accidental in Unit 3, and the renewed emphasis on not being her own self after all. It is revealing that the text ends with reference to *my other half.*

What makes this text typical for the way academic women tackle the question posed is the ease with which a central point in her biography is selected, described and foregrounded, without removing any of its ambiguity. This ability to express and resolve in the narrative what is described as a central dilemma, differentiates the women's texts from those of their male counterparts. Nowhere is this more obvious than in the texts where academic women wrote about childbirth.

The Birth of my Daughter

(Female academic, 39 years)

Selection/Relativization

> I had been *intensely ambivalent* about the prospect of becoming a mother, indeed *very inclined not to do so*. I feared a *loss of identity* and my *hard-earned professional status*; was *dismal* about the prospect of an endless round of domesticity and confinement. I *loathed* the doctor and nurses at the pre-natal clinics when they called me "Mum" and implied that it was time to "grow up" and abandon my penis-envying intellectual ambitions. I'd thought so hard about the *disadvantages* I couldn't conceive of the pleasures: *my self* was at stake. The *conflicts* were more than anything *I'd suffered* during a tortured, anorexic adolescence.

Description/Complication

> So when A. was born I was *unprepared for the joy*, not of childbirth which hurt, but of her. She was like a *plump fruit*. She smelled good and was intelligent, and endlessly lovely. She looked at me, *and was other*. I was *still me*, but *enriched* by a passion and terror I could scarcely cope with. Every morning was full of the exhilaration I'd felt as a child on X-mas day, full of anticipation and a warmth which was physical and could be felt from toes upwards. It got better and better, and my second child was just as good.

Evaluation

> Both daughters were, always and continue to be, *my greatest joys* and *greatest vulnerabilities* in life.

This text is equally controlled, and stylistically as impressive as the preceding one. There is very clear selection of an event – becoming a mother – with all the concomitant conflicts and tensions openly acknowledged. Unit 1 shows the woman's fear of becoming a mother, which she describes as a fear of losing her identity and independence, achieved in a world of intellectual competitiveness. Against this perceived threat, Unit 2 describes her exuberance at having a child. This is all done in terms of physical release; the language is one of emotions and passion, of physical pleasure. The resolution in Unit 3 signals total acceptance of the inherent and undeniable conflict in her life. The children are both her *greatest joy* and her *greatest vulnerability*.

The following narrative also speaks of childbirth, as did several others by academic women, and one by an academic man. But this text takes a very different perspective:

The Birth of my Son

(Female academic, 44 years)

Selection/Relativization

> The most important event of my life was the birth of my son. It was and has remained, the *only experience* in my life which was *unmarred by any taint of disappointment or compromise*.

Description/Complication

> Far from the *usual mismatch between expectation and reality*, the *fulfilment I experienced* was beyond my most ardent imaginings. Looking back, I am amazed at the *strength of my compulsion* throughout my teenage years to

have a son. It *clouded my judgement*. I married one of my lecturers. My perception of him as lovable – *distorted*, alas, by *my subconscious drive* to find a husband able to provide the financial support I needed to devote myself full-time to having and raising my son – *was remorselessly eroded* by his *unloveable reality*, and *I came to despise him.*

Evaluation

But despite the *prolonged pain of an unhappy marriage*, the birth *of the son of that marriage* remains the *supreme experience* of my life.

Again, what is impressive is the boldness in the narration – here in the acknowledgement that the woman's life contains a great deal of pain, disappointment and compromise, and an acceptance of her own lack of judgement. The language is openly bitter, not only about her husband and his *unloveable reality*, but also about herself, and her motives for marrying. This bitterness is offset by what is perceived as, paradoxically, her only worthwhile experience, that of having her son. The resolution in Unit 3 openly accepts this contradiction in her life.

The last female text I want to select from the corpus is even more traumatic than the previous one, but again shares all the features of the others. Like the preceding texts it uses poetic devices, here a form of syntactic parallelism, in order to foreground the essential paradox between the love for a father and the dependency this entails, the rage against the betrayal by the father's suicide, and the freedom which the suicide nonetheless implies.

My Father's Suicide

(Female professional, 39 years)

Selection/Relativization

My father's suicide.
Description/Complication

the shock – that I had lived for 23 and a half years with this waiting to happen to me and not known
the horror – that the man I loved the most, who'd given me life, could take it away from himself
the freedom, that the man who had dominated my life was no longer there

Evaluation

Leaving me able to discover myself professionally, and to relate to men, trying not to compare them with him.

If the underlying assumption of the research is correct, that the ability to focus on, and narrate oneself indicates a coming to terms with and a control over one's life, then these women's narratives make very optimistic reading. This is true even – or perhaps especially – where the events themselves are upsetting or traumatic. The readiness with which tensions, ambiguities and traumas are acknowledged, and the way in which the women come to terms with them, is echoed linguistically in the clarity of the language, the openness of the 'I'-narrations, and in the balanced patterning of the three discourse units of selection, description and evaluation.

The Men's Texts

Having Children

(Male academic, 44 years)

Selection/Relativization

    1) HAVING CHILDREN

Description/Complication

    2) FOR *MY WIFE AND I*, BOTH WITH CAREERS, THE DECISION TO HAVE (OR NOT TO HAVE) CHILDREN WAS ONE OF THE MOST DIFFICULT *WE* EVER FACED.

Evaluation

    IN PROSPECT, *ONE* CAN SEE ALL THE DISADVANTAGES AND ONLY A HANDFUL OF BENEFITS. IN RETROSPECT *IT* ANCHORS *ONE'S* WHOLE LIFE. ABOVE ALL IT IS, *AS SO OFTEN STATED, ONE'S* PLACE IN ETERNITY. BUT NO WORDS OF WHICH *I* AM CAPABLE CAN EXPRESS THE EMOTIONS UNLEASHED BY THE MOMENT OF BIRTH, EVEN IF *THE MALE'S* PERSONAL PHYSICAL CONTRIBUTION WAS SO LIMITED.

This text is the only piece written by a man that mentions children, whereas this was the case with more than half of the academic women's texts. It provides an interesting parallel to the text 'The Birth of my Daughter' in acknowledging the difficult decision which women and men face if they want to have careers and raise a family in equal partnership. The man writing this piece is clearly aware of his responsibility, as the choice of pronouns in Unit 2 shows.

Both Units 1 and 2 are brief in comparison with Unit 3, the evalua-tion of the event in question for the man's life. Here, an intriguing shift takes place in the use of pronouns. Unit 2 is written in terms of 'we' and 'us', but Unit 3 begins with an impersonal pronoun, *one can see, one's life, one's place in eternity*, almost as if the perspective on the man's life is already that of the future looking back. This impersonal validation is further strengthened by making the observation part of a general truth – *as so often stated* – and by making the experience part of a general male one: *the male's contribution*. Inserted into this recourse to generalizable, impersonal truths, however, is one moment where the writer asserts his own self. The brief switch to an 'I' posi-tion is used to express the impossibility of finding words to express the emotions felt at the moment of birth.

This tension in pronoun use in such a brief text – the subjective 'I', the collective personal 'we', the impersonal 'one' – the generalized truth of the passive construction, and the reference to 'the male', seem to suggest some unease in the way the self is perceived, even though the selection of the event is expressing pleasure at having made the right choice in his life. But in contrast to the women's texts, this ambivalence about the role of the self is embedded in the gram-mar, rather than foregrounded in the theme itself.

The Anti-Climax

(Male academic, 60 years)

Selection/Relativization

> *Most important?* That would mean birth or death, both difficult to describe on half a page. But *plain 'important'*: I can think of several and to my sur-prise find myself thinking of *internal* rather than *external* dramas. What fol-lows is not different in kind from certain others, only earlier – and, being earlier, perhaps of greater importance.

Description/Complication

> A *town boy*, aged perhaps four, I am *in a wood*. The *sun is shining* and it's a *warm* day: the *wood* is *dark and cool by contrast*, excitingly so. It fills me with a sense of drama, not as of *danger* but as of something *interesting* to come. I wander on, directionless and temporarily separate from friends and family. Something in the distance *beckons secretly*: light, a shining something, and I respond to it as to a *promise of happiness*. *My heart beats*: I run towards the brightness, the need to get there becoming *more urgent* as I run. *I get closer and closer, I arrive.* It is a *road* cut through the wood, *ordinary, newish, met-alled, straight*; nothing paradisiacal about it. And soon my companions reach it too.

Evaluation

> *An anti-climax* but I don't mind it too much because the *sense of the marvel-*
> *lous* outlasts the mean fact, and lingers still.

This text is highly poetic, and stylistically one of the most impressive from my corpus. It begins, in Unit 1, with a relativization of the question itself: *most important* v. *plain important*. Such qualifications of the question before answering it are typical for several of the academic men's texts (see also 'Change of Orientation' below). The writer then expresses his surprise at wanting to choose an internal rather than an external event, and one taken from his youth.

Unit 2, the descriptive part, sets up a series of highly charged oppositions, between the town boy in the open warm sunshine as against the dark, cool, exciting, sensuous woods. The description becomes tenser and more erotic as the boy goes on exploring the woods – *something* [. . .] *beckons secretly* – a mysterious offer seems to loom. The text achieves an almost orgiastic rhythm: *My heart beats* [. . .] *I get closer and closer* [. . .] *I arrive.* But at the moment of climax comes the total anti-climax: nothing is there but a straight road, no secrets, no mystery, no fulfilment. End of story.

Unit 3 then brings a surprising turn-around: the narrator settles for the memory, the feeling of anticipation, rather than allowing himself to be upset by the absence of any fulfilment.

The text suggests a deeper disappointment; the man was 60 years old at the time of writing, and it could be the story of someone who did not find the fulfilment in life which he had hoped for. Whatever the events were that caused such melancholy resignation is not mentioned. The moment described in the text may be an allegory for such events, with the aestheticized, poetic language acting as a shield to hide the source of the sadness in the man's life.

Change of Orientation

(Male academic, 44 years)

Selection/Relativization

> The problem is obviously: important to what? *I could easily decide* to outline
> my relationship with my family or aspects of my school life. *Accidents of my*
> *birth* (English, liberal/left middle-class parents etc.) *might logically take*
> *precedence.* I will however pick as an important event in my life a visit to
> *Algeria* to take part in a relief project after the Algerian War when I was
> about 18 or 19.

Description/Complication

> A *number of features* of my 5 months there *led to a major depression* and a break-up with my first love.

Evaluation

> These experiences fundamentally changed my *orientation to life*. I came to depend much less on *intuition and beliefs* and to accept the importance of *more formal knowledge*. This led to my decision to do 'A' levels and go to University *etc.*

This text, like the previous one, also begins by relativizing the question. Here, a long preamble preceding the choice of an event makes Unit 1 the longest of the three discourse units. However, in Unit 2, the descriptive part, it remains unclear what the actual event consisted of. Instead of a description of the event itself, we are told the result of this – unnamed – event: a major depression, and the break-up with his first love. The third unit explains the importance of these consequences in terms of a total redirection in the man's life in favour of one set of oppositions, which are aligned through the text with rationality:

- rationality v. irrationality
- logic v. intuition
- formal knowledge, A-levels, university v. depression
- liberal, left, middle-class parents v. first love

The text is torn between these two poles. The man here clearly states his preference for the rational and logical decisions, against the irrational, uncertain and accidental. But this decision in favour of rationality is made as a consequence of an unnamed event – an *irrational* moment – a major crisis, which is not formulated in the text.

Both the 'anti-climax' and the 'rationality' texts share, in spite of their differences in style and selection of event, something that is typical for the majority of the male academics' texts, and highly atypical for those of the women: the event that is perceived as major is not actually named at all. In the case of the older man, it is hidden behind an allegorical narrative; in the other, the event is suppressed behind its consequences. The last text from my corpus which I want to discuss is one that takes this avoidance of naming important moments in one's life to an extreme. It is a very witty, clever and entirely evasive narrative, which celebrates the fact that importance in one's life escapes any attempt at being put into words.

Telling Lies

(Male academic, 31 years)

Selection/Relativization

> The most important event in my life can make no immodest claim to being unique, but does make the immodest claim to being the most important event in anybody's life: the repeated telling of that life in a story.

Description/Complication

> Mother-supervised discovery, in a derelict air shelter cool and rank in its suburban garden, of a toad in my pre-loathing childhood, first exposures to atheism, music, sex, injustice and anxiety only ever could proclaim priority or idiosyncrasy in the tellings they already called for and must have had before this time.

Evaluation

> Importance slips into what can't be told about those tellings, and makes the event escape again in ways that make irrelevant the indubitable fact that I've spent most of my life telling lies.

This last text, the most self-conscious of all, epitomizes what could be seen as a tendency in all the other texts by male academics: that for whatever reason – unease, dislike, unwillingness, repression, conde-scension, playfulness etc. – most men found it easier to reject or bypass the question than use it to explore a genuine moment of their lives.

Conclusion

In most cases, the avoidance of an intensely personal question in the academic men's texts produced elegant and suggestive writing. Nevertheless, the majority of the narratives still contained enough traces of paradox in their language to suggest where hidden sources of conflicts may lie. Whether discourse analysis of the kind I have employed for these strictly anonymous texts could help to uncover genuine biographical repressions and tensions can only be surmised. Such a project would need to be extended by methods more familiar to psychoanalysis than linguistics. The main aim of this chapter has been to explore potentially different linguistic orientations of academic women and men towards the narration of self. The analysis would appear to imply that academic women's acceptance of the difficulties and ambivalences of their everyday existence is not just an unconscious compromise they may be forced to make, but a consciously experienced life-choice, which can be narrated and shared in all its ambiguity. My analysis of texts by male academics, on the other hand, suggests that this might not be an option that men are comfortable with. In this sense, my chapter can be seen to complement those contributions in this volume (e.g. Heywood, chapter 11; Pujolar, chapter 5; Talbot, chapter 10) which similarly highlight the difficulties experienced by modern men with the fragmentation of self, and its dissolution into multiple identities –.something which women have learned, or had to learn, to embrace with confidence.

Notes

1 Freud's account of how repressed names can be reconstituted in memory by association leads him to propose the following: 'What is possible in the case of forgotten names must be also possible in the interpretation of dreams: starting from the substitute we must be able to arrive at the real object of our search by means of a train of associations.' (Freud, 1922, p. 93) (German original: Freud, 1916–17, pp. 126–7; also quoted in Hartig, 1984).
2 For the analysis of linguistic patterning in other forms of narratives, see also Labov and Waletzky (1967); for conversational storytelling, see Jefferson (1979); Polanyi, (1985a, 1985b).

Bibliography

Adler, M. K. 1978: *Sex Differences in Human Speech: a Sociolinguistic Study.* Hamburg: Buske.

Aries, Elizabeth 1976: Interaction patterns and themes of male, female and mixed groups. *Small Group Behaviour* 7 (1), 7–18.

Aries, Elizabeth and Johnson, Fern 1983: Close friendship in adulthood: conversational conduct between same-sex friends. *Sex Roles* 9 (12), 183–96.

Austin, J. L. 1961: *How To Do Things With Words.* Oxford: Clarendon Press.

Bailey, L. A. and Timm, L. A. 1976: More on women's and men's expletives. *Anthropological Linguistics* 18, 438–49.

Bakhtin, Mikhail 1981: *The Dialogic Imagination*, ed. M. Holquist, trans. C. Emerson and M. Holquist. Austin: University of Texas Press.

Bakhtin, Mikhail 1986: *Speech Genres and Other Late Essays*, ed. M. Holquist, trans. C. Emerson and M. Holquist. Austin: University of Texas Press.

Bate, Barbara 1988: *Communication and the Sexes.* New York: Harper & Row.

Bateson, G. 1985: A theory of play and fantasy. In R. Innis (ed.), *Semiotics: an Introductory Reader.* London: Hutchinson, 131–44.

Bernstein, B. 1959: A public language: some sociological implications of a linguistic form. *British Journal of Sociology* 10, 311–26.

Bernstein, B. 1962: Social class and linguistic codes. *Language and Speech* 5, 21–40.

Biesele, M. 1976: Folklore and ritual of !Kung hunter–gatherers. Unpublished Ph.D. thesis, Cambridge, MA, Harvard University.

Bly, Robert 1990: *Iron John: a Book about Men.* Shaftsbury: Element Books.

Bourdieu, Pierre 1991: Did you say 'popular'? In P. Bourdieu, *Language and Symbolic Power.* London: Polity Press, 90–102.

Breen, Marcus 1991: A stairway to heaven or a highway to hell? Heavy metal rock music in the 1990s. *Cultural Studies* 5 (2), 191–204.

Brittan, Arthur 1989: *Masculinity and Power.* Oxford: Blackwell.

Brouwer, Dede, Gerritsen, Marinel and De Haan, Dorian 1979: Speech differences between men and women: on the wrong track? *Language in Society* 9, 111–36.

Brown, Gillian 1977: *Listening to Spoken English.* London: Longman.

Brown, P. 1980: How and why women are more polite. Some evidence from a Mayan community. In S. McConnell-Ginet, Ruth Borker and Nelly Furman (eds), *Women and Language in Literature and Society*. New York: Praeger, 111–36.

Brown, P. and Levinson, S. 1987: *Politeness. Some Universals in Language Use*. Studies in Interactional Sociolinguistics 4. Cambridge: Cambridge University Press.

Bublitz, Wolfram 1988: *Supportive Fellow-Speakers and Cooperative Conversations*. Amsterdam: John Benjamins.

Burgoon, M. and Stewart, D. 1975: Empirical investigations of language intensity: the effect of sex of source, receiver and language intensity on attitude change. *Human Communication Research* 1, 244–8.

Burgoon, M., Dillard, J. and Doran, N. 1983: Friendly or unfriendly persuasion. *Human Communication Research* 10 (2), 283–94.

Butler, Judith 1990: *Gender Trouble: Feminism and the Subversion of Identity*. New York: Routledge.

Cameron, Deborah 1990: *The Feminist Critique of Language*. London: Routledge.

Cameron, Deborah 1992a: *Feminism and Linguistic Theory*, 2nd edition. London: Macmillan.

Cameron, Deborah 1992b: Not gender difference but the difference gender makes – explanation in research on sex and language. *International Journal of the Sociology of Language* 94, 13–26.

Cameron, Deborah 1995a: *Verbal Hygiene*. London: Routledge.

Cameron, Deborah 1995b: Rethinking language and gender studies: some issues for the 1990s. In Sara Mills (ed.), *Language and Gender. Interdisciplinary Perspectives*. London: Longman, 31–44.

Cameron, Deborah, McAlinden, Fiona and O'Leary, Kathy 1989: Lakoff in context: the social and linguistic functions of tag questions. In Jennifer Coates and Deborah Cameron (eds), *Women in their Speech Communities*. Harlow: Longman, 74–93.

Candlin, C. E. 1987: Beyond description to explanation in cross-cultural discourse. In L. E. Smith (ed.), *Discourse across Cultures*. New York: Prentice Hall, 22–35.

Chafe, Wallace 1994: *Discourse, Consciousness and Time: The Flow and Displacement of Conscious Experience in Speaking and Writing*. Chicago: University of Chicago Press.

Chafe, Wallace 1995: Polyphonic topic development. Paper given at the Symposium on Conversation, University of New Mexico, Albuquerque, 12–14 July.

Chapman, Rowena and Rutherford, Jonathan (eds) 1988: *Male Order: Unwrapping Masculinity*. London: Lawrence & Wishart.

Cheshire, Jenny 1978: Present tense verbs in Reading English. In P. Trudgill (ed.), *Sociolinguistic Patterns in British English*. London: Edward Arnold, 52–68.

Cheshire, Jenny 1982a: *Variation in an English Dialect*. Cambridge: Cambridge University Press.

Cheshire, Jenny 1982b: Linguistic variation and social function. In S. Romaine (ed.), *Sociolinguistic Variation in Speech Communities*. London: Edward Arnold, 153–66.

Cheshire, Jenny 1984: Indigenous non-standard varieties and education. In P. Trudgill (ed.), *Applied Sociolinguistics*. London: Academic Press, 564–88.

Chomsky, Noam 1965: *Aspects of the Theory of Syntax*. Cambridge, MA: MIT Press.

Clark, Kate 1990: The linguistics of blame: representations of women in *The Sun*'s reporting of crimes of sexual violence. In Michael Toolan (ed.), *Language, Text and Context: Essays in Stylistics*. London: Routledge, 209–24.

Coates, Jennifer 1986: *Women, Men and Language*. London: Longman.

Coates, Jennifer 1987: Epistemic modality and spoken discourse. *Transactions of the Philological Society*, 110–31.

Coates, Jennifer 1989: Gossip revisited: language in all-female groups. In Jennifer Coates and Deborah Cameron (eds), *Women in their Speech Communities*. Harlow: Longman, 94–121.

Coates, Jennifer 1991: Women's cooperative talk: a new kind of conversational duet? In Claus Uhlig and Rudiger Zimmermann (eds), *Proceedings of the Anglistentag 1990 Marburg*, Tübingen: Max Niemeyer Verlag, 196–211.

Coates, Jennifer 1993: *Women, Men and Language*, 2nd edition. London: Longman.

Coates, Jennifer 1994: No gap, lots of overlap: turn-taking patterns in the talk of women friends. In David Graddol, Janet Maybin and Barry Stierer (eds), *Researching Language and Literacy in Social Context*. Cleveland: Multilingual Matters, 177–92.

Coates, Jennifer 1995a: Language, gender and career. In Sara Mills (ed.), *Language and Gender. Interdisciplinary Perspectives*. London: Longman, 13–30.

Coates, Jennifer 1995b: The construction of a collaborative floor in women's friendly talk. Paper given at the Symposium on Conversation, University of New Mexico, Albuquerque, 12–14 July.

Coates, Jennifer 1996: *Women Talk. Conversations between Women Friends*. Oxford: Blackwell.

Coates, Jennifer and Cameron, Deborah (eds) 1989: *Women in their Speech Communities*. Harlow: Longman.

Coates, Jennifer and Jordan, Mary Ellen, in press: Que(e)rying friendship: discourses of resistance and the construction of gendered subjectivity. In Anna Livia and Kira Hall (eds), *Queerly Phrased: Language, Gender and Sexuality*. Oxford: Oxford University Press.

Connell, R. W. 1987: *Gender and Power*. Stanford, CA: Stanford University Press.

Connell, R. W. 1995: *Masculinities*. Oxford: Polity Press.

Crosby, F. and Nyquist, L. 1977: The female register: an empirical study of Lakoff's hypotheses. *Language in Society* 6, 313–22.

Darnton, Robert, 1994: Sex for thought. In *New York Review of Books* XLI, Number 21, 65–74.

Davidson, L. R. and Duberman, L. 1982: Friendship: communication and interactional patterns in same-sex dyads. *Sex Roles* 8, 809–22.

Davies, Bronwyn 1989: The discursive production of the male/female dualism in school settings. *Oxford Review of Education* 15 (3), 229–41.

Dorval, Bruce (ed.) 1990: *Conversational Organization and its Development*. Norwood, NJ: Ablex.

Easthope, Antony 1986: *What a Man's Gotta Do. The Masculine Myth in Popular Culture*. Boston: Unwin Hyman.

Eckert, Penelope and McConnell-Ginet, Sally 1992: Think practically and look locally: language and gender as community based practice. *Annual Review of Anthropology* 21, 461–90.

Edelsky, Carole 1981: Who's got the floor? *Language in Society* 10 (3), 383–422.

Edley, Nigel and Wetherell, Margaret 1995: *Men in Perspective. Practice, Power and Identity*. London: Prentice Hall.

Edwards, Tim 1994: *Erotics and Politics. Gay Male Sexuality, Masculinity and Feminism*. London: Routledge.

Ehrlich, Susan and King, Ruth 1994: Feminist meanings and the (de)politicization of the lexicon. *Language and Society* 23, 59–76.

Epstein, Cynthia Fuchs 1988: *Deceptive Distinctions: Sex, Gender and the Social Order*. New Haven, CT: Yale University Press.

Evans-Pritchard, E. 1967: *The Zande Trickster*. Oxford: Clarendon Press.

Fairclough, N. 1989: *Language and Power*. London: Longman.

Fairclough, N. 1992a: *Discourse and Social Change*. Cambridge: Polity Press.

Fairclough, N. (ed.) 1992b: *Critical Language Awareness*. London: Longman.

Falk, Jane 1980: The conversational duet. *Proceedings of the 6th Annual Meeting of the Berkeley Linguistics Society* 6, 507–14.

Farley, Lin 1978: *Sexual Shakedown: the Sexual Harassment of Women on the Job*. New York: McGraw-Hill.

Feigen Fasteau, Marc 1975: *The Male Machine*. New York: Delta.

Fejes, F. 1992: Masculinity as fact: a review of empirical mass communication research on masculinity. In Steve Craig (ed.), *Men, Masculinity and the Media*. Newbury Park/London: Sage, 9–22.

Fishman, Pamela 1983: Interaction: the work women do. In B. Thorne, C. Kramarae and N. Henley (eds), *Language, Gender and Society*. Cambridge, MA: Newbury House, 89–101.

Flexner, S. B. and Wentworth, H. 1975: *Dictionary of American Slang*. New York: Crowell.

Foucault, Michel 1971: *L'ordre du Discours*. Paris: Gallimard.

Foucault, Michel 1972: *The Archaeology of Knowledge*. London: Tavistock.

Foucault, Michel 1980: *Power/Knowledge: Selected Interviews and Other Writings*. New York: Pantheon Books.

Foucault, Michel 1982: The subject and power. *Critical Inquiry* 8, 777–95.

Fowler, Roger 1991: *Language in the News*. London: Routledge.

Fowler, R., Hodge, B., Kress, G. and Trew, T. 1979: *Language and Control*. London: Routledge.

Frank, Karsta 1992: *Sprachgewalt: die sprachliche Reproduktion der Geschlechterhierarchie*. Tübingen: Max Niemeyer Verlag.

Fraser, N. 1989: *Unruly Practices: Power, Discourse and Gender in Contemporary Social Theory*. Cambridge: Polity Press.

Freud, S. 1901: *Zur Psychopathologie des Alltagslebens*. Frankfurt: Fischer.

Freud, S. 1916–17: Vorlesungen zur Einführung in die Psychoanalyse. In *Vorlesungen zur Einführung in die Psychoanalyse und Neue Folgen*, 1989, Volume 1. Frankfurt: Fischer.

Freud, S. 1922 [1916–17]: *Introductory Lectures on Psycho-Analysis*, trans. J. Riviere. London: George Allen & Unwin.

Fuente de la, I. 1993: Hombres. *El País* (Madrid edition), 28 February, 8–9.

Fuss, Diana 1989: *Essentially Speaking. Feminism, Nature and Difference*. London: Routledge.

Garnica, O. 1979: The boys have the muscles and the girls have the sexy legs. In O. Garnica and M. King (eds), *Language, Children and Society: the Effect of Social Factors on Children Learning to Communicate*. Ohio: Pergamon Press.

Gergen, M. C. (ed.) 1988: *Feminist Thought and the Structure of Knowledge*. New York: New York University Press.

Gill, Rosalind 1993: Justifying injustice: broadcasters' accounts of inequality in radio. In Erica Burman and Ian Parker (eds), *Discourse Analytic Research*. London: Routledge, 75 93.

Goffman, Erving 1967: *Interaction Ritual*. New York: Anchor Books.

Goffman, Erving 1974: *Frame Analysis. An Essay on the Organisation of Experience*. Harmondsworth: Penguin.

Goffman, Erving 1976: Replies and responses. *Language in Society* 5, 257–313.

Goffman, Erving 1977: The arrangement between the sexes. *Theory and Society* 4, 301–31.

Goffman, Erving 1979: *Gender Advertisements*. London: Macmillan.

Goffman, Erving 1981: *Forms of Talk*. Philadelphia: University of Pennsylvania Press.

Goodwin, M. H. 1980: Directive-response sequences in girls' and boys' task activities. In S. McConnell-Ginet, R. Borker and N. Furman (eds), *Women and Language in Literature and Society*. New York: Praeger, 157–73.

Goodwin, Marjorie 1990: *He-Said-She-Said. Talk as Social Organization among Black Children*. Bloomington and Indianapolis: Indiana University Press.

Gough, Val and Talbot, Mary M. 1993: Guilt over games boys play: coherence as a focus for examining the constitution of heterosexual subjectivity on a prob lem page. *Liverpool Papers in Language and Discourse* 1, 3–20.

Gouldner, Helen and Strong, Mary Symons 1987: *Speaking of Friendship*. New York: Greenwood Press.

Graddol, D. and Swann, J. 1989: *Gender Voices*. Oxford: Blackwell.

Grice, H. P. 1975: Logic and conversation. In P. Cole and J. Morgan (eds), *Syntax and Semantics*, Volume III, *Speech Acts*. New York: Academic Press, 41–58.

Griffin, Christine 1989: Review of Brod, Kimmel and Connell. *Feminist Review* 33, Autumn, 103–5.

Griffiths, Sian 1992: A knock at the men's room door. *The Higher*, 4 September, 36.

Gumperz, John 1982: *Discourse Strategies*. Cambridge: Cambridge University Press.

Gumperz, John and Hymes, Dell 1972: Preface. In John Gumperz and Dell Hymes (eds), *Sociolinguistics: the Ethnography of Communication*. New York: Holt, Rinehart & Winston.

Haas, Adelaide 1979: Male and female spoken language differences: stereotypes and evidence. *Psychological Bulletin* 86, 616–26.

Hartig, M. 1984: Sprache und Biographie. Die Bedeutung der sprachlichen Rekonstruktion der Biographie. In E. Oksar (ed.), *Spracherwerb, Sprachkontakt, Sprachkonflikt*. Berlin: de Gruyter, 205–19.

Hatch, E. and Farhady, H. 1982: *Research Design and Statistics for Applied Linguistics*. Cambridge, MA: Newbury House.

Hearn, Jeff 1992: *Men in the Public Eye*. Critical Studies on Men and Masculinities 4. London: Unwin Hyman.

Hertzler, J. O. 1965: *A Sociology of Language*. New York: Random House.

Hewitt, Roger 1986: *White Talk, Black Talk. Inter-racial Friendship and Communication Amongst Adolescents*. Cambridge. Cambridge University Press.

Hewlett, Sylvia Ann 1986: *A Lesser Life: The Myth of Women's Liberation in America*. New York: Warner Books.

Hey, Valerie 1984: The company she keeps. Unpublished Ph.D. thesis. Canterbury: University of Kent.

Hirschman, L. 1994: Female–male differences in conversational interaction. *Language in Society* 23, 427–42.

Hodge, Robert and Kress, Gunther 1988: *Social Semiotics*. Cambridge: Polity Press.

Hollway, Wendy 1984: Gender difference and the production of subjectivity. In Julian Henriques, Wendy Hollway, Cathy Urwin, C. Venn and Valerie Walkerdine (eds), *Changing the Subject: Psychology, Social Regulation and Subjectivity*. London: Methuen, 227–63.

Holmes, Janet 1984a: Hedging your bets and sitting on the fence: some evidence for hedges as support structures. *Te Reo* 27, 47–62.

Holmes, Janet 1984b: Women's language: a functional approach. *General Linguistics* 24 (3), 149–78.

Horvath, B. 1985: *Variation in Australian English*. Cambridge: Cambridge University Press.

Hoyles, C. and Sutherland, R. 1989: *Logo Mathematics in the Classroom*. London/New York: Routledge.

Hughes, Linda 1988: 'But that's not REALLY mean': competing in a cooperative mode. *Sex Roles* 19, 669–87.

Hymes, Dell 1964: Directions in (ethno-) linguistic theory. *American Anthropologist* 66, 6–56.

Jefferson, G. 1979: Sequential aspects of storytelling in conversation. In J. Schenkein (ed.), *Studies in the Organization of Conversational Interaction*. New York: Academic Press, 219–48.

Jespersen, O. 1922: *Language: its Nature, Development and Origin*. London: Allen & Unwin.

Johnson, Anthony 1990: Couples talking: conversational duets and conversational style. Paper given at Sociolinguistics Symposium 8, Roehampton Institute, London.

Johnson, Anthony 1996: *Couples Talking*. London: Longman.

Johnson, Fern and Aries, Elizabeth 1983a: The talk of women friends. *Women's Studies International Forum* 6 (4), 353–61.

Johnson, Fern and Aries, Elizabeth 1983b: Conversational patterns among same-sex pairs of late-adolescent close friends. *Journal of Genetic Psychology* 142, 225–38.

Johnson, Sally A. 1995: *Gender, Group Identity, and Variation in the Berlin Urban Vernacular*. Zurich: Peter Lang.

Jones, Deborah 1980: Gossip: notes on women's oral culture. *Women's Studies International Quarterly* 3, 193–8. Reprinted in D. Cameron (ed.), 1990, *The Feminist Critique of Language*. London: Routledge, 242–50.

Kalcik, S. 1975: '. . .like Ann's gynecologist or the time I was almost raped': personal narratives in women's rape groups. *Journal of American Folklore* 88, 3–11.

Keenan, E. 1974: Norm-makers, norm-breakers: use of speech by men and women in a Malagasy community. In R. Bauman and I. Scherzer (eds), *Explorations in the Ethnography of Speaking*. New York: Russell Sage, 125–43.

Kessler, S. and McKenna, W. 1978: *Gender: an Ethnomethodological Approach*. New York: John Wiley & Sons.

Key, M. R. 1975: *Male/Female Language*. Metuchen, NJ: Scarecrow Press.

Kotler, P. and Roberto, E. 1989: *Social Marketing: Strategies for Changing Public Behavior*. New York: The Free Press.

Kramarae, Cheris 1981: *Women and Men Speaking: Frameworks for Analysis*. Cambridge, MA: Newbury House.

Kreckel, M. 1981: *Communicative Acts and Shared Knowledge in Natural Discourse*. London: Academic Press.

Kress, Gunther 1985: *Linguistic Processes in Sociocultural Practice*. Victoria, Australia: Deakin University Press.

Kristeva, Julia 1970: *Le Texte du Roman*. The Hague: Mouton.

Kristeva, Julia 1981: Women's time. *Signs* 7 (1), 13–35.

Kuiper, Koenraad 1991: Sporting formulae in New Zealand English: two models of male solidarity. In Jenny Cheshire (ed.), *English around the World*. Cambridge, Cambridge University Press.

Labov, William 1966: *The Social Stratification of English in New York City*. Washington, DC: Center for Applied Linguistics.

Labov, William 1972a: *Sociolinguistic Patterns*. Philadelphia: University of Pennsylvania Press.

Labov, William 1972b: *Language in the Inner City*. Oxford: Blackwell.

Labov, W. and Fanshel, D. 1977: *Therapeutic Discourse· Psychotherapy as Conversation*. New York: Academic Press.

Labov, W. and Waletzky, J. 1967: Narrative analysis: oral versions of personal experience. In J. Helms (ed.), *Essays on the Verbal and Visual Arts*. Seattle: University of Washington Press.

Lakoff, Robin 1973: Language and woman's place. *Language in Society* 2, 45–80. Reprinted in 1975 by Harper Colophon Books, New York.

Layard, J. 1958: Note on the autonomous psyche and the ambivalence of the trickster concept. *Journal of Analytical Psychology* 3, 21–3.

Leet-Pellegrini, H. M. 1980: Conversational dominance as a function of gender and expertise. In H. Giles, W.P. Robertson and P.M. Smith (eds), *Language: Social Psychological Perspectives*. Oxford: Pergamon.

Lichterman, Paul 1992: Self-help reading as a thin culture. *Media, Culture and Society* 14, 421–47.

Lloyd, G. 1993: *The Man of Reason*. London: Routledge.

McCabe, T. 1981: Girls and leisure. In A. Tomlinson (ed.), *Leisure and Social Control*. Brighton Polytechnic: Chelsea School of Human Movement.

McConnell-Ginet, Sally, Borker, Ruth and Furman, Nelly (eds) 1980: *Women and Language in Literature and Society*. New York: Praeger.

McElhinny, Bonnie 1993: We all wear the blue: language, gender and police work. Unpublished Ph.D. dissertation. Stanford, CA: Stanford University.

Mackinnon, Catherine 1979: *Sexual Harassment of Working Women: a Case of Sex Discrimination*. New Haven, CT: Yale University Press.

McLemore, Cynthia 1991: The pragmatic interpretation of English intonation: sorority speech. Unpublished Ph.D. dissertation. Austin: University of Texas at Austin.

Maltz, D. and Borker, R. 1982: A cultural approach to male–female miscommunication. In J. Gumperz (ed.), *Language and Social Identity*. Cambridge: Cambridge University Press.

Maurer, D. W. 1976: Language and the sex revolution: World War 1 through World War 2. *American Speech* 51 (2), 5–24.

Meadow, R. 1989: Political campaigns. In R. E. Rice and C. Atkin (eds), *Public Communication Campaigns*. Newbury Park, CA: Sage, 253–72.

Metman, P. 1958: The trickster figure in schizophrenia. *Journal of Analytical Psychology* 3, 5–21.

Meyers, Kathy 1986: *Understains*. London: Comedia Publishing Group.

Miller, Stuart 1983: *Men and Friendship*. San Leandro, CA: Gateway Books.

Mills, Sara (ed.) 1995: *Language and Gender. Interdisciplinary Perspectives*. London: Longman.

Milroy, Lesley 1980: *Language and Social Networks*. Oxford: Blackwell.

Misra, R. B. 1980: The social stratification and linguistic diversity of the Bhojpuri speech community. Unpublished Ph.D. dissertation, University of Poona.

Moerman, Michael and Sacks, Harvey 1971: On 'understanding' in the analysis of natural conversation. Paper given at the 70th Annual Meeting of the American Anthropological Association. Reprinted in M. Moerman, 1988, *Talking Culture: Ethnography and Conversation Analysis*. Philadelphia: University of Pennsylvania Press.

Moi, Toril 1985: *Sexual/Textual Politics*. London: Routledge.

Moreau, N. B. 1984: Education, ideology and class/sex identity. In C. Kramarae, M. Schulz and W. O'Barr (eds), *Language and Power*. Newbury Park, CA: Sage, 43–61.

Morgan, David H. J. 1992: *Discovering Men*. Critical Studies on Men and Masculinities 3. London: Routledge.

Mulac, A. and Lundell, T. 1980: Differences in perceptions created by syntactic–semantic productions of male and female speakers. *Communication Monographs* 47, 111–18.

Mulac, A., Incontro, C. and James, M. 1985: Comparison of the gender-linked language effect and sex-role stereotypes. *Journal of Personality and Social Psychology* 49, 1098–1109.

O'Barr, W. and Atkins, B. A. 1980: 'Women's language' or 'powerless language'? In S. McConnell-Ginet, R. Borker and N. Furman (eds), *Women and Language in Literature and Society*. New York: Praeger, 93–110.

O'Connor, Pat 1992: *Friendships between Women: a Critical Review*. London: Harvester Wheatsheaf.

Oliver, M. and Rubin, J. 1975: The use of expletives by some American women. *Journal of Anthropological Linguistics* 17, 191–7.

Pateman, C. and Gross, E. 1986: *Feminist Challenges: Social and Political Theory*. Boston: Northeastern University.

Philips, Susan U., Steele, Susan and Tanz, Christine (eds) 1987: *Language, Gender and Sex in Comparative Perspective*. New York: Cambridge University Press.

Pickford, G. R. 1956: American linguistic geography: a sociological appraisal. *Word* 12, 211–33.

Pilkington, Jane 1992: 'Don't try and make out that I'm nice.' The different strategies women and men use when gossiping. *Wellington Working Papers in Linguistics* 5, 37–60.

Pleck, Joseph 1975: Man to man: is brotherhood possible? In N. Glazer-Malbin (ed.), *Old Family, New Family*. New York: Van Nostrand.

Polanyi, L. 1985a: *The American Story*. Norwood, NJ: Ablex.

Polanyi, L. 1985b: Conversational storytelling. In T. van Dijk (ed.), *Handbook of Discourse Analysis: Discourse and Dialogue*. New York: Academic Press, 183–201.

Preisler, B. 1986: *Linguistic Sex Roles in Conversation*. Berlin: Mouton de Gruyter.

Pujolar, Joan 1995: The identities of *'la penya'*: voices and struggles of young working-class people in Barcelona. Unpublished Ph.D. dissertation. Lancaster: Lancaster University.

Rabinow, Paul (ed.) 1986: *The Foucault Reader*. London: Peregrine.

Radin, P. 1956: *The Trickster*. London: Routledge & Kegan Paul.

Rampton, M. B. H. 1991: Interracial Panjabi in a British adolescent peer group. *Language in Society* 20 (3), 391–422.

Reid, Euan 1978: Social and stylistic variation in the speech of children: some evidence from Edinburgh. In P. Trudgill (ed.), *Sociolinguistic Patterns in British English*. London: Edward Arnold, 158–71.

Roper, Michael and Tosh, John (eds) 1991: *Manful Assertions*. London: Routledge.

Rubin, Lilian 1985: *Just Friends: the Role of Friendship in Our Lives*. New York: Harper & Row.

Rutherford, Jonathan 1988: Who's that man? In R. Chapman and J. Rutherford (eds), *Male Order: Unwrapping Masculinity*. London: Lawrence & Wishart, 21–67.

Rutherford, Jonathan 1992: *Men's Silences*. London: Routledge.

Sabo, Donald and Jansen, Sue Curry 1992: Images of men in sport media: the social reproduction of gender order. In Steve Craig (ed.), *Men, Masculinity and the Media*. Newbury Park, CA: Sage, 169–84.

Sacks, Harvey, Schlegoff, Emanuel A. and Jefferson, Gail 1974: A simplest systematics for the organization of turn-taking in conversation. *Language* 50, 696–735.

Sattel, Jack 1983: Men, inexpressiveness and power. In B. Thorne, C. Kramarae and N.Henley (eds), *Language, Gender and Society*. Cambridge, MA: Newbury House, 119–24.

Scheibman, Joanne 1995: Two-at-a-time: the intimacy of simultaneous speech in sister talk. *LGSO Working Papers 1995*. Albuquerque: University of New Mexico Linguistics Department.

Schlauch, M. 1943: *The Gift of Tongues*. London: Allen & Unwin.

Segal, L. 1990: *Slow Motion: Changing Masculinities, Changing Men*. London: Virago.

Seidler, V. 1989: *Rediscovering Masculinity: Reason, Language and Sexuality*. London: Routledge.

Seidman, Steven 1993: Identity and politics in a 'postmodern' gay culture: some historical and conceptual notes. In M. Warner (ed.), *Fear of a Queer Planet. Queer Politics and Social Theory*. Minneapolis/London: University of Minneapolis Press, 105–42.

Sheldon, A. 1993: Pickle fights: gendered talk in pre-school disputes. In D. Tannen (ed.), *Gender and Conversational Interaction*. Oxford Studies in Sociolinguistics. Oxford/New York: Oxford University Press, 83–109.

Sherrod, Drury 1987: The bonds of men: problems and possibilities in close male relationships. In Harry Brod (ed.), *The Making of Masculinities*. Boston: Allen & Unwin, 213–39.

Silverman, Kaja 1992: *Male Subjectivity at the Margins*. London: Routledge.

Simonds, Wendy 1992: *Women and Self-help Culture: Reading Between the Lines*. New Brunswick, NJ: Rutgers University Press.

Simpson, Mark, 1994: *Male Impersonators: Men Performing Masculinity*. London/New York: Cassell.

Skeggs, Beverley 1993: Theorizing masculinity. *Nykykulttuurin Tutkimusyksikkö,* 39 Jyväslaylän, Finland, 13–36.

Smith, Dorothy 1988: Femininity as discourse. In Leslie Roman and Linda Christian-Smith with Elizabeth Ellsworth (eds), *Becoming Feminine: The Politics of Popular Culture.* London/New York/Philadelphia: Falmer, 27–60.

Smith-Hefner, N. J. 1988: Women and politeness: the Javanese example. *Language in Society* 17, 535–54.

Spangler, Lynn C. 1992: Buddies and pals: a history of male friendships on prime-time television. In Steve Craig (ed.), *Men, Masculinity and the Media.* Newbury Park, CA: Sage, 93–110.

Spender, Dale 1980: *Man Made Language.* London: Routledge & Kegan Paul.

Sperber, D. and Wilson, D. 1986: *Relevance. Culture and Cognition.* Oxford: Blackwell.

Staley, C. M. 1978: Male–female use of expletives: a heck of a difference in expectations. *Anthropological Linguistics* 20 (8), 367–80.

Stanko, Elizabeth 1985: *Intimate Intrusions: Women's Experience of Male Violence.* London: Routledge & Kegan Paul.

Stearns, P. N. 1979: *Be a Man.* New York: Homes & Meier Publications.

Stein, Edward (ed.) 1992: *Forms of Desire. Sexual Orientation and the Social Constructionist Controversy.* London: Routledge.

Strate, Lance 1992: Beer commercials: a manual on masculinity. In Steve Craig (ed.), *Men, Masculinity and the Media.* Newbury Park, CA: Sage, 78–92.

Street, Brian V. 1993: Culture is a verb: anthropological aspects of language and cultural process. In *Language and Culture.* British Studies in Applied Linguistics 7. Clevedon: Multilingual Matters, 23–43.

Swann, Joan 1992: *Girls, Boys and Language.* Oxford: Blackwell.

Talbot, Mary M. 1990: Language, intertextuality and subjectivity: voices in the construction of consumer femininity. Unpublished Ph.D. thesis. Lancaster: Lancaster University.

Talbot, Mary M. 1992a: The construction of gender in a teenage magazine. In N. Fairclough (ed.), *Critical Language Awareness.* London: Longman, 174–99.

Talbot, Mary 1992b: 'I wish you'd stop interrupting me': interruptions and asymmetries in speaker-rights in equal encounters. *Journal of Pragmatics* 18, 451–66.

Talbot, Mary M. 1995a: *Fictions at Work: Language and Social Practice in Fiction.* London: Longman.

Talbot, Mary M. 1995b: A synthetic sisterhood: false friends in a teenage magazine. In Kira Hall and Mary Bucholtz (eds), *Gender Articulated: Language and the Socially Constructed Self.* London: Routledge.

Tannen, Deborah 1984: *Conversational Style. Analysing Talk among Friends.* Norwood, NJ: Ablex.

Tannen, Deborah 1990: *You Just Don't Understand: Women and Men in Conversation.* New York: Ballantine Books.

Thorne, Barrie 1993: *Gender Play. Girls and Boys in School.* Buckingham: Open University Press.

Thorne, Barrie and Henley, Nancy (eds) 1975: *Language and Sex: Difference and Dominance.* Cambridge, MA: Newbury House.

Thorne, Barrie, Kramarae, Cheris and Henley, Nancy (eds) 1983: *Language, Gender and Society.* Cambridge, MA: Newbury House.

Trudgill, Peter 1974: *The Social Differentiation of English in Norwich*. Cambridge: Cambridge University Press.

Tucker, S. 1961: *English Examined*. Cambridge: Cambridge University Press.

Tusón, Amparo 1985: Language, community and school in Barcelona. Unpublished Ph.D. thesis. Berkeley: University of California.

Van Leeuwen, Theo 1994: Grammar, identity and the press. Paper presented at Sociolinguistics Symposium 10, Lancaster University, Lancaster.

Viner, Katherine 1993: Calling the shots. The *Guardian*, 4 January.

Watney, Simon 1987: *Policing Desire. Pornography, Aids and the Media*. London: Methuen.

Weber, M. 1969: *The Theory of Social and Economic Organisation*. New York: The Free Press.

Weedon, Chris 1987: *Feminist Practice and Poststructuralist Theory*. Oxford: Blackwell.

West, Candice and Zimmerman, Don H. 1983: Interruptions in cross-sex conversations. In B. Thorne, C. Kramarae and N. Henley (eds), *Language, Gender and Society*. Cambridge, MA: Newbury House, 103–18.

Wetzel, P. J. 1988: Are 'powerless' communication strategies the Japanese norm? *Language in Society* 17, 555–64.

Williams, Glyn 1992: *Sociolinguistics. A Sociological Critique*. London: Routledge.

Willis, Paul 1977: *Learning to Labour*. Westmead: Saxon House.

Wilson, J. 1956: *Language and the Pursuit of Truth*. Cambridge: Cambridge University Press.

Wodak, R. 1980: *Das Wort in der Gruppe. Linguistische Studien zur therapeutischen Kommunikation*. Vienna: Österreichische Akademie der Wissenschaften.

Woolard, Kathryn 1989: *Doubletalk: Bilingualism and the Politics of Ethnicity in Catalonia*. Stanford: Stanford University Press.

Wulff, Helena 1988: Twenty girls growing up: ethnicity and excitement in a south London microculture. *Stockholm Studies in Social Anthropology* 21.

Zahn, C. J. 1989: The bases for differing evaluations of male and female speech: evidence from ratings of transcribed conversation. *Communication Monographs* 56, 59–74.

Zimmerman, Don H. and West, Candice 1975: Sex roles, interruptions and silences in conversation. In B. Thorne and N. Henley (eds), *Language and Sex: Difference and Dominance*. Cambridge, MA: Newbury House, 105–29.

Index

academe/academia 16, 22, 105
adolescence 3, 4, 153–4
advertising/advertisements 5, 135,
 160–1
aggression 91–4, 148
AIDS 189, 197, 204
alcohol 100
  see also drinking
anonymity 151, 191, 194, 212
appearance 51, 53–4, 191
attitudes 86, 99, 103, 144, 150, 153–4,
 189
authority 8, 68, 72, 76–7, 99, 147, 154,
 200, 201

Bakhtin, Mikhail 87, 95–6
banter 136
binary opposition 11, 14, 22, 126
bonds 4, 8, 42–4, 58
boys 32, 27–46, 154–5
Brittan, Arthur 141
Brown, P. 29

Cameron, Deborah 3, 4, 9, 10, 11, 30,
 107, 142
Cheshire, Jenny 10, 107, 149
child-care 65
class 19
  class antagonism 183–4

social class 150, 154, 175, 180–2,
 183, 185–6, 195
Coates, Jennifer 4, 10, 29, 55, 130, 134,
 140, 210
code-switching 4, 86, 99, 101
coherence 31, 38–9, 173–87
comics 159–72
communication 11
  face-to-face communication 28
community 69
competition 9, 27–32, 57–8
conflict 27
Connell, Robert 16, 19, 155, 156
context 10
conversation 47, 62
cooperation 9, 27–32, 42–5, 55–7,
 108–9, 200
  see also floor, collaborative
cultural studies 16

data 9, 12, 34–8, 42–3, 45, 51–4, 66,
 72–81, 88–90, 100, 109–16, 119,
 121–4, 131–2, 149–50, 157–8, 162–3,
 177, 192–3, 196, 198, 200, 209,
 212–27
deficit 10
dialectical
  view of gender 22
  view of language 15
difference 9, 15, 48

discourse
    class discourse   174–5
    critical discourse analysis   15, 174–5
    discourse frame   190–5
    discourse genre   15, 130, 139, 174–5,
        178–9
    discourse norms   8, 146–7
    discourse unit   209–12
    feminist discourse   6, 184–6
    gay discourse   188–207
    political discourse   159–72
    private discourse   140, 168–9
    public discourse   140, 168–9
domain
    private domain   18, 133–4, 169
    public domain   18, 133, 169
    see also setting
dominance   9
    male dominance   145
drinking   94
    see also alcohol
drugs   92

Easthope, Antony   16, 137, 188, 199
Eckert, Penelope   66
Edelsky, Carole   55, 109
education   69, 149–50
essentialism   1, 15, 197–8
ethnography   31
expletives   144–58

Fairclough, Norman   15, 87, 133, 146
Fanshel, D.   209
feminism   8, 12, 18, 156, 183–4
    see also discourse; linguistics
femininity   12
Finlay, Frank   4
Fishman, Pamela   29
floor   9
    collaborative floor   58, 108–9,
        117–18
    one-at-a-time floor   108–9, 117–18
form   10
Foucault, Michel   31, 87, 174
Fowler, Roger   146, 179–80
fraternities   21, 65–85
Freud, Sigmund   209, 228
friendship   117

men and friendship   107, 119
    women and friendship   117, 125
function   10

game   32–40
gay men   52, 194–5
    Gay Liberation   194–5
    gay press   189–90
    gay studies   15
    see also identity; men
gender   8–26
    gender construction   23, 65–6, 144,
        159, 199
    gender crossing   92–3, 103
    gender displays   88
    gender order   13
    see also identity; men; roles; women
genderlect   9, 15
genre   15
    see also discourse
girls   31, 154–5
Goffman, Erving   31, 39–40, 87
gossip   15, 60–2, 130–43
Graddol, David   28, 107, 145, 146
Grice, H. P.   31, 58

Hartig, M.   209–11
Hearn, Jeff   16
hedging   55
Henley, Nancy   9
heterosexuality   47, 184–6, 201
    see also masculinity/masculinities;
        men
Hewitt, Roger   3, 90
Heywood, John   6
hierarchy   71, 169–71
Hodge, Robert   201
Holmes, Janet   10, 55, 148
homophobia   104
homosexuality   51–4
housework   65
Hymes, Dell   8

identity
    ethnic identity   192–3, 197
    gay identity   194–6
    gender identity   23, 145, 152,
        159–60, 170–1, 181–2

identity – *contd.*
  identity crisis   156, 171
  identity work   23
  male construction of identity   3, 95,
    141–3, 155–6, 199
  politicized identity   93, 159
  poststructuralist identity   87–8, 176
  public and private identity   163–8
ideology   67
inequality   144, 159
  women's inequality   15
informants   11
information   123
interaction   47, 87
  face-to-face interaction   86
  social interaction   87
interruption   9
intertextuality   175–6, 178, 184–6
interviews   90
intimacy   136–7, 166
  see also men and intimacy

Johnson, Sally   1, 4
jokes   71
Jones, Deborah   130–1

Kiesling, Scott Fabius   3
de Klerk, Vivian   5
Kress, Gunther   201
Kristeva, Julia   176

Labov, William   14, 149, 209
Lakoff, Robin   8, 147
language
  dialogical approach to language   95
  language change   24
  language choice   86
  powerless language   9, 12
  symbolic order of language   22
  see also interaction; linguistics;
    speech; talk
laughter   117
Levinson, S.   29
linguistics
  androcentric approaches to
    linguistics   12
  feminist linguistics   1, 8, 21
  mainstream linguistics   11

  Marxist approaches to
    linguistics   15
  poststructuralist approaches to
    linguistics   14
  structuralist approaches to
    linguistics   13
  variationist approaches to
    linguistics   14
  see also sociolinguistics

McConnell-Ginet, Sally   66, 148
masculinity/masculinities   19, 199
  crisis in masculinity   13
  hegemonic/hierarchical
    masculinity   19, 173, 175
  heterosexual masculinity   47
  simplified masculinity   92–3
media   132–5
  see also newspapers; television
men
  academic men   211, 215–16, 223–7
  Black men   107
  gay men   52, 194–5
  heterosexual men   192–4
  men and confessionalism   18
  men and effeminacy   17
  men and expertism   120–4
  men and intimacy   90–1, 139–40
  men's movement   18
  men and rationality   17
  men's studies   13
  middle-class men   50
  students   47–8, 66–7, 211, 213, 217
  white men   50
  working-class men   86–7
  young men   47
metalanguage   210
monologues   120–3
Morgan, David   16
multilingualism   86–7
music   94

narratives   195–203
  written narratives   208–28
Neff van Aertselaer, JoAnne   5
newspapers
  The Sun   173–87
normalization   12

oppression 13, 131
overlap 112–15, 117

paralinguistic features 136
participants 51
patriarchy 13
peer groups 87, 99
performance/performativity 47, 49–50, 59–60
politeness 30
pornography 188–207
postmodernism 49
poststructuralism 87
  see also linguistics, poststructuralist approaches
power 12, 65–85, 159, 165, 169, 198–201
  male power 12, 146–8
prosody 90
psychoanalysis 19
Pujolar i Cos, Joan 4

question 9, 123–4
  tag questions 9
questionnaire 149–50, 153–5, 210–12

race 19, 192–3
racism 104
roles
  female/women's roles 130, 134, 163
  gender roles 164
  male/men's roles 18, 159, 163, 171
  sexual roles 198–201

Saint and Greavsie 4, 130–43
Sattel, Jack 17
Saussure, Ferdinand de 14
school 27, 87, 152
Segal, Lynne 16
Seidler, Victor J. 16
self/Self 27–8
setting 134–5
  college setting 3
  multilingual setting 4, 86–106
  see also domain
sexism 21
sexuality 19
  see also heterosexuality; homosexuality

similarity 11
slang 94, 147–8
social networks 10
sociolinguistics 11
sociology 16
solidarity 139
Spain 86–106, 159–72
speech
  speech genres 96–8
  speech styles 49, 86, 96–8, 145–6
Spender, Dale 148
sport 47, 134
  football 130–43
status 48, 59
stereotype 44, 47–8, 147–8, 150–2, 188–9
Straight to Hell magazine 189–207
Street, Brian 23
structuralism 13
  see also linguistics, structuralist approaches
subculture 11, 148–9
subjectivity 19
Swann, Joan 28, 107, 145, 146
swearing 94

taboo 120, 147–9, 152–3
Talbot, Mary 5, 117, 175, 176
talk 38
  all-male talk 107–29
  all-female talk 54–5
  cross-sex talk 107
  goals of talk 124–5
  organization of talk 107
  polyphonic talk 98, 109, 119
  single-sex talk 107
Tannen, Deborah 48, 140, 146
television 50
  BBC 135
  ITV 132
  Sky TV 132
text
  text consumers 189
  text production 189
  visual texts 23
  written texts 23
Thorne, Barrie 9
topic 47

turn-taking   4, 9, 55, 58, 111

university   66

verbal play   96, 179
voices   95

West, Candice   9
women
    academic women   211, 213–14,
        219–22
    marginalization of women   12

middle-class women   108
problematization of women
    8, 10
students   211
white women   108
women's movement *see* feminism
women's studies   16
working-class women   102–3
work   65
working classes   86

Zimmerman, Don   9